DATE DUE

MAR 2 1 1997	
JUN - 2 1999	
SEP 2 4 2000	
SEP 2 5 2000	

BRODART   Cat. No. 23-221

CLINICAL
CASE
MANAGEMENT

OTHER RECENT VOLUMES IN THE
SAGE FOCUS EDITIONS

CLINICAL
CASE
MANAGEMENT

A Guide to Comprehensive Treatment of Serious Mental Illness

Robert W. Surber
editor

SAGE PUBLICATIONS
The International Educational and Professional Publisher
Thousand Oaks   London   New Delhi

For information address:

SAGE Publications, Inc.
2455 Teller Road
Thousand Oaks, California 91320

SAGE Publications Ltd.
6 Bonhill Street
London EC2A 4PU
United Kingdom

SAGE Publications India Pvt. Ltd.
M-32 Market
Greater Kailash I
New Delhi 110 048 India

Printed in the United States of America

Library of Congress Cataloging-in-Publication Data

Main entry under title:

Clinical case management : a guide to comprehensive treatment of
    serious mental illness / edited by Robert W. Surber
        p.   cm.   —   (Sage focus editions ; v. 167)
    Includes bibliographical references.
    ISBN 0-8039-4386-5 (cl.)   —   ISBN 0-8039-4387-3 (pb)
    1. Mentally ill—Care. 2. Chronically ill—Care. I. Surber,
Robert W.   II. Series: Sage focus editions, vol. 167.
    [DNLM: 1. Psychology, Clinical—methods. 2. Mental Disorders—
therapy. WM 400 C6405 1994]
RC480.53.C55 1994
362.2'0425—dc20
DNLM/DLC
for Library of Congress   93-34552
                                                                  CIP
94 95 96 97 10 9 8 7 6 5 4 3 2 1

Sage Production Editor: Yvonne Könneker

Contents

This book is dedicated to our clients,
on whom we depend for so much.

Preface

Over the past decade, case management has been recognized as one of the core approaches in the treatment of persons with severe mental illness. In an era of biological psychiatry, we have learned that psychotropic medications have considerable limitations in alleviating mental illness unless supported by comprehensive environmental interventions. In a concurrent era of deinstitutionalization, we have also learned that reducing hospital censuses will neither improve quality of life nor provide stable housing unless such environmental supports are available.

As is evident in the streets of all American cities, discharging mentally ill persons with only a prescription for medications has been neither effective psychiatry or compassionate social policy. Increasingly, mental health professionals, public officials, and concerned citizens have begun to recognize that persons with long-term mental illnesses require hands-on personal assistance to create safe and secure living arrangements and obtain appropriate treatment.

Thus, across the nation, a myriad of case management programs have sprouted in recent years to address these concerns. Although these programs' philosophies and practices echoed the sometimes-forgotten traditions of professional social work, interdisciplinary staffing patterns and the unique problems posed by mental illness contributed to the emergence of a "new" practice modality called "case management." Responding to pressing social needs, case management programs were begun before conceptual frameworks or practice methodologies were developed.

"Something" needed to be done to address these problems, so case managers were hired before we began to understand how "something" could be done.

This volume is one of the first comprehensive efforts to describe how this "something" can be accomplished, that is, how case management can be practiced in a complex urban environment. As a pioneer in the case management field, the Citywide Case Management Team at San Francisco General Hospital has struggled with some of the most difficult problems imaginable. Beyond the formidable challenges of long-term mental illness, the majority of their clients suffer from severe difficulties with alcohol and substance abuse. Many also have significant medical conditions, including HIV disorders and the related infections. Furthermore, many clients have migrated to the Bay Area, seeking a temperate climate, drugs, and a high tolerance for "deviant" behavior; thus they often have no families or support systems beyond their acquaintances on the streets. Finally, housing costs in the Bay Area are among the highest in the nation, adding to the difficulty of establishing a stable living situation for clients on public entitlements.

I specifically mention these social factors because case managers in different locales often struggle with very different problems and resources. For example, in some economically depressed rural communities, inexpensive housing options are plentiful while job opportunities are in short supply. On the other hand, in my community of metropolitan Washington, DC, a robust economy has encouraged many employers to provide jobs for persons recovering from mental illness while reducing the supply of affordable housing. Like Bob Surber and his colleagues, effective case managers tailor their interventions to the specific needs and resources of both their clients and communities (Florentine & Grusky, 1990).

The title of this volume, *Clinical Case Management: A Guide to Comprehensive Treatment of Serious Mental Illness*, raises the semantic problems that have plagued this field since its inception. The term *case management* connotes an impersonal power relationship between case managers and clients, implying that clients/cases are managed by their case managers. This semantic confusion has been exacerbated by the increasing use of the term *case management* to describe the corporate rationing of medical services.

To differentiate our work from these other activities, we introduced the term *clinical case management* to emphasize a personal intervention strategy that integrates therapeutic and environmental perspectives (Harris & Bachrach, 1988; Kanter, 1989). In turn, we found that this term elicited its own confusion as some of our colleagues interpreted the term *clinical* as connoting an elitist and classical psychotherapeutic approach that could only be implemented by professionals with advanced degrees. Although we agree that this work requires a high degree of clinical skill, we also recognize that none of the mental health professions offer adequate training for this work. Thus skilled clinical case managers inevitably develop the bulk of their expertise through their ongoing work experience supported by appropriate supervision, consultation, and in-service training experiences.

In our view, clinical case management requires a wide range of clinical skills. These may include evaluating dangerousness, a need for rehospitalization, or a referral for psychiatric or medical consultation. They may also involve understanding whether offering a client a ride to an appointment is providing support or promoting dependency; or whether a client's rage toward his landlord should be addressed with empathic support, pragmatic problem solving, transference interpretations, environmental advocacy, or psychopharmacological adjustments. The clinical challenges of this work are still not appreciated by most mental health administrators and policy planners.

The term *management* still leaves us with the impersonal connotation that all of us involved in this work find inadequate. A number of alternative terms have been suggested, but no consensus on an improved phrasing has emerged. As this term will remain in use for the foreseeable future, this volume continues a process of recontextualization, discussing case management as a form of caring and empowering instead of a form of manipulation and dehumanization. Elsewhere, I have outlined how D. W. Winnicott, a psychoanalyst, began using the term *management* in the 1940s to describe a personal process of providing growth-enhancing environmental support in child rearing and clinical interventions (Kanter, 1990). In his writings, management assumes a very different coloration. If we are unable to change the language, perhaps we can begin to change the connotations these terms evoke.

Finally, throughout this volume, the authors realistically describe the accomplishments and limitations of their own years of work with persons with very severe, long-term difficulties. This honesty is courageous, as we all may be tempted to make exaggerated claims for clinical success. Unfortunately, the relatively new approach of case management is coming of age in an era in which there are tremendous pressures to demonstrate efficacy and provide immediate solutions to sometimes intractable social problems.

Unfortunately, too much of the literature in our field is written by academics, administrators, and policymakers whose primary experience with case management involves preparing policy guidelines, evaluating grant applications, and presenting workshops. Too often, these case management experts convey an image of a simplistic practice technology that can be mastered by case managers within months. We must remember that clinical case management is a relatively young, evolving modality, perhaps as sophisticated as the field of psychotherapy in 1920 or psychopharmacology in 1965.

The evocative case reports in this volume remind us that we are only beginning to learn what happens in case management with different types of clients with different problems in different types of environments. It is my hope that readers of this volume will be inspired by the efforts and ideas of the authors to view their own work as an educational process. In doing so, case managers can learn from both success and failure without succumbing to the despair our clients experience on a daily basis. With such a perspective, our collective expertise can continue to accumulate while avoiding the cycle of promise and disappointment that have characterized other experiments in addressing social problems.

—*Joel S. Kanter*
August 1993
Silver Spring, Maryland

References

Florentine, R., & Grusky, O. (1990). When case managers manage the seriously mentally ill: A role-contingency approach. *Social Service Review, 54*, 77-93.

Harris, M., & Bachrach, L. (Eds.). (1988). *Clinical case management* (New Directions for Mental Health Services, Vol. 40). San Francisco: Jossey-Bass.

Kanter, J. (1989). Clinical case management: Definition, principles, components. *Hospital and Community Psychiatry, 40*, 361-368.

Kanter, J. (1990). Community-based management of psychotic clients: The contributions of D. W. and Clare Winnicott. *Clinical Social Work Journal, 18*, 23-41.

Acknowledgments

There are literally hundreds of people who have contributed to this book. They include the staff and clients of the Citywide Case Management Team, and the families of the authors, who have put up with the stress of living with the authors during its writing. In addition, there are very few "new" ideas in this volume, and much of what is said is based on the work and experience of many others who have written about their work with seriously mentally ill adults.

There are a few individuals, however, who deserve special recognition. Stephen M. Goldfinger, who is now Clinical Director at the Massachusetts Mental Health Center and Assistant Professor of Psychiatry at the Harvard Medical School, collaborated with me in designing and developing the program on which this book is based. Margaret A. Watson, who is now Lecturer at the School of Social Welfare at the University of California at Berkeley, on the faculty of the California Institute for Clinical Social Work, and in private practice in San Francisco, provided many of the conceptualizations on which the work of the program is based, and helped me keep the dream of this book alive for a decade.

John T. Hopkin and Robert L. Okin, the former and current Chiefs of the Department of Psychiatry at San Francisco General Hospital, have consistently supported me in the development and management of the Citywide Case Management Team. Linda Wang and John Riggs with the Division of Mental Health and Substance Services of the San Francisco Department of Public Health have trusted and encouraged me over the years to implement innovations in care.

Finally, Marquita Flemming of Sage Publications, Inc., has consistently provided encouragement from the conception of the book through its completion.

—Robert W. Surber

Introduction

It was at a memorial service for Dottie Turner in 1983 that this book was born. Dottie had been a Field Coordinator for the School of Social Welfare at the University of California at Berkeley for many years and was known and respected throughout the San Francisco Bay Area. Her untimely death, shortly after her retirement, brought the social work community together in her honor.

At the reception, Margaret Watson and I shared with each other that we both had a wish to write a book on case management. Although we felt that the concept of case management held significant promise in caring for seriously mentally ill individuals, we had concerns about how it was being understood and implemented. In much of the literature on case management at that time, it was considered to be simply a coordinating role that neither incorporated mental health treatment nor required professional skill or training. Additionally, the literature on case management was largely written from a service system perspective and offered little practical help for case managers who were working with clients.

We knew that working with this population required considerable knowledge and skill. We thought there was a need for a book that would be a practical guide both for case managers and for mental health students who were learning to work with seriously mentally ill adults. We envisioned a book that conceptualized a comprehensive approach to care and described the integration of a broad array of interventions. We hoped to provide information that practitioners could use to help solve the day-to-day problems they faced in serving their clients. Finally, we agreed that the book should use a great deal of case material for illustration.

For 10 years we have been reading the case management literature, and attending professional meetings, with an eye toward whether someone else had written "our book." The literature has developed dramatically in this decade, and much in the way of useful concepts, models, and research findings has come forth. Yet, there continues to be a need for a detailed discussion of what it is that case managers do, and what it is that case managers have learned about providing these services. It is hoped that this book will fill that need, providing valuable information and support both for case managers working in the field, and for those who are learning to work with clients with mental illness.

Other obligations have prevented Margaret from participating in the writing of this book. Nevertheless, through discussions, presentations, papers, and in-service trainings, she has contributed to both its conception and its content.

I have mixed feelings as this work is now completed. Certainly one of these feelings is relief that it is finished. Ten years of thinking and planning and more than 2 years of writing are enough. I am pleased that it is being completed at this time. It is certainly a better work than if it had been written several years ago. It has taken all these years to gather the knowledge, expertise, and understanding that are included within it.

On the other hand, it is not finished. Our understanding of this work grows daily, and there is always the temptation to add more material. This is particularly true in relation to the role of consumers in the delivery of case management services.

I must admit that 10 years ago I did not consider that there might be a role for mental health consumers as providers of case management services. Today, I believe that consumers have a significant and important role in the delivery of all mental health services. Yet, our experience is too new with this role in case management to fully understand or describe its potential.

This book has been authored by current and former staff of the Citywide Case Management Team in San Francisco, California. It draws on the experience of a multidisciplinary staff with clients who suffer from severe mental illnesses, as evidenced by multiple psychiatric hospitalizations, and who struggle with serious and disabling problems in a challenging urban environment with few economic or social resources. It also draws on long experience with many individuals, through which it is understood that clients may take many months to engage, years to achieve stability in community settings, and a decade or more to develop interdependent relationships and meaningful activities. Finally, it draws on the painful experience of having clients do poorly in spite the best efforts.

This book could only have been written as an edited volume. This is for two reasons. First of all, no one person has the breadth or depth of clinical experience that is recounted in all of the chapters. More important, the authors are a very diverse group of individuals in terms of professional discipline, ethnicity, gender, and sexual orientation. This diversity brings a variety of perspectives that enhances the case management approach described.

Despite this diversity, the authors share a common philosophy or approach to care that is outlined in the first chapter. They have also attempted to incorporate the themes of the first section of the book throughout the remaining chapters. The initial theme is that psychological and practical issues are inextricably intertwined, and that clinical and practical interventions must be delivered concurrently. Therefore, psychotherapeutic interventions are integrated into a variety of activities with clients. The second theme is that understanding and utilizing the strengths and resources of the client's culture is critical to the successful implementation of care. The third theme emphasizes the importance of families and natural support systems as essential components of the system of care that case managers are responsible for supporting and developing. By sharing an approach to care and by acknowledging these common themes, it is hoped that a diverse group of authors have written a volume that is both coherent and cohesive.

Nevertheless, inconsistencies are inherent in an edited volume. At the most basic level, the authors use different terms to describe themselves and their clients. They refer to themselves as case managers, or clinical case managers, or clinicians, or therapists. They refer to the population they work with as chronically mentally ill individuals, or seriously mentally ill clients, or severely mentally ill people. The authors also describe somewhat different interventions for dealing with similar problems.

There has been no effort to edit out these inconsistencies. Rather, I believe that it will be appreciated that a comprehensive approach with a complex clientele must engender a variety of views and approaches.

In any case, I trust that the dedication, commitment, and hard work of all of these authors is evident throughout the pages of this book. I hope that it will serve as an inspiration to you, the readers, in your work to both serve and understand the needs of these challenging but rewarding clients.

PART I

Clinical Case Management Themes

1

An Approach to Care

ROBERT W. SURBER

Providing effective care for individuals with serious mental illness can be a humbling endeavor. There are no simple formulas. There are no easy answers. There is no correct way to approach treating any particular client. The best interventions are only somewhat effective, with some people, sometimes. The severity and multiplicity of the client's problems can feel overwhelming, and the process is often fraught with frustration.

On the other hand, providing effective care for seriously mentally ill people is quite possible. When the treatment is successful it can be exceptionally rewarding. It is proposed here that success is based on understanding and on providing care in keeping with several conceptions of both mentally ill individuals and treatment. It is not based on implementing specific interventions at particular times.

Therefore, clinical case management, as described in this book, is a process that is defined by a set of premises and principles of care. It is not a specific intervention that can be easily described, or a program with clear boundaries. Simply, clinical case management is as much a way of thinking about care as it is providing specific interventions.

There are many reasons why case management services are now being developed and funded within public mental health services. These include reducing inappropriate use of acute care and institutional resources, encouraging more appropriate use of community-based treatment and supportive services, improving the coordination of services, and limiting costs. While these are important goals, they are not particularly compelling reasons for clients to accept or utilize services, because case management services must usually be accepted voluntarily by the clients, and the purpose of these services must speak to the clients' understanding of their needs and wishes. Therefore, it is suggested that a primary purpose of care must be to assist clients in working toward achieving their own goals, aspirations, and dreams.

Frequently conflicts arise between clients' wishes and their families' goals, program goals, and community goals. These conflicts create a natural tension for case managers that must be continuously monitored so that services are balanced to provide care that is useful and acceptable to the clients and will still be supported by the larger community.

Three premises underpin an effective approach for serving the seriously mentally ill population. The first is that clients are a heterogeneous group of people, each of whom struggles with the illness in a unique context. The second is that the definition of what is therapeutic must be very broad, and implies that care for this population integrate a diverse array of approaches and interventions. The third is that care and treatment are provided through and are dependent upon the relationship between client and clinician. These premises reflect the thinking of Margaret A. Watson on working with seriously mentally ill clients, as she has described through a series of papers and presentations (Watson, 1983a, 1983b, 1987).

This chapter will describe these three premises and 11 principles of care as they relate to providing clinical case management services to seriously mentally ill clients.

Heterogeneity of Clients

Perhaps it is because it is so obvious, that it is so often forgotten by service planners and service providers that those with mental illness are an extremely heterogeneous group. Yet a clinician's acknowledgement of this simple fact can greatly determine the outcome of treatment.

At the simplest level, clients suffer from very different illnesses, which cause different symptoms and different forms of disability. But even within a particular diagnostic group there are wide variations. Clients carefully diagnosed with schizophrenia all have different symptom patterns, different kinds and degrees of disability resulting from their symptoms, and different understandings of and affective responses to the symptoms; and the symptoms respond differently to the same interventions.

Although auditory hallucinations are common with schizophrenia, they may be hostile or friendly, ego syntonic or dystonic, continuous or sporadic, consistent and clearly situational or highly unpredictable, medication responsive or nonresponsive. Their content and meaning are as varied as the life experiences of those who hear them.

Just as important as the different ways the illnesses are experienced, are the differences in the ways that individuals respond to them. With other disabilities, such as blindness, one person may be completely incapacitated while another may compensate with other senses and live a creative and fulfilling life. The response of people with mental illnesses is equally varied. It is also important to note that people with mental illness have different responses to treatment. This includes differences in their capacity to avail themselves of treatment and supportive services, and differences in the effects of various interventions.

Problems associated with the illnesses, or merely caused by the vicissitudes of life, also vary by individual. These can include problems in obtaining basic resources, difficulties in developing and maintaining interdependent relationships, substance abuse, medical problems, legal problems, or any other human dilemma. These occur with differing degrees of severity and in differing combinations.

With all of the problems experienced by mentally ill individuals, it is easy to overlook their strengths. These are as varied as their problems. Like the general population they can be intelligent, strong, determined, hard-working, responsible, skilled, persistent, creative, organized, musical, humorous, and lovable. They can also be inspiring and charismatic.

Heterogeneity is not limited to personal characteristics. The context in which individuals live is equally variable. A most immediate difference can be the availability of family, and the family's response to the client and the illness. Different communities also offer differing resources and differing attitudes toward those with mental illness. Similarly, clients from different cultural backgrounds experience different types and levels of support, depending on their own culture's understanding of and tolerance for mental illness. Finally, mentally ill individuals can be wealthy or poor, although few have great resources, and most are distinguished by the degree of their impoverishment.

Perhaps this heterogeneity is just too obvious to be worth describing so thoroughly. Yet if one carefully observes services for those with serious mental illness, the acknowledgement of or response to this variety is anything but obvious. All too often clinicians and programs design interventions or services for typical clients or a narrow range of clients. Because there is no such thing as a typical client, and because clients vary dramatically, these efforts are often unsuccessful with significant numbers of clients. Similarly, care providers can be tempted to intervene with the next client by utilizing interventions that worked with previous ones. Given the heterogeneity of the clients, it is better to see each new client as a challenge of individual discovery.

Defining What Is Therapeutic

For the purposes of this discussion, what is therapeutic is what is helpful. This clearly goes beyond the concept of curing an illness to include efforts that are palliative by alleviating symptoms and suffering when outright cure might not be possible. It also includes treatment efforts to reduce pathology and disability, and rehabilitative efforts to increase functioning and meaningful interdependent relationships. Finally, it includes whatever increases an individual's sense of well-being.

From this perspective, mental health treatments are therapeutic for many people with serious mental illnesses. Medications have certainly had a dramatic and positive effect in helping mentally ill clients live successfully in community settings. Residential treatment, day treatment, and outpatient treatment—in individual, group, and family formats—have provided necessary support, skill development, education, and useful insights for many clients. Hospitalization is also useful in helping clients regain control in a safe and structured setting.

As useful as formal mental health treatments can be, they represent only a small portion of what is defined as therapeutic for a severely mentally ill population. Clearly, emotional stability can be achieved only when the survival needs of personal safety, housing, food, and clothing are met. Resolving or ameliorating other problems that cause suffering and anxiety can also improve a person's mental status. These include health, financial, legal, and other problems.

A core disability often caused by mental illness is the difficulty in establishing and maintaining relationships. Yet positive relationships are central to the concept of mental health for all people. Therefore, any efforts that help clients establish or rebuild constructive interdependent relationships with family, friends, or any other members of the community must be considered therapeutic interventions. This includes the ongoing struggle to love and be loved.

Mental health consumers indicate that well-being is achieved through opportunities to work, to be creative, and to contribute to the lives of others (Campbell & Schraiber, 1989). In this light therapeutic interventions can be those that support clients' efforts to develop constructive uses of their time. This may include paid and volunteer work; recreational, educational, and socialization activities; and artistic and other creative efforts. Last, it is suggested that spirituality is also an important component of well-being. Therefore, recovery can be enhanced by activities that range from participating in formal religious programs, to searching for meaning in life, to prayer.

Responding to this broad definition of what is therapeutic requires implementation of a broad array of interventions and approaches. These include psychological, psychopharmacological, rehabilitative, educational, social, spiritual, and practical approaches that must be integrated to serve a particular client.

The Primacy of the Relationship

Clinical case management is an approach to care that depends on the relationship between an individual clinician and an individual client (Bachrach, 1992). A case manager is working for change: change within the client, change within the client's environment, and change in the relationship between the client and the environment. The clinical relationship is a vehicle for change.

Through the clinical relationship a case manager becomes the tool that helps a client change, grow, reexamine relationships, and pursue goals. It is through a relationship that clients can overcome their resistance to both accepting treatment and accepting practical supports. The relationship can also help them understand and master their illnesses, develop meaningful goals and activities, and develop the capacity to relate to others. The relationship, in and of itself, can have therapeutic benefits.

Although many individuals in a case management program and throughout the service system may work with a client, it is the clinical case manager who has responsibility for implementing or coordinating all aspects of care over an indefinite period of time. This makes the relationship between client and case manager the primary treatment relationship. This offers many opportunities and, at the same time, creates great responsibility. Case managers must have not only considerable skills to make the most effective use of these opportunities but also considerable support to manage the responsibility. The remainder of this book is intended to help clinical case managers obtain the necessary skills and support.

Principles of Care

The heterogeneity of clients and their needs, and the broad definition of what is therapeutic, suggest that services for seriously mentally ill clients must necessarily be complex and respond to a large array of considerations. It is clear that no specific program, intervention, or activity can define adequate care for any particular person. Rather, care must be organized according to a number of principles.

The principles for organizing services for seriously mentally ill people described here have evolved over time. Although they reflect traditional human service concepts, they were first proposed as a group for serving those with serious mental illness by Bachrach (1978, 1981). They were later expanded by Goldfinger, Hopkin, and Surber (1984), and are further expanded here through the experience of the Citywide Case Management Team in San Francisco, California. They suggest that care must be organized and provided so as to be comprehensive, continuous, individualized, flexible, capable, meaningful, willing and accepting, culturally competent, participatory, resourceful, and accessible. These principles are overlapping and no one of them can be considered or implemented in isolation. They do, however, provide a context for approaching care to a population that can be highly vulnerable and severely disabled.

Comprehensive

If one accepts the broad definition of what is therapeutic, it follows that the approach to treatment must encompass all efforts that are likely to be helpful. This is necessary not just to ensure that all areas of possible benefit are addressed but also because many interventions can be helpful only if other areas of the client's life are also attended to. For instance, the best medication regimen may not be effective at reducing symptoms if the client is highly stressed as a result of homelessness and a severe medical illness, or is suspicious of the prescribing physician and refuses to take the medication. Another way of looking at it is that one of the reasons community-based mental health services are often unsuccessful at serving seriously mentally ill people is because they are not prepared to respond to clients' multiple problems and multiple needs.

Comprehensive care encompasses all of the above-described components of what is therapeutic and includes mental health treatment, interventions to provide basic supports and resolve health and social problems, as well as efforts to help clients grow and achieve their goals.

A case manager will need to be prepared to address all of these areas of need. It is a tenet of this approach that it is necessary to have one point of responsibility for comprehensive care, so that no important aspect of a client's life is overlooked, and also because success in one area is dependent on success in other areas. This single point of responsibility means that one individual, or possibly one team, has clear responsibility and authority for developing and implementing a comprehensive service plan. It is also a tenet of this approach that psychological difficulties and practical problems are inextricably intertwined, and that their resolution is best resolved by skillful intervention in both arenas by the same clinician at the same time.

Continuous

Continuity of care has been a central concept of the community mental health movement since its inception. However, it has been observed that this concept is more distinguished by its absence than its presence in many public mental health service systems (Turner, TenHoor, & Schiffren, 1979). Nevertheless, it is a concept that must be successfully implemented if care to a severely mentally disabled population is to be effective.

Continuous care has several meanings. First of all, it means that care must be available over time. Serious mental illness tends to persist, and individuals may need care for an indefinitely long period of time. This means that care must be available in an uninterrupted manner for as long as it is needed.

Continuity of care means that care is consistent and coordinated wherever the client is served in the system. When care and treatment are given by different programs, the effect can be as discontinuous as if treatment were interrupted. This is because, without the strong clinical presence of a core provider, different providers, with different approaches to care, will tend to totally reassess the client and begin treatment anew. Therefore, a role of case management is to provide continuity by providing not only a thorough history of the client, but also a coherent and consistent treatment plan to every program that works with the client.

Continuity also means that care is to be continuously available. This requires that clients not be excluded from services if they otherwise meet the criteria for the case management program. Implementing this concept requires developing strategies to engage clients who are reluctant to use the services they need to survive in the community. Helen Harris Perlman (1986) has remarked that the consummate clinical skill is finding a way to help a person who is in desperate need, but is unable to use the help that is available.

Continuously being available involves finding ways to keep clients within the care system no matter how difficult their behaviors. Although dangerous and unpalatable behavior may require that services be available in restricted settings and with limited scope, it is still necessary to assure that care, in some form, is always available for there to be any hope that it might be helpful. This requires continuing to be available, even when the client clearly and consistently rejects care. This may be done by making it clear that services will be available when the client is ready and willing to accept them, and again offering services when the client is in a crisis or is hospitalized.

Finally, continuity means that care is constantly available at all times, every day. This may involve staff of the case management program being on duty or on call at all hours or, at a minimum, may include backup provided by an emergency service that collaborates closely with the case managers.

Individualized

The principles of comprehensive and continuous care derive from a broad conceptualization of what is therapeutic. The heterogeneity of the clients provides the rationale for the principles of individualization and flexibility.

Quite simply, individualized services are those that are designed to respond to the unique needs, strengths, resources, and context of each client, as detailed in the section on the heterogeneity of clients.

Since each client is different, each client's care plan must reflect the differences. This means, of course, that clients will need to have the goals and interventions of the care plan individualized to their needs, problems, strengths, and resources. It also means that the clinical approach to engaging and coming to understand the client and the client's support system must be individualized. It means that the priority and emphasis in implementing a particular plan will vary according to such parameters as the dangerousness of the client's immediate situation, the ability and willingness of the client to participate in treatment, the client's goals and dreams, the client's attitude about care and previous experience with human services, and the views of the client's support system about mental illness. In short, the implementation of the plan must be as individualized as the plan itself.

For the purposes of this discussion, individualized has another meaning. It also means that one individual clinician is primarily responsible for planning, coordinating, and delivering care for an individual client. This individual approach requires the clinician to establish a trusting relationship through which an individualized service plan can be developed and implemented. As noted above, the greatest clinical skill is required to establish a relationship with a population that has, by the nature of the illnesses, serious deficits in establishing and maintaining useful relationships.

Flexible

The concept of flexibility is a variation on the theme of individualized services. Like continuity of care, flexible services are often described as being provided within public mental health services, but are seldom delivered. Yet the ability to be flexible in providing care may be the most important factor for a successful outcome.

Flexibility begins with both a willingness to provide services that are acceptable to the client and providing them in a manner that is acceptable to the client. Examples include providing services in the community if the client cannot or will not go to the clinic; or providing survival services, even if the client does not accept medications or agree to remain sober; or being available to see clients when they appear at the office, even if at unscheduled times or a day late; or making exceptions to bureaucratic requirements that, by definition, are inflexible.

Being flexible means treating each client differently, even though some clients may complain that they are being treated differently from others in the program. However, being flexible should not be interpreted as always doing what the client wants or demands. Being flexible includes the ability to provide clear structure, even rigid enforcement of the rules, when this is what the client needs.

Another way of considering flexibility is that the ideal is to make every intervention based on the best assessment of what the client needs, rather than on other considerations such as program design, regulations, staff needs, and so forth. As client needs necessarily compete and conflict with other needs, it is understandable why the principle of flexibility is so difficult to implement.

A key element in developing a flexible approach is professional staff that have a flexible definition of what distinguishes professional practice. In other words, mental health professionals must not only understand the broad definition of what is therapeutic, but must also accept responsibility for developing an array of interventions in a variety of settings, as determined by client needs.

Capable

In one sense capable means having the ability to implement all of the principles described here. Practically, it means having the resources to provide adequate care and an organizational structure to utilize these resources most effectively.

Since the primary resource within a case management program is staff time, it is critical that clinicians have enough time to serve each client according to the client's needs. Primarily, this means having a manageable caseload. The larger the caseload, the more the staff must restrict the types of services offered and the settings where care is delivered. Larger caseloads are likely to make care reactive rather than proactive and, therefore, less likely to be effective.

Being capable requires that staff are sanctioned to provide care as clients need it. Staff mobility to provide care where the client will accept it must be supported with both transportation resources and administrative confirmation that this is an expectation. The flexibility to provide care as needed and acceptable must also be sanctioned and supported as a priority over regulatory and bureaucratic needs.

This level of capability represents an ideal that might not be able to be met in reality. Yet it must be recognized that funding requirements and expectations often severely limit a case manager's ability to deliver needed services. This recognition is required so that unnecessary and unproductive impediments are constantly questioned, challenged, and modified in an effort to maximize client services and minimize wasting limited resources.

Adequate capability involves having resources in the community to meet client needs. These resources include housing, financial resources, medical and dental care, legal supports, and particularly, resources to assist clients in achieving their goals. Therefore, one important role of case managers and case management programs is assuring the availability of or participation in the development of these resources.

The last component of capability has to do with staff members who have the expertise and personal resources to effectively serve their clients with severe mental illness. Primarily, this requires not only good clinical and administrative supervision but also educational opportunities to help further develop knowledge and skills.

Meaningful

This means meaningful to the clients. As stated above, one purpose of case management services must be to assist clients in working toward their own goals and dreams as they define them. It follows then that services for the clients must be meaningful to the clients.

In addition, case management services are usually provided on a voluntary basis. That is, clients usually have the option of rejecting case management services. Even if clients agree to work with a case manager, they can still accept or reject any component of the service plan they wish to. The exception to this voluntary acceptance of services is when clients have a conservator and are required by the court to accept services. However, the goal with conserved clients is to assist them to live more independently in the least restrictive settings. Also, while the client is in the community, a conservator has very limited practical authority to require that a client use services appropriately.

All of this means that services are most effective if the client participates actively in the treatment process. This active participation means that the services offered must be of interest to the client. Services must respond to the clients' definition of what they want, what they say they need, what they want to get out of life, and what they are willing to work on or cooperate with.

Willing and Accepting

People who suffer from severe mental illness can be very difficult to treat. The illnesses are persistent, and the available techniques, technologies, and resources are frequently less than adequate. In addition, the conditions, situations, and behaviors of these people can be quite unpalatable and overwhelming. Clients can be threatening or even violent. They can be unclean, smell, and carry infectious diseases. They often deny their illnesses and problems and may actively work to defeat efforts to treat them, while at the same time demanding some form of help. They may even exhibit self-destructive behaviors, such as suicide attempts, substance abuse, self-mutilation, and unsafe sexual practices that jeopardize themselves or others. Finally, they may be downright rude, hostile, and demeaning to those who are doing their best to care for them.

One solution to these qualities and behaviors within mental health services has been to describe the clients as manipulative or untreatable and exclude them from care. Yet, because these individuals are seriously disabled as a result of their mental illnesses, they only recycle into costly institutional care in psychiatric and medical hospitals, and jails. They also become homeless and they not infrequently die. This lack of care is expensive in financial and human costs. The financial costs are troubling because limited resources are wasted. That is, they are spent in expensive programs that do not serve to ameliorate any of the problems that caused the need for the expensive services, nor do they help clients live more effectively in the community. The human costs are troubling because unnecessary suffering is compounded, both for the clients and for those who care about them.

This is a long way of saying that it is imperative that case managers be willing to take on the needs of these clients. Difficult behaviors must not exclude clients from care. Attempts must be made both to understand these behaviors and to develop strategies to treat clients in spite of them. This willingness to serve clients must continue indefinitely, as long as the client does not actively refuse care.

Acceptance is required for staff to continue being willing to provide services. Acceptance does not mean that staff must approve of client behaviors. Rather it implies that they must try to find a way to understand all clients and accept them into care. This is a population that must be seen as legitimately disabled and deserving of the best efforts to help them.

Culturally Competent

Culture offers one way to provide understanding. Culture provides a collective framework through which people interpret and understand their world. Culture is partly determinative of the way people behave, partly determinative of the way people feel, and partly determinative of the way people think. Culture, therefore, must be of great interest and concern to mental health professionals who are specifically working with patterns of behavior, feelings, and thinking.

For a case manager this requires that assessment and care be provided from a cultural context. This involves understanding the client's culture and using this understanding of cultural norms and values to support treatment. Therefore, an assessment of a client is incomplete unless it includes an understanding of the client and the client's illness from a cultural perspective. In developing a service plan the client's cultural heritage must be seen as a strength to be both supported and built upon.

There is an argument to be made that care is best provided by clinicians who are from the same cultural background as the client. Certainly, clients are more likely to engage with staff who they perceive as similar to themselves. It is also more likely that a same-culture clinician will be able to correctly identify cultural traits and not pathologize strengths. Nevertheless, most clinicians, regardless of their ethnicity, will, at some time, work with clients from ethnic backgrounds different from their own. This requires that all clinicians become culturally competent. Cultural competence means coming to understand the cultural values and norms of one's clients, and knowing when to obtain consultation to learn more about how these cultural values may be relevant to the treatment of specific clients. It also means understanding one's own cultural values and norms so that they can be set aside when assessing and intervening with a client from another background, thereby not imposing them on the client. Finally, it means supporting the client's culture as a strength and using it to enhance care and treatment.

Resourceful

Mentally ill individuals cannot depend solely on the formal human service system to meet their needs in the community. Not only will there never be sufficient human services to meet human needs, but organized services are often not the best way for those with mental illness to receive the support they require.

Being resourceful means utilizing all of the resources of the community to implement a service plan. This does include the formal service system, but it also includes family, others who care about the client, religious organizations, cultural affiliations, local businesses, landlords, parks, tourist attractions, the climate, and any other resource, feature, or quality of the community that can further the clients' goals.

A major resource to many clients is their families. For the purposes of this discussion, family is defined very broadly to include anyone who cares for the client, but it is emphasized that blood and marital relationships can be a profoundly helpful resource.

However, families often experience a great burden by having a seriously mentally ill family member (Hatfield, 1978). Consequently, families often require considerable support so that they can, in turn, support the client. This support can include education about mental illnesses and their treatment, information about available resources and how to use them, consultation on handling difficult behaviors, mobilization of resources during a crisis, encouragement for them to achieve their own goals, genuine empathy for their own plight, respite from providing continuous care, and hope that the mentally ill family member can improve. With sufficient support, family can be an excellent ally in serving the client. The support, of the family might make it possible to reduce the direct involvement of a case manager, but more important, family can often provide stronger, longer, and more comprehensive support than any service provider can.

Family is only one resource in the community. It has been suggested that case managers view the community as an oasis of resources for the clients (Rapp, 1992). Simply, this means that there are many opportunities within the natural resources of the community. It is a case manager's role to bring the client and these resources together, through a variety of strategies, both to help the clients avail themselves of the resources and to prepare the resources to be accepting of the client.

Comprehensive care implies that a case manager is responsible for assuring that anything that needs to be done for a client will be done. Being resourceful means that a case manager will not do anything that someone else can and will do for the client.

Participatory

Case management is not done to clients or done for clients; rather, it is done with clients. Indeed, the clients must participate in the process for it to be meaningful. This involves including clients in both developing and implementing the service plan. Which services will be offered, how they will be offered, and when they will be offered are as much the client's decisions as they are the case manager's.

Client participation also means that clients will be expected to do all that they can for themselves in meeting their needs. Taking over for clients when they can manage on their own undermines self-esteem, breeds unnecessary dependence, and reduces clients' reliance on their own strengths. Rather, one aspect of participation is to support clients' strengths and work to empower them to pursue their own goals.

Participation is usually possible, even when involuntary treatment is necessary. At this time the case manager can work closely with the client to explain what is occurring and why, and to give the client those options that are available. In addition, there are always aspects of involuntary treatment in which the client can make decisions. These may include where the treatment is to be provided, which medications will be used and how, what other resources will be utilized, and where the client will be discharged. It is helpful to give the clients as much control over as many decisions as possible.

It should be noted that it is just as important not to give the client the sense that the process is participatory when it is not. There are times that case managers must make decisions on behalf of the clients, because of safety needs or legal requirements, when the clients are not capable of making decisions on their own. It is useful to make clear at the outset of treatment these responsibilities of the case manager and the circumstances when the client's wishes must be overridden.

Participation also includes enjoining the client's family, other human service providers, and community resources in caring for the client. Again, the process for including these resources is not completely determined either by the case manager or by the client. Rather, those providing support must also participate in the process of determining what they can offer, what they wish to offer, and the expectations they have of the client and the case manager in order to provide the support.

Accessible

Care and treatment of serious mental illness can be effective only if the clients reach it, or if it reaches the clients. Accessibility, for the purposes of this discussion, is defined in physical, cultural, linguistic, and psychological terms.

In the simplest sense, accessibility means that case management services must be located where clients can get to them. Case managers are best located in the communities and neighborhoods where clients live. It is also helpful if case management and other services are on or near public transportation routes.

Physical accessibility also involves providing services in the community whenever this will best serve the clients. This means that case managers must be able and willing to go where the clients are when the clients are unable or unwilling to go where care is provided. There are also a number of circumstances when care and treatment are best provided in the clients' homes or other community settings. As examples, a client may be too frightened from paranoia to leave home; or the case manager may need to assess the client's home situation to determine if the client can meet basic survival needs; or the client may need help and support at the Social Security office to apply for entitlements; or the client may be more comfortable meeting in a coffee shop or park than in the office. In all of these situations, and many others, the case manager must provide care where it is needed and is likely to be most effective.

Cultural accessibility also has several aspects. It involves supporting the client's cultural values and norms to assist in engagement and development of ongoing treatment. As mentioned above, this requires staff who represent the cultural backgrounds of the clients, and staff who are trained and experienced in working cross-culturally with clients. In recent years a number of mental health services have developed programs that focus on providing treatment for particular ethnic minorities or other special need populations. In these settings in-depth cultural programming can be developed (Lu, 1987).

Linguistic accessibility is one aspect of cultural accessibility. Obviously, it is necessary to provide care in a language the client can speak. In many cases it is best to provide care in the client's native language, even though the client might have a good grasp of English, because many emotional issues are best explored in the client's native language. In the case described in the Epilogue (Chapter 15) of this book, the use of both English and Spanish was useful in providing different aspects of care. Therefore, it is necessary that case managers who are working with clients who do not speak English or who have a primary language other than English be fluent in both the client's primary language and English.

Psychological accessibility involves using a human relationship to provide treatment that is meaningful and relevant so that the client can accept it. This requires responding to the client's goals and wishes, as well as developing trust, so that the client can understand and accept care for needs that the case manager identifies. It also involves the ability to explore and intervene with psychological needs when the client is able to work on these issues.

Summary

All of the principles described here represent ideals. Therefore, they can never be fully achieved. Nevertheless, as a whole, they represent a way to approach care and a way to approach mentally ill clients in offering and implementing care.

It is clear that implementing care in keeping with these principles requires considerable knowledge and skills. It requires knowledge of mental illness and how to treat it, knowledge of human behavior and how to influence it, knowledge of culture and how to support it, knowledge of families and how to involve them, and knowledge of community resources and how to use them.

Some of the skills required include the ability to engage clients in trusting and helpful relationships, to motivate clients toward growth, and to determine when to provide active help and when to allow clients to venture forth on their own. In addition to skills required with the clients, there are equally important skills required to develop and utilize the community resources that could be available to the client.

The following chapters describe the implementation of these principles in providing care to clients with serious mental illness. The intent is to provide a practical discussion that will be helpful to mental health professionals and others who are striving to effectively serve this population. The first section focuses on themes that underlie the treatment of this population. These include defining and utilizing clinical interventions, the role of culture in providing care, and developing a partnership with clients' families and natural support systems. The second section describes in detail the traditional activities of case management—comprehensive assessment, treatment planning, linkage, monitoring, and advocacy—in a manner that is consistent with this approach to care. The third section responds to a variety of treatment issues that impinge on the care of mentally ill individuals. These include the treatment of mentally ill substance abusers and personality disordered clients, the management of difficult behaviors, and the perspective of the psychiatrist. The third section also includes methods to support clients in achieving their goals and dreams, a discussion of value conflicts that can impede care, and a description of the organizational requirements for implementing a case management program. Finally, the Epilogue is a case study that illustrates the principles and approaches described throughout the book.

This approach to care has been derived from more than a decade of experience in working with clients who have had multiple psychiatric hospitalizations in San Francisco, California. It is offered here to assist case managers in developing services that improve the lives of their clients while enjoying challenging and rewarding careers.

References

Bachrach, L. L. (1978). A conceptual approach to deinstitutionalization. *Hospital and Community Psychiatry, 29*, 573-578.

Bachrach, L. L. (1981). Continuity of care for chronic mental health patients: A conceptual analysis. *American Journal of Psychiatry, 138*, 1449-1456.

Bachrach, L. L. (1992). Case management revisited. *Hospital and Community Psychiatry, 43*(3), 209-210.

Campbell, J., & Schraiber, R. (1989). *The well-being project: Mental health clients speak for themselves. Pursuit of wellness: Vol. 6.* Sacramento, CA: The California Network of Mental Health Clients.

Goldfinger, S. M., Hopkin, J. T., & Surber, R. W. (1984). Treatment resisters or system resisters?: Toward a better service system for acute care recidivists. In B. Pepper & H. Ryglewicz

(Eds.), *New directions for mental health services: Advances in treating the young adult chronic patient* (pp. 17-27). San Francisco: Jossey-Bass.

Hatfield, A. B. (1978). Psychological costs of schizophrenia to the family. *Social Work, 23*(5), 355-359.

Lu, F. G. (1987). Culturally relevant inpatient care for minority and ethnic patients. *Hospital and Community Psychiatry, 38,* 1216-1217.

Perlman, H. H. (1986). Presentation at National Association of Social Work Annual Meeting, San Francisco, CA.

Rapp, C. A. (1992). The strengths perspective of care management with persons suffering from severe mental illness. In D. Saleesby (Ed.), *The strengths model of social work practice: Power in the people* (pp. 445-458). New York: Longman.

Turner, J. A., TenHoor, W. J., & Schiffren, I. (1979). The NIMH community support program: Pilot approach to needed social reform. *Schizophrenia Bulletin, 4*(3), 319-348.

Watson, M. A. (1983a). *Chronic schizophrenics: A heterogeneous population.* Unpublished manuscript.

Watson, M. A. (1983b). *The working relationship in social work service to the chronically mentally ill.* Unpublished manuscript.

Watson, M. A. (1987). *Working therapeutically with chronically mentally ill adults.* Keynote presentation for Conference on Treating the Severely Mentally Ill, Division of Mental Health Substance Abuse and Forensic Services, Department of Public Health, San Francisco, CA.

2

Clinical Case Management

EVELYN F. BALANCIO

Deinstitutionalization began in the 1960s after mental health professionals and social reformers became aware of the iatrogenic effects of institutionalization. This was shortly after medications to treat psychotic symptoms were discovered. There have been many efforts since to find effective treatments and service delivery models that will help severely mentally ill individuals to live successfully in the community. Studies have investigated the interactive effects of medications and psychosocial treatments in reducing hospitalizations, in improving functioning, and in enhancing the participation of clients in the community (Hogarty, Solomon, & Schooler, 1974; Marx, Test, & Stein, 1973; Stein, Test, & Marx, 1975). All of them have contributed to the present-day understanding of community-based treatments for individuals with severe mental illness. Many conceptualizations and approaches have gradually emerged—biological treatments, social skills training, family treatments, support systems development, behavioral and cognitive interventions, psychotherapeutic models, and rehabilitation programs—all of which benefit clients as they experience debilitating symptoms, as they react to having a mental illness, and as society reacts to them.

A significant number of clients, however, continue to go through the revolving doors of psychiatric emergency rooms and inpatient wards. Many are unable to utilize existing community services as they are provided. Many are unable to maintain stable lives in the community, where they face tremendous stressors and risks of homelessness, victimization, problems with the law, and further estrangement from their families and community.

Fierce debates continue within ideological, theoretical, and practice realms in an effort to understand what could be effective community-based care for severely mentally ill clients. There are four general problems in serving this population:

1. There is a lack of integration of knowledge and approaches on the treatment of severely mentally ill clients.
2. The organization, administration, and delivery of mental health and human services are fragmented. Programs are specialized and disconnected from one another. The lack of integration of programs within a system makes it difficult to address the complex needs of severely mentally ill individuals with multiple problems.
3. The academic preparation of mental health practitioners seldom addresses how clinical practice is affected by the health economy, health policy, and administrative systems. A clinician who treats a client with multiple needs, deals with difficult countertransference reactions, and has to provide care within a limited and fragmented mental health system often becomes overwhelmed by what can and cannot be done. To provide effective care to a difficult clientele within a complex human services system requires a knowledge and skills base that includes both clinical and resource management considerations.
4. The ever-changing political and economic factors affecting public health in general, and mental health in particular, indicate society's ambivalent commitment to serving severely mentally ill clients. In the face of economic and political constraints, funding for human services is generally the first to get cut. The resulting reduction of resources, higher clinician/client ratio, higher productivity expectations, and increased clinical and administrative documentation can dilute the quality of care.

In response to these issues, case management emerged in the 1970s. The case management concept was mainly used in mental health administration and planning in the attempts to organize and integrate services. The components of case management—comprehensive assessment, continuity of services, planning, linkage, monitoring, advocacy, and resource development—were articulated as activities for services coordination. Case management was not considered treatment, but was seen as an adjunctive service. A case manager was a broker of services, not a treatment provider (Intagliata & Baker, 1983). The brokerage model of case management describes activities or interventions directed to a client's environment. While these activities are important in service delivery, the brokerage model is focused on systematizing services and is impersonal. It understates the unique, complex needs of a client for whom services are being coordinated. It overlooks the importance of the case manager/client relationship, where service provision includes a therapeutic dimension. Case management then evolved to include clinical and therapeutic considerations. The clinical case management model articulates the therapeutic activities directed to the client and the client-in-the-environment. It includes treating a client's symptoms or addressing a client's psychological difficulties that inhibit optimal functioning and social participation. It also includes intervening in the client's environment when real impairments compromise a client's ability to independently obtain what is needed from the environment. A clinical case manager uses clinical skills in dealing with a client and uses brokering or resource management skills in dealing with the client's environment. Clinical case management integrates treatment with coordination of services. The brokerage model is incorporated within the clinical case management model.

Defining Clinical Case Management

Clinical case management, as an approach to care, has been generally described in Chapter 1 as a process defined by a conceptualization of mental illness and treatment and by a set of principles for implementing care. It acknowledges the heterogeneity of clients who each experience their illness in a unique manner, and it calls for a broad definition of what is therapeutic. Such acknowledgments require no less than an individualized approach, where a client's comprehensive needs are taken into consideration and where treatment is participatory for it to be meaningful and effective. Specifically, clinical case management can be defined as a process of providing comprehensive treatment to individuals with severe mental illness who, either at some stage of their illness or over a long period of time, are unable to function autonomously. It is a treatment modality that integrates psychological treatment, medication, psychosocial rehabilitation, and environmental support (Kanter, 1989). All interventions are based on clinical assessments of the individual's strengths, vulnerabilities, impairments, capacity for growth, and external resources. All interventions are effected within the context of a therapeutic relationship.

An individual's adaptive functioning involves the interaction of internal and external processes. A comprehensive assessment that integrates the psychological, biological, psychosocial, and environmental factors affecting the individual, as well as an understanding of the dynamic interplay of all these factors, is essential. Comprehensive assessments and dynamic formulations are continuous throughout the process of treatment—as clients improve or decompensate, as they are confronted with predictable and unpredictable stressors, as they maintain their lives in the community, as they show increasing capacities for growth, and as they go through maturational changes.

Psychological Treatment

An understanding of a client's psychological makeup informs a clinical case manager's decisions on what therapeutic stance to take or what intervention to apply. Even the most concrete of interventions (e.g., helping a client find housing) is guided by clinical information. It is important to have a working hypothesis on what psychological factors may be operating underneath a client's behaviors. Although psychological explorations are not possible or appropriate for those who are disorganized, psychotic, or anxious, information can be obtained from records, and much can be inferred from observations of behaviors and transference and countertransference reactions.

Major Impairments of Severely Mentally Ill Clients

Regardless of theoretical orientation, there is agreement that clients with severe mental illness often have major difficulties in forming attachments and have compromised capacities for functional adaptation. From an ego psychology perspective, clients with severe mental illness are often unable to develop or maintain ego boundaries. The lack of ego boundaries affects identity formation, capacity for attachments or relationships, and ability to differentiate internal from external states. The maturation of thought processes is likewise often affected. Secondary process thinking that is reality-oriented, logical, organized, and goal-directed may not be well developed. Primary process thinking that is illogical, contradictory, fantasy-filled, and confusing frequently dominates and is manifested in the way a severely mentally ill client communicates. Other ego functions, such as judgment, regulation and control of drives, affects and impulses, capacity to protect the self (defenses), stimulus modulation, autonomy, mastery, and synthesis, are also affected in varying degrees (Goldstein, 1984, pp. 43-84). However, regardless of the degree of impairment, there is always an intact part of the ego that can be engaged in treatment (Lamb, 1982, pp. 121-122).

The Therapeutic Relationship

Establishing an affective connection, engagement in treatment, and maintenance of a stable relationship throughout the course of treatment are crucial and difficult tasks in working with severely mentally ill clients (Harris & Bergman, 1988). It is difficult because clients often feel a deep sense of isolation and are fearful of relationships. Without a relationship, case management interventions can become ineffective and meaningless to clients. At worst, clients can feel intruded upon, increasing their fears and driving them deeper into their isolation.

The importance of having a positive connection with a client is emphasized by many authors, especially from the object relations approach. It is considered that a positive connection is therapeutic in itself. Improvements in the capacity to bond facilitate adaptation. The relationship becomes the "sustaining link" between a client and an external world that is often experienced as confusing and chaotic (Munich, 1987). It allows for identification and internalization to occur, processes that help a client form a sense of self (Harris & Bergman, 1987). These processes also help a client learn ways of handling problems through the role modeling of a clinical case manager. Winnicott (1965) describes the therapeutic relationship as a "holding environment" where a client is provided with a sense of trust and a sense of safety that anxieties are understood.

Difficulties in Communication

A client with severe mental illness often communicates in a fragmented, illogical, fantasy-filled manner because of disruptions in secondary thought processes. Thoughts or feelings may not be clearly communicated to others because they may not be a part of the client's awareness. These illogical thoughts, delusions, hallucinations, and bizarre behaviors, however, are reactions to stimuli or experiences that are real to the client. These reactions, no matter how incomprehensible, are attended to by a clinical case manager in a manner that does not encourage more fantasy but addresses the source of the anxiety. A clinical case manager listens empathically for the meaning behind a client's fragmented thoughts. The approach is supportive, focusing on the here and now. Past events may be used to understand the present and may be explored to identify other ways by which a client might cope with stressful situations. A clinical case manager contains a client's chaotic thoughts and deep anxieties. This successful containment provides the client with an ego corrective experience in trust and safety, and increases tolerance for closeness.

Ambivalence About Relationships

Clients with severe mental illness are often ambivalent about relationships. Depending on the disruption of ego functions, they may simultaneously have a deep sense of isolation and profound dependency needs. Burnham (1969) best describes this ambivalence with the concept of the *need-fear dilemma*: "the need for an object from which to borrow ego strength, and the fear of the same object because of its threat to ego organization." Some common examples of this dilemma encountered by clinical case managers are:

1. A client may be very disorganized, but if the clinical case manager gives structure, the client may experience this as a threat to autonomy.
2. A client may be helpless, but if the clinical case manager gives direct help, the client may feel incompetent.
3. A client may have poor impulse control, but if the clinical case manager sets limits, the client may experience this as punitive and rejecting.

These dilemmas need to be understood as part of the illness and dealt with therapeutically. If they are seen as lack of either motivation or interest in treatment, the therapeutic relationship may fail.

Helping Clients Manage Their Illness

During more stable periods, a clinical case manager teaches the client how to manage the symptoms of the illness, how to cope with the client's and others' reactions to the illness, and how to adjust to the social environment. The clinical case manager assists the client in making informed decisions regarding the use of medications. The client is helped to recognize stressful events, to identify ensuing feelings, and to recognize signals— "red flags"—that the client may be losing control. The case manager also helps the client learn to directly communicate distress in the best possible way, as well as help identify people and places where support and help could be sought. Harmful behaviors are identified and discouraged.

The process of helping a client gain mastery over the illness and the environment does not happen in a mechanical manner. Neither does it happen by merely giving rote lectures on "how to." The learning occurs within an empathic, nurturing environment, where a clinical case manager imparts objective knowledge in a manner that is meaningful to the client, and at a time when the client is prepared to receive it. The teaching-learning interaction is unique to the relationship of the clinical case manager and the client. It is an interaction that addresses not only cognitions, but also the affects, ambivalence, impairments, and growing capacities of a particular client.

A Note on Countertransference

Working with a severely mentally ill client often evokes strong feelings and reactions or countertransference in a clinical case manager. In a therapeutic relationship, a case manager's awareness of these feelings or countertransference is just as important as the awareness of the client's difficulties. Countertransference reactions may stem from a case manager's unresolved conflicts around issues presented by a client. If these conflicts are not acknowledged as one's own, a case manager may become judgmental, may displace feelings toward the client, or may become subtly punitive toward the client. Countertransference may also be due to a client's behaviors that elicit reactions in the case manager that are similar to those of the client's early caregivers. If recognized as such, these reactions could be used in further understanding the client, and could therefore inform the case manager's choices of effective interventions. Culturally derived differences between case manager and client may often account for countertransference reactions. Differences in ethnicity, race, gender, class— variables that shape one's worldview and manner of being and relating —are often overlooked. The failure to examine cultural assumptions (both the case manager's and the client's) in assessment and treatment can constrain engagement or cause the client to withdraw. Cultural factors in treatment will be discussed further in Chapter 3.

The Use of Medications

The discovery of medications to treat psychotic symptoms, and the advancements in psychosocial treatments, made it possible for clients with long-term illness to return to their communities. Medications alone are often not enough to maintain clients in the community, but, in combination with psychosocial treatments, can be more effective in reducing relapses and hospitalizations. Current thinking around the causes of mental illness includes biochemical imbalances that can be treated by medications.

While medications are known to have positive effects on managing symptoms and decreasing relapses, they are also known to cause uncomfortable side effects. At times, these side effects are difficult to distinguish from the symptoms of the illness, making treatment more complicated. The long-term use of antipsychotic medications could also cause tardive dyskinesia, a serious neurological condition (Strauss & Carpenter, 1981, pp. 182-190). Side effects must be closely monitored so that necessary changes in medication regimens can be made to decrease their negative effects.

A clinical case manager works in tandem with the psychiatrist regarding the client's medications. Periodic consultations with the psychiatrist ensure coordination of treatment. Although usually a nonmedical practitioner, a clinical case manager integrates medications in the treatment plan and discusses the effects of pharmacological treatment.

Psychiatric medications, their therapeutic ranges, the symptoms they target, and their common side effects must be part of a clinical case manager's knowledge. It is important to know the client's medications and how the client is responding to them. Generally speaking, a clinical case manager sees the client more often than the psychiatrist does. Giving the psychiatrist information on the client's psychological and social functioning, current and impending stressors, observable side effects, and sudden changes in mental status can be useful in decisions related to changes in medication dosages.

A client must be given information about medications, their effects and side effects. A clinical case manager is open to discussing medication compliance and is interested in knowing the client's beliefs and attitudes about medications. Discussions of beliefs and attitudes about medications are particularly important with clients of different cultural backgrounds, because other cultures may have different views about mental illness, its causes, and its cure.

A clinical case manager is also sensitive to what the medications may mean symbolically to a client. Issues of control, dependency, acceptance or denial of mental illness, and feelings of dehumanization are common examples of issues that arise. These issues are approached therapeutically. It is useful to inform the psychiatrist about these issues so that medications can be discussed and given in contexts that are meaningful to the client.

Special attention must be paid to the effects of medications on pregnant women, on clients who have other medical problems, and on clients who are substance abusers. Further discussion of medication issues is found in Chapter 11.

Psychosocial Rehabilitation and the Development of Environmental Supports

As mentioned earlier, the comprehensive treatment approach of clinical case management focuses on the client and the client-in-the-environment. The reduction of a client's debilitating symptoms, maintenance of psychiatric stability, and improved psychological well-being free a client's potentials in acquiring skills for living a better quality of life. The general therapeutic stance of a clinical case manager is directed toward supporting a client's adaptive functioning and mastery of the environment. It is in relationships and in the client's natural environment where adaptive functioning is both nurtured and tested. The learning of independent living skills and community living skills, and the development of a social support system, are crucial in a client's process of growth and mastery. The psychosocial rehabilitation aspect of clinical case management focuses on skill building and the development of a client's social/environmental supports (Anthony, 1988). Psychosocial rehabilitation is concerned with the reentry, reintegration, and participation of a client in the community.

A clinical case manager works with a client in the clinic, in the client's home, and in the community. Working in the community gives a direct picture of both how a client reacts and functions in the environment and how the environment reacts to the client. Work outside the clinic is focused on providing in vivo training in independent and community living skills, and in helping the client develop a social support system. The appropriate type and intensity of intervention and training depend upon the client's goals, guided by the clinical case manager's assessments. For example, a case manager taught a mental health client with developmental disability how to use public transportation. The case manager actually took bus rides with the client and showed the client where to wait for the bus and where to get off. After several bus rides with the case manager, the client learned how to take the bus alone from home, to the clinic and back. Another client who was functioning at a higher level was taught how to utilize public transportation using a transit map. Unlike with the former client, it was not necessary for the case manager to actually take bus rides with this client.

Utilizing Formal Psychosocial Rehabilitation Programs

There is an array of formal programs that specialize in rehabilitation and related services. They range from day treatment programs, socialization programs, and clubhouses to vocational rehabilitation agencies, volunteer bureaus, and community colleges. Many residential treatment facilities also operate with psychosocial rehabilitation philosophies. In some communities there are now specialized vocational programs for mental health clients that operate small businesses where clients receive on-the-job training in areas such as food preparation, janitorial skills, or clerical skills.

All of these programs provide valuable services to clients and are important community resources. A clinical case manager encourages the client to use these programs, and an individualized plan can be made to gradually move a client through the spectrum of services, depending on the client's interests, goals, and growing capacities. For example, a client may start with a socialization program, move to a day treatment program after 6 months, and transition to a volunteer job after one year of day treatment. Another client may have the interest and capability to hold a volunteer job after 3 months of day treatment. Another client may be able to attend classes at a community college instead of a day treatment program.

A familiarity with the expectations of such programs is important so that an appropriate match between client and program can be made. Finding an appropriate match is important so that the client is "set up" to succeed. Other treatment or service providers involved with the client participate in developing a coordinated treatment plan through periodic case conferences. Although each service provider has a specific focus in the client's coordinated treatment plan, each should know what others are doing to avoid both a duplication of services and working across one another's purposes. A duplication of services, aside from wasting resources, can confuse the client. Working across one another's purposes can create tensions among workers, causing the client to be at risk for absorbing the tensions and for receiving compromised care. The clinical case manager remains the primary therapist (Lamb, 1980), and is ultimately responsible for the treatment plan. This is because the case manager maintains a long-term relationship, which continues regardless of the other services a client may utilize. The relationship of a client with a halfway house counselor or a day treatment counselor ends when the client leaves the program. The client's relationship with the case manager continues.

Although a client may be receiving formal rehabilitation services from another agency, skills taught in a structured setting may not generalize to practical life. The clinical case manager provides in vivo training in the client's natural environment. Independent living skills like doing laundry, budgeting, grocery shopping, and cooking meals are taught by a clinical case manager in varying degrees of involvement, depending on the client's clinical circumstances. It must be underscored that the goal is *to teach* the client, not *to do* for the client. Even a concrete task of helping a client shop for groceries is informed by a sound clinical assessment. Regardless of good intentions, any intervention that is not given clinical thought could be countertherapeutic. For example, a client with a severe borderline personality disorder was experiencing paranoid feelings. He had not left his apartment for 3 days and had just run out of food. His brother, who accompanies him to the store at times of difficulty, was out of town. The client was feeling increasingly more anxious and paranoid, and no verbal intervention was helping him mobilize to attend to his grocery shopping. It was clinically appropriate to help the client with his grocery shopping at that time. Two months later he was functioning at baseline, was not paranoid, but was asking for assistance in grocery shopping. He felt entitled to his case manager's assistance. Helping him directly with grocery shopping at this time might have been clinically inappropriate because this would have been a collusion with his entitlement and narcissistic issues. An appropriate intervention might be to explore his feelings for wanting such assistance when he is able to do the task on his own. Addressing his sense of competence and autonomy will be ego fostering.

Utilizing Informal Resources for Psychosocial Rehabilitation

Many clients benefit from existing formal rehabilitation programs. However, there are also many who are unable to use them because of stringent program expectations or because they do not have the tolerance to be around other people. Many clients are so isolated that the only contact they have is with their case managers. These clients require intensive work in the community. With the client's consent, the clinical case manager works to develop an informal support system for the client and teaches the client how to use it. This demands creativity, resourcefulness, and community organizing skills in addition to clinical skills. An informal support system may include a friendly restaurant manager and a grocer who are willing to run a tab for the client, a caring neighbor and a hotel manager who are willing to call the case manager when they see changes in the client's behavior, a pastor who notices the client in church on Sundays, the mailman, or the policeman who patrols the neighborhood who can be watchful of the client's needs.

The following example shows how informal support from the community can be helpful. A client who had difficulty budgeting her money usually found herself without any means to provide for food during the last week of every month. She would become very anxious and in the past year had been hospitalized for grave disability because of this problem. The client and her case manager had worked on her budget several times, but the client was not organized enough to stay within budget. She wished to be more efficient with her money in order to avoid worrying about food toward the end of every month. She was willing to try other solutions to the problem. The case manager and the client found a restaurant in the neighborhood where the owner was willing to give the client dinner of a specified amount every day. The restaurant bill was paid on the first day of every month, when the client received her check. The client initially had to adjust to having less cash to handle, but liked not having to worry about being hungry.

Developing an informal support system includes giving members of the support system information on mental illness, clarifying common misconceptions about mental illness, and recommending ways of interacting with a particular client. A clinical case manager bridges a relationship between the client and the community. Throughout this process, the clinical case manager gets the client's permission, is sensitive to the client's reactions, and makes sure that this is not experienced by the client as intrusive, controlling, or infantilizing. Likewise, through the process, the clinical case manager maintains an awareness of countertransference reactions that may negatively affect the client. For example, a lack of awareness of one's rescue fantasies may lead a case manager to do more than what the client needs, reinforcing the client's feelings of helplessness and incompetence. A case manager who is fearful of others' dependencies and is not aware of it might inadvertently reject or abandon a client possibly in need of critical help.

Psychosocial rehabilitation attempts to increase the participation of clients in the community, and reciprocally attempts to increase the community's willingness to accept individuals with mental illness as members of the community. There is research evidence that community acceptance affects the course of mental illness. In an international pilot study on the role of individuals with schizophrenia in society, Carpenter and his colleagues found that in developing countries (Nigeria, India, and Colombia), patients with schizophrenia tended to have a more benign course of illness compared to those in developed countries (Denmark, United States, Soviet Union, England, and Czechoslovakia). Carpenter says, "In general, cultures that were more socio-centric provided a more supportive, less demanding ambiance. So someone with schizophrenia was not put in such a disadvantage as in more egocentric countries where there's such a focus on accomplishment" (Worthington, 1992, p. 3).

To increase community participation, a clinical case manager develops resources outside the mental health system—church-sponsored social activities, neighborhood recreation groups, activities in parks, cultural groups, and ethnic organizations. Encouraging clients to use resources outside the mental health system prevents unnecessary dependency on the system, and provides opportunities for participation in "normal" activities and settings. For example, an athletically inclined client who attended day treatment daily wished to play basketball on a regular basis, but basketball was not one of the activities offered at the center. The client had mentioned that there was a basketball court in his neighborhood where residents played about twice a week. Anyone who happened to be there on a given afternoon could play. The client had watched many games and felt that he could play just as well as the others, but never participated because he was afraid he would not be welcome. The case manager first helped the client overcome his fear of not being accepted by the players and continually encouraged him to participate. The client started to participate and actually was easily accepted by the others. The client currently plays basketball regularly and has made a couple of friends among the neighborhood players. He has decreased his day treatment attendance to half-time to be able to participate in the neighborhood games regularly.

A growing resource for psychosocial rehabilitation is self-help groups. Self-determination and empowerment are the underlying values of self-help, values that are consistent with the client-centered approach of clinical case management. The availability of mutual support in independent living through self-help enhances the viability of clients' having meaningful relationships and community participation. A clinical case manager works with self-help groups and supports the empowering effects of individuals with mental illness supporting each other.

In recent years several mental health programs have included consumers of mental health services as providers of care. They work as volunteer peer counselors or are hired as part of the program staff. Hired consumers function as case management aides (Sherman & Porter, 1991) or as peer case managers (Balancio et al., 1992). To clients, peer case managers serve as role models, provide assistance in independent living skills, and provide help in identifying community resources. Within an interdisciplinary program staff, peer case managers represent a consumer perspective in discussions around treatment issues. In their roles, peer case managers help strengthen the engagement of clients in treatment by helping bridge empathy gaps that may exist between professionals and clients.

Working With Clients' Primary Support System

Families continue to be the primary support system for most clients. The thinking on the role of families in the lives of severely mentally ill individuals has dramatically changed from "causing the illness" to being "allies in treatment." There have also been increased efforts among treatment providers to give support to families of mentally ill individuals. As life-styles change, the definition of "family" beyond the traditional nuclear family is also being given significant attention. Chapter 4 will discuss the importance of working with families and natural support systems in case management.

A Case Example: Sam

The following case illustrates the integration of the psychological, biological, psychosocial, and environmental interventions described in this chapter.

Sam is a 43-year-old Caucasian male, with a seventh-grade education, who receives public entitlements and lives alone in a hotel. He has not had contact with his family of origin since age 19 and has been separated from his wife and son for 17 years. He was referred for clinical case management services by a hospital after a serious suicide attempt, where he cut his wrists and his neck. The attempt happened after he was robbed of all his money for that month. He was drunk when he did it.

Sam is well known in the community mental health system. Prior to his referral, he had 26 psychiatric emergency contacts within a period of 12 months and numerous psychiatric hospitalizations, mostly due to psychotic symptoms, depression, and suicide attempts. He was not welcome in two outpatient clinics and a day treatment center because of provocative and verbally abusive behavior and a concomitant alcohol problem. He was considered a serious problem in the mental health system and had a reputation as someone whose needs just could not be met. Treaters who had worked with him in the past commented on their feelings of helplessness while working with him. They thought that Sam's psychiatric problems, severe interpersonal difficulties, and alcohol problem would eventually lead to his being killed, or that it was only a matter of time before he would successfully kill himself.

Sam has a history of refusing medications and not following through with outpatient treatment referrals. Upon referral by a hospital social worker, a case manager went to the hospital to meet Sam and start engaging him in treatment. The case manager had feelings of fear and felt that she had been dumped upon by the system. She wondered how she could work with a client whom the system had already grieved.

Sam was first seen in the inpatient ward. He was a disheveled, long-haired man who looked much older than his age. He greeted the case manager quietly, anxiously rocked himself throughout the meeting, did not look at her, and rambled about how depressed he was about his life and angry about the world in general. He was not specific about why he was depressed. He stated that this world bored him, and society made him angry. He admitted to hearing voices often and being paranoid most of the time. Even though he was slightly incoherent, his intelligence was apparent. He admitted to being alcoholic and having been through detox several times. He said he had given up on self-help groups because he ends up arguing with others and is eventually thrown out of meetings. He made it clear during the first meeting that he was not interested in talking about his past, but that the case manager was free to read his past treatment records. Sam said he had been in psychiatric hospitals and in mental health treatment even before he became alcoholic.

The case manager proceeded to tell him about the case management program and expressed her availability to work with him. He was cynical about what she could really do for him, and derisively commented that she looked like she wouldn't understand the culture of the streets. She restated her availability and acknowledged that she would not do things for him but would work with him, if he would give it a chance. He tentatively agreed to work with her and gave her permission to work closely with the hospital social worker around discharge plans.

Sam's discharge medication was Haldol 10 mg. *bid*, and Cogentin 1 mg. *bid*. He was discharged to a hotel with 2 weeks' temporary housing and a 10-day supply of medication. Given his many crisis presentations, the case manager arranged for a closer coordination with the psychiatric emergency services. They would inform her of Sam's emergency contacts, and she would inform them when she sensed a high probability that he would show up in crisis.

Sam did not show up for his first clinic appointment and did not return the case manager's phone calls. Knowing that he was going to run out of medications and a place to stay, she visited him at his hotel.

He said he had forgotten all about his appointment. He had been drinking almost every day since his discharge and was anxious about his money and housing. He was not feeling suicidal "yet." The case manager said she would help him with these concerns at his next appointment in the clinic the next day. He said he would make it this time, and showed mixed suspicion and appreciation for the visit.

Sam started going to the clinic. The case manager proposed a weekly visit and encouraged him to drop in whenever he felt the need. He was inconsistent with his weekly appointments, but dropped in as often as he needed—at times three times a week. The focus of the work over the first 6 months was his inability to maintain housing, his difficulties with managing his own money, and his alcohol problem. He hesitantly agreed to see a psychiatrist, did not promise to take his medications as prescribed, but promised not to harm himself. He felt that medications "stripped [him] of all emotions, even the good ones." The case manager worked closely with the psychiatrist around Sam's medication issues.

Sam's crises were almost always precipitated by not having money or not having a place to stay. He was caught in a cycle where he would spend his money on food and alcohol, then not have enough money to pay rent. He would become anxious, depressed, and confused about losing his room, would cope with his anxiety and depression by drinking more, eventually becoming paranoid and suicidal and presenting in the psychiatric emergency room.

Sam had stayed in and had been evicted from almost all of the hotels in town because he was inconsistent with rent. It was difficult for him to get a hotel room on his own. Sam mismanaged his money—spent it treating strangers he would meet on the streets to food and alcohol. He had also been robbed while drunk several times. Knowing his concerns and difficulties around these practical aspects of his life, the case manager decided to work actively with him on these problems in an effort to forge a good working alliance. She offered to help negotiate for a place to stay if he would consider a referral to a money management agency. Sam became angry and suspicious of this recommendation. He was rageful and berating in the succeeding two sessions and attempted to engage the case manager in a power struggle. He demanded immediate help but saw all alternatives presented as controlling. Through this rageful period, there were limits set around the use of abusive language. He was asked to leave the clinic several times because of inappropriate behavior, but the case manager saw to it that he always left with a card for his next appointment. She actively sought him out by phone or outreach when he missed his appointments. She arranged a meeting with a money manager to explain the service and to make it clear to Sam that the service is like a bank. After his rent is paid, he is free to make arrangements for daily, every other day, weekly, or biweekly disbursements. He could terminate with the service anytime. Sam agreed to use the service on a trial basis. The case manager continues to work closely with Sam's money manager, who not only disburses Sam's checks but also helps him with budgeting. He also encourages Sam to see the case manager when he is going through periods of feeling angry, or when he is threatened by the increasing feelings of closeness with his case manager. The money manager is a very real part of Sam's support system. Sam continues to use money management services to this day and acknowledges how helpful they have been.

It was difficult to find a hotel manager who would accept Sam. One hotel manager finally agreed to accept him, as long as rent was paid on time and as long as the case manager was willing to help out when Sam became disruptive or difficult. On his end, the hotel manager was willing to be watchful of Sam and to deliver the case manager's phone messages promptly. Sam participated in all these negotiations. He raised his objections until an acceptable plan was reached, and was able to accept responsibility. Sam stayed in this hotel for 2½ years without any major incident. He moved to another hotel with better accommodations and has been living there for about 4 years. Sam's drinking problem, the underlying anxieties that lead him to drink, and his lack of adaptive skills in coping with these anxieties were addressed gradually, simultaneously, as the case manager actively worked with him around his practical problems on housing and money management.

Around the third month of working with him, as his housing and money problems started to show hope for resolution, the case manager took a firm stance on his alcohol use. From the very start, given every opportunity, the case manager gave the opinion that Sam's judgment was completely compromised by his alcohol abuse, to the extent that he failed to manage his basic needs. He disagreed with this opinion, saying that alcohol was the only way by which he could withstand the sadness and anger in his life. He was also feeling in a bind with the recommendation that he seek alcohol treatment or use self-help groups in conjunction with his work with the case manager. He said he had attempted alcohol treatment in the past, but was not understood by others and was thrown out of meetings or groups. Capitalizing on his growing trust from the help he had been given around housing and money management, the case manager stood firm with his going to Alcoholics Anonymous. She acknowledged his real interpersonal difficulties and allowed him to leave AA meetings as soon as he started feeling irritated or angry. Ten minutes in an AA meeting were better than none. She also helped him identify AA groups that were more tolerant of people with psychiatric problems. As Sam started attending AA, she gave him education on alcohol use, the symptoms of alcohol dependence, its similarities with psychiatric symptoms, and the difficulty of differentiating which symptoms were attributed to alcohol abuse and which to psychiatric problems.

Sam made noticeable changes in his alcohol use. He started to drink less, would go without alcohol for 2 weeks, drink again, abstain for a week, drink again. His longest period of sobriety in the first year of treatment was 3 months. So far, the longest period of sobriety in the 6 years of work with the case manager is 6 months. As Sam experienced periods of sobriety, he felt less depressed, less paranoid, and slept better. What he heard about alcohol abuse from the education, he started to experience. He also became more receptive to taking his medications regularly and felt their calming effects.

Despite a decrease in his depression and paranoia due to a decrease in alcohol use, Sam's anxiety, rageful outbursts, provocativeness, impulsiveness, manipulativeness, and chaotic interpersonal relationships were always there. It was around the third month of treatment that he started to talk about his past. At the age of 5, when his parents divorced, Sam had been passed around to different caregivers—aunts, grandparents, boarding schools, foster homes. The many separations did not provide him a chance to experience a constant other, from whom he could expect consistent nurturance and with whom he could establish deep, long-lasting bonds. In his words, "Just when I'm starting to like my new home and my new friends, they were ready to send me away." Sam has deep-seated feelings that he was sent away because he was bad. The incident at age 12, when he killed a boy in a gang fight—which resulted in 6½ years of reform school with maximum security—did damage to Sam's process of identity formation. When he left reform school at the age of 19, he sought refuge in the subculture of the sixties, where the implications of his wanderings, casual and brief relationships, and drug experimentation were not put to a test. They were somehow reinforced.

Sam's alcohol problem, his narrow range of adaptive skills, and his compromised ego strengths do not allow for explorations into his past. Explorations would raise his anxieties, which could lead to further alcohol abuse. The case manager takes a supportive stance, mostly dealing with the day-to-day issues that arise, validating the anger and sadness he has about his past. The case manager reorients him cognitively to other ways he could view the many separations in his life, the gang fight, and reform school. Most important, she provides him with a safe place and a secure relationship where he can vent his fears, anger, and rage within reasonable limits. The case manager continuously learns not to be afraid of his anger, not to act out her hatred when he talks about others in a vile and hateful way, not to be exasperated when he is needy and clinging. She continues to learn to do this through her deeper understanding of him and through her clinical supervision.

Most of Sam's day-to-day problems are interpersonal. He makes friends easily and becomes oversolicitous in his effort to keep them. He expects a lot from his friends in return. At the slightest hint of rejection, he reacts so strongly that his friends will abandon him. He is left feeling used and victimized, oftentimes plunging into a depression.

Sam depends on others too much because he does not have enough in himself to depend on. One of the continuing interventions is to help him find pleasurable things he can do on his own. For example, Sam is well read in the literature of the sixties, but had not read in the past 15 years. In the past 2 years he has started to read again. He used to spend a lot of time in the park during his hippie days, had not been in the park for 8 years, but rediscovered it 2 years ago and actually finds warm and positive memories from it. Every opportunity is taken to reflect to him his growing capacity to take care of himself and his decreasing need to be defined by others. Sam has not been in a street brawl or a physical fight in more than 2 years. Unlike in the past, when Sam spent most of his days either hanging out drunk on street corners or isolated in his room, he now takes walks in quieter parts of the city and spends much time in the library.

The manner of working with Sam has changed over time. The case manager has not made a single outreach in the past 3 years, except to visit him in the psychiatric emergency room. For the past 2 years, he has been keeping his clinic appointments fairly consistently. He drops in frequently when he is feeling suicidal or when he is feeling victimized. He occasionally asks for concrete help, like a letter of endorsement for free clothes from thrift shops. His contacts with the psychiatric emergency service have decreased per year from 26, to 6, 2, 2, 1, and 1 for the past

6 years, respectively. He has not been psychiatrically hospitalized in the past 3 years. In many of his sessions, Sam talks about the books he reads, comments on current events with wit and humor, and is able to reflect on what could be the personal significance of events outside of himself. When he talks about his day-to-day interpersonal interactions that may have failed, he shows an increasing capacity to recognize what he could have done better.

Sam continues to be provocative, rageful, and manipulative, but to a lesser frequency and intensity. He is also increasingly able to control himself and actually walks away from situations that agitate him. He still gets depressed, but can be specific about its cause. He still hears voices, but is able to connect them with current stressful events in his life. He still drinks alcohol, but is able to go without for longer intervals of time.

Most recently, he has been talking more about his ambivalent desire to reconnect with his son and his estranged wife. He wonders where his sisters are and whether his father is still alive. Sam and his case manager are exploring the possible emotional gains or risks should he decide to reconnect with family. He fantasizes about the possibility of communes in these "yuppie" times. He has been looking back at his life, at times feeling he is a total failure and at times feeling it hasn't been so bad. It is becoming clearer that Sam is experiencing the maturational strains of midlife. He has made many improvements, but is still considered to be at risk as he starts to negotiate the psychological tasks of midlife.

References

Anthony, W. A. (1988). Rehabilitation programs in the 1980s: Laying the groundwork for the 1990s. In L. G. Perlman & C. E. Hansen (Eds.), *Rehabilitation of persons with long-term mental illness in the 1990s: A report of the 12th Mary E. Switzer memorial seminar* (pp. 9-17). Alexandria, VA: National Rehabilitation Association.

Balancio, E. B., Tape, A., Morales, C., Crew, R., Morgan, A., Imperiale, V., Song-Hawkins, S. H., Atkins, S., & Kelly, D. (1992). *Consumers and case managers: Partners in delivering community based mental health services.* A panel presentation at the Third Annual Case Management Training Conference of the California Case Management Council, Pacific Grove, CA.

Burnham, D. (1969). Schizophrenia and object relations. In D. Burnham, A. Gladstone, & R. Gibson (Eds.), *Schizophrenia and the need-fear dilemma* (pp. 15-41). New York: Jason Aronson.

Goldstein, E. G. (1984). *Ego psychology and social work practice.* New York: Free Press.

Harris, M., & Bergman, H. C. (1987). Case management with the chronically mentally ill: A clinical perspective. *American Journal of Orthopsychiatry, 57*(2), 296-302.

Harris, M., & Bergman, H. C. (1988). Clinical case management for the chronically mentally ill: A conceptual analysis. In M. Harris & L. L. Bachrach (Eds.), *New directions for mental health services: Clinical case management* (pp. 5-13). San Francisco: Jossey-Bass.

Hogarty, G., Solomon, G., & Schooler, N. (1974). Drug and sociotherapy in the aftercare of schizophrenic patients: Adjustment of non-relapsed patients. *Archives of General Psychiatry, 31*, 609-618.

Intagliata, J., & Baker, F. (1983). Factors influencing the delivery of community mental health services to the chronically mentally ill. *Administration and Mental Health, 11*, 73-91.

Kanter, J. S. (1989). Clinical case management: Definition, principles, components. *Hospital and Community Psychiatry, 40*(4), 361-368.

Lamb, H. R. (1980). Therapist-case managers: More than brokers of services. *Hospital and Community Psychiatry, 31*(11), 762-764.

Lamb, H. R. (1982). *Treating the long-term mentally ill.* San Francisco: Jossey-Bass.

Marx, A., Test, M., & Stein, L. (1973). Extrahospital management of severe mental illness. *Archives of General Psychiatry, 29*, 505-511.

Munich, R. L. (1987). Conceptual trends and issues in the psychotherapy of schizophrenia. *American Journal of Psychotherapy, 41*(1), 23-37.

Sherman, P. S., & Porter, R. (1991). Mental health consumers as case management aides. *Hospital and Community Psychiatry, 42*(5), 494-498.

Stein, L., Test, M., & Marx, A. (1975). Alternative to the hospital: A controlled study. *American Journal of Psychiatry, 132*, 417-422.

Strauss, J. S., & Carpenter, W. T. (1981). *Schizophrenia.* New York: Plenum.

Winnicott, D. (1965). *The maturational process and the facilitating environment.* New York: International Universities Press.

Worthington, J. F. (1992, August). Shaping schizophrenia research, portrait of William T. Carpenter, Jr., M.D. *National Alliance for Research on Schizophrenia and Depression Research Newsletter*, pp. 1-5.

3

Understanding Culture as a Process

VALERIE ROXANNE EDWARDS

There is a growing recognition that differences of culture have much broader manifestations than variance in color, class, and creed. This, as well as the increasing diversity of our society, most significantly with greater diversity among the middle and professional classes, has fueled the exploration of multicultural work. Evidence of this can be found in the business world, on college campuses, and in the social service fields, including community mental health. Despite this increased focus there is little common understanding of why and how to consider a client's culture when making assessments and providing interventions (Sue & Sue, 1990). A provider's cultural proficiency is more salient when attempting a case management approach to clinical work. Effective case management requires that clinicians not take a generic approach to providing services. Rather, they must look beyond the problems confronting clients—severe mental illness, poverty, and disorganization—to include in the treatment plan the clients' unique set of resources and the principles by which they are guided. A clinician must fully appreciate interaction with the client's support network, including family, friends, SRO hotel managers, inpatient ward staff, and others. Understanding the various worldviews and values that guide the client's orbit is essential to excellent clinical work. Effective clinical case management is reliant on awareness and appreciation of the texture and richness that culture offers human life. This chapter will present a definition of culture within the context of providing mental health services; explore ways it is expressed; and explain what is meant by cultural competence. In doing so, it will illustrate the breadth of culture as it pervades clinical work.

Culture Defined

Culture can be defined by two concepts that in sum represent the meaning of life and being. It is one's worldview; where one came from, why one is here, where one is going. It also represents the values, principles, and beliefs by which one tries to live. Thus, it guides both every giant and every minute aspect of one's behavior: rites of passage, the color of one's clothing, how one greets others, and when and how to retire for the night. When considering the magnitude of its reach it is not surprising that the extent of its significance is elusive most of the time. The effectiveness of a culture as a process for living requires that it be expressed automatically, without prejudice. Unfortunately, the flip side to this is that it also promotes unconscious prejudice against attitudes and beliefs that differ from one's own, creating the tendency to label alternative perspectives, or whole lifestyles, as bad or wrong. No wonder contacts one perceives as intercultural are often experienced as negative. Often laden with fears of either being branded a racist or sustaining a barrage of racist remarks, an individual may leave these situations angry and defeated. This only perpetuates the anxiety and denial experienced when confronted with cultural differences. However, most people also have frequent positive intercultural experiences without recognizing them as such. Adopting a different cuisine as part of the usual diet, enjoying a foreign film, developing affection for others because of their "unusual" or even "eccentric" outlook are definitely positive intercultural experiences. Once previous successes are recognized, an individual has reason to be much more optimistic about charting unfamiliar cultural waters. At worst, specific aspects of culture may be neutral, only a vestige of a practical purpose. But mostly they are an opportunity to experience the best of culture, the rich texture it brings to life and the strength that can be found in diversity. Clinicians' understanding of their own culture facilitates the use of formal support networks within their communities. Again, much of this understanding is so automatic as to be largely unconscious. Without necessarily knowing a specific agency, most urban social workers are certain services such as shelters or soup kitchens exist, based on a tacit understanding of our society's culture and its expression in governmental and community polices. Features of the culture also indicate what is not to be expected, such as perinatal care for all who need it, or equally accessible services to the disabled. But how can a clinician tap into the unique resources offered by a client's culture? A first step is to make conscious that which is unconscious about one's own culture. Though culture's permutations of expression seem limitless, the boundaries, dimensions, and codes that guide it are universal, based on the similarities found throughout human nature.

The Boundaries of Culture

There is a range of overlapping boundaries that define culture. The manner in which culture is typically understood and most broadly defined is by race or ethnicity. Rites of passage, codes of communication, ways of being, are most usually defined by nations or regions of the world. Nationality and ethnicity have the most identifiable distinctions, and have historically the greatest utility as a means of defining rights and resources within societies. One consequence of racism is that it can strengthen the significance of such boundaries. Shared racial identity means sharing much of the same worldview and values and, for people of color, sharing the wide range of ramifications of racism and oppression as well. This greater sense of camaraderie strengthens the cultural bond. It also facilitates a greater psychological distance between races than between other cultural boundaries, and is fueled by the social tenet that discussion of racial issues, like sex and politics, is verboten. It is this boundary that is the most intimidating when attempting cross-cultural therapy. When clients declare, "You can't understand because you don't have to live in this crummy hotel . . ." or "on such a limited income . . ." the response to such statements is typically one of inquiry, "Tell me what it is like for you." However, when the statement is, "You can't understand because you are not black," the verbal and nonverbal responses of the clinician often communicate tension, indecisiveness, even guilt, and above all, "this is something we can't talk about." As with sexual concerns, it is incumbent on the clinician to assure the client in a variety of ways that racial issues are an accepted topic in clinical work. How much race influences the other boundaries discussed below is a function of the level of racism prevalent in the society.

There are many other ways in which worldview and values are bound. Recognizing them has great clinical importance because this recognition gives a sense of how they are used. Generational differences are often identified by variance in sexual mores, dress, slang, and style of entertainment. Years ago a case manager revised a client's mental status and treatment plan to accurately reflect his level of functioning, which was much higher than assessed previously. The case manager had thought his dress bizarre, a symptom of his illness. In fact his outfit was consistent with popular youth culture. He was a 19-year-old male who was diagnosed with schizophrenia. His case manager found his dress to be foreign and odd: overalls with the bib drooping over his waist, basketball shoes that were never tied, a porkpie hat; and he walked with his shoulders drooped to one side. While watching a TV show on the emerging rap music scene, the case manager discovered that the client's dress was patterned after one of the most popular rap stars. This had important implications with regard to his capacity for peer relationships, his ability to engage, and his ego strength. By considering his dress odd, rather than a style appropriately identifying him with his generational peer group, the clinician failed to recognize many more opportunities to motivate him, increase his insight, improve his social skills, help involve himself in a life that was meaningful to him, and thus increase his experience of happiness.

Geographical boundaries influence such daily rituals as when to rise and how to best feed and shelter oneself, given the local climate. They also shape accents. Rivers and ridges most often determine the difference in the sound of language. In the U.S. Midwest one can travel hundreds of miles before there is a discernible difference between the accents of the residents. But in many urban areas such as New York City, distinctly different accents can be found within a few city blocks of one another. This is a clue as to how insulated the communities are and to what degree the residents are culture bound and sensitive to cultural difference. Accent development is a function of the degree of socializing within a select group. This can be significant when weighing which residential program a client is most likely to adapt to. Though one may prefer to take the color-blind or culture-blind approach to placement, no one would consider entering a living arrangement without regard for differences in lifestyle. There is no reason to expect a person with a severe mental illness to be any different. Instead, a clinician should expect that the stress of unfamiliarity would be much more significant for those with psychiatric disabilities.

A 55-year-old woman with bipolar illness, who was referred to a case management program after spending 2 years in a long-term psychiatric skilled nursing facility, was discharged to a residential care home. In the weeks following she was evicted from several placements and had several acute care contacts per month due to her inability to adapt to community living. Finally, a residential care home was found in which the operator was able to manage the client despite her irritability, anxiety, and insomnia. Discussions with this client revealed basic cultural incentives for her: "The food is so good," she said gleefully. "Beans and greens . . . such good soul food."

A home visit revealed another critical difference. When the client began escalating, yelling and becoming increasingly disorganized, the residential care operator pulled her close and beseeched her to "pray to the Lord for strength." The client did, calmed herself down, and a crisis was averted.

Clients' religions not only can determine what is restricted from their diet, what holidays they observe and how, with whom they will socialize, and especially whom they may marry, but can also provide, and often prescribe, methods for handling stress. It is lamentable how rarely a client's religious beliefs are explored and utilized when therapy or any other mental health service is provided. No degree of psychiatric care can replace the role spirituality has in life. The client has lived in this residential care home now for more than 2 years, the longest she has been able to stay in the community in more than 10 years. For the past year she has also worked an average of 8 to 20 hours a week, as a home health care provider. She has not needed acute inpatient care in this time. Though medication and supportive therapy played an essential role, it was a case management approach responsive to the client's cultural needs that made the critical difference between community and institutional care.

Variance in courtship rituals is found across a variety of boundaries, including sexual orientation. This, along with the surreptitious expression of homosexuality that arises from the oppression of gay and lesbian lifestyles, creates some of the significant cultural differences between heterosexual and homosexual communities. The more persecution resulting from being open with one's sexuality, the more codes are needed to communicate. Particular dress, vernacular, even gestures and accents are used to communicate interest or attraction. There is a much higher rate of estrangement from family of origin for members of lesbian and gay communities. The consequential emotional loss is mitigated by creating emotional ties in the friendship network that for many people are similar in quality to those in the kinship network. This dynamic should be considered when determining who in the gay client's support system will be included in the treatment plan.

The devastation of the community by the AIDS epidemic is another important feature to consider when assessing gay clients. Chronic dsyphoria and poverty of social support can often be misdiagnosed as indicative of a severe character disorder, rather than the tragic consequence of multiple deaths within a personal network. Once there is recognition that the lack of social support is caused by a social crisis rather than a personal deficit, the logic in using community linkage as the primary intervention becomes clear. Helping clients engage in appropriate community-based organizations that serve people who are HIV positive, and their caretakers, can be a critical aspect to treatment.

Like other fields, the field of mental health is culture bound. Clients are considered not motivated for treatment if they do not anticipate being enriched by the process of appearing at a business office at a prescribed time weekly, to pay a virtual stranger to listen and respond to their most intimate thoughts and history, then leaving at a prescribed time and returning at the next appointed time. Instead, clients are rejected for being unappreciative of this helping style and are labeled as "not psychologically minded." Yet setting aside time to explain to prospective clients both the assumed value of this practice and the expected outcomes does not happen often enough.

There are numerous other examples of how cultures are bound. There have been hundreds of articles and books written on this for mental health professionals alone. It is within this context that most professionals receive didactic training of cultural awareness: the role of family in the African-American community, the religious practices of Asian-Americans, and so on. The difficulty in this content approach to culture is that, used alone, it does not allow professionals to escape from relying on stereotypes and generalities. This would be adequate if all clinicians needed to know was the probability of certain behaviors. However, to reach a therapeutic standard, professionals must be able to respond to the uniqueness of the individuals or families they are working with. For that, there must also be an understanding of the process of culture, how it is defined and how it is expressed. In gaining this understanding, the clinician is equipped to engage cross-culturally with clients well enough to both gain insight into how culture shapes their experiences and to address how culture is tailored to their experiences.

The Codes of Culture

There are many codes by which culture is expressed. The degree of *personal space,* how much physical distance a person feels comfortable with when speaking with another, is a distinctive expression (Hall, 1966). Too close, and the other person is perceived as intrusive and inconsiderate;

too far, and that person is perceived as unemotional to the point of being cold or icy. It is important to allow the client latitude in determining how to sit in relationship to the clinician in meetings. Kinesthesis, or body movement, is another way culture is expressed and is also a dramatic way the cultural variance between men and women is expressed. Relaxed body language, distancing of one's limbs when sitting or standing, which is consistent with an outgoing personality, is more prevalent with males of most cultures than with females. Females are also socialized to insert more passive or submissive messages into communication, such as tilting the head, smiling, or limiting eye contact in conversation. To diminish the potential of intimidating their audience, women also tend to raise their pitch as they finish a sentence, as if posing a question when making an assertion. Paradoxically, this can also lead to their being defined as weak and indecisive.

Existential perspectives are also rooted in cultural belief. The perception that personhood is most completely expressed by who one is, versus what one does, is a function of culture. Defining oneself in relation to who the parents are, how many siblings there are, and the land in which one's ancestors were born is how most individuals in the world identify themselves. The practice of U.S. culture is to identify by unenduring features, such as occupation and possessions. Appreciation of such differences aids the case manager in addressing the existential and spiritual concerns of the client.

A prominent code of expression in all cultures, however, is the relationship with time (Hall, 1959). A client's promptness for an appointment is often considered, in the culture of mental health, as a strong sign of interest in getting help. It can be another example of how lack of appreciation for cultural differences impairs clinical judgment. Contrary to most European cultures, particularly the northern region where promptness is more the norm (no wonder the Swiss have a reputation for precision watches), many cultures of the world give accuracy in timing far less importance. But the relationship to the past, present, and future is central to one's worldview, and its priority varies across cultures. In the United States the dominant culture places a high value on things being done quickly, and focuses on the future. This is expressed in terms of fast food, fast cars, and fast growth. In most Asian cultures greater attention is paid to the past, on the spirit of ancestors, attendance, and proper respect. Native American, Latin, and African cultures place significant emphasis on the past as well as the present and the future. A rigid concept of how time is experienced leads the therapist to expect to apply a prescribed range to emotional time, without consideration for cultural influence. Time has an objective measure. But events that happened months or years ago may be only hours away emotionally to some clients. This kind of disparity, and the pain associated with it, are often what drive clients into therapy. For example, a man may come into therapy haunted by the experiences in combat he had half a lifetime earlier. It is extremely important that clinicians not only be aware that cultural values influence how time affects an individual's emotional investments in events, but also use this to shape what clients could or would want to expect of themselves.

The Effects of Not Acknowledging Culture

Once there is acknowledgment that the mental health profession possesses its own culture, it is not surprising that historical attempts to deal with cultural differences within the field parallel the struggles of the greater society. What hasn't worked on the community level has also been tried, and has failed, within mental health (Barbarin, 1984). It has been made abundantly clear that imposing values on others does not work. A color-blind approach, the belief that the only difference is in our skin pigmentation, does not work (Thomas & Sillen, 1972). Nor does assimilation, funneling everyone together and expecting peaceful homogenization of cultures (Sager, Brayboy, & Waxenburg, 1970). These approaches have fueled misdiagnosis due to differences in modes of communication and value systems, missing relevant issues and resources; and such approaches alienate clients (Sue, 1977).

The denial of or the inability to address cultural difference in a therapeutic relationship has also contributed to many countertransference issues. The racial conflicts existing in our society often contribute to clinicians' fear of confrontation. This results in lack of empathy, false alliance, discomfort, and awkwardness. All this because one is unsure how to communicate, fearing revelation of ignorance or disrespect. This inevitably leads to insincerity and often resentment on the part of the clinician as well as the client.

These approaches have resulted in dismal rates of engagement between client and clinician in cross-cultural relationships; this, in a field that more often than not fails to engage with clients. Cultural difference has the least effect on treatment when the treatment is defined as brokering of concrete services. However, to provide effective clinical case management, the clinician has to be at least as effective in providing interpersonal support as in linking to practical services.

If a comprehensive approach emphasize cultural competence, then it greatly increases the opportunities for successful treatment within cross-cultural relationships.

The Process of Cultural Competence

Cultural competence has become a popular term for describing effective cross-cultural work (Cross, 1988; Green, 1982); however, it is rarely defined. The best definition reflects its complexity. Many, such as Terry Cross, conceptualize it as stages along a continuum that, as with other clinical tools such as theory or intervention techniques, must be continually developed and sharpened.

Critical to every aspect of cultural competence is the willingness to learn and to change. This is a much greater challenge than it may first appear. Discourse is an essential part of learning; yet there has been little experience in exploring in a constructive manner cultural differences in a multiracial group. European-Americans have very little experience discussing racial conflict and other cultural differences, even among themselves. This seems to be particularly true for those who identify as being against racial prejudice, perceiving acknowledgement of racial difference as tantamount to racism. People of color habitually discuss the ways of white folks. This discussion is an artifact of oppression; and vigilance is essential for avoiding abuse. For example, literature outlining the dynamics of domestic violence describes how much the safety of victimized women and children is predicated on their ability to anticipate anger and attack. White Americans may agonize greatly about racism, may refer to it often, but rarely explore the subject, possibly out of allegiance to the color-blind approach of "one's race shouldn't matter." Ironically, this perception unwittingly fuels much racist practice. For example, ignorance of the dynamics of vigilance vis-à-vis oppression contributes to an overdiagnosis of paranoia, particularly in African-American males.

Another aspect of the challenge is that there are few tools with which to work. There is little language available to explore the range, let alone the nuances, of discrimination. The term *racism* is all that is available to describe actions ranging from an insensitive remark to a lynching. This greatly impedes communication and any opportunity for learning. It is important to keep in mind these formidable difficulties when instituting the following plan.

The first step in developing cultural competence is to build cultural awareness. This includes exploring one's own culture with brutal honesty while confronting one's own value conflicts and prejudices. This step is essential for any clinician, but may be of particular importance to European-Americans. Racism victimizes the dominant culture by obliterating any distinction or glory to its heritage, in an effort to define difference as negative and undesirable and its own ways as standard. Consequently, the pride of identifying with a culture of one's own is lost. This is why it is essential to understand what culture is and how it is manifested. All clinicians need to be able to identify what culture means for their own lives as well as those of their clients.

The next level of development is committing to valuing diversity, not just tolerating it. This includes developing a broad perspective that results from learning more about the differences between cultures and revealing this knowledge in a respectful fashion. Key to this process is to never, ever, regardless of how many years one has lived abroad or to whom one is married, assume to be an expert on any aspect of another person's culture. If it is clear to the client that the clinician has more understanding of cultural ways than was expected, this can only enhance the therapeutic relationship. But one must be humble, otherwise any advantage experience gives the clinician in building an alliance is lost.

Once oriented to one's own culture and how it differs from others, it is possible to appreciate how events influence culture. The third stage is developing an awareness of these events. One way is for clinicians to learn the social history of the people with whom they are working. This is an enormous task, which needs to include learning how racism and other forms of oppression have been practiced and experienced in the communities the clients have lived in. It particularly means understanding what social events prompted the clients or families to action. Nothing impacts culture more than entering a new community, physically or by marriage. Especially if the whole client population is composed of a particular ethnic group, it is important to learn more about the group's history through reading and consultation. The most difficult stage of development in cultural competence is the willingness to acknowledge and address valid cultural differences between oneself and the client. It is akin to the difference between understanding a second language and being able to speak it. It is important for the therapist to be skilled in recognizing the appropriate time to introduce or address the subject of difference, and also be able to respond to the client's explicit and implied references to difference. The therapist has to also be willing to address possible conflict resulting from this. Doing this requires that the case manager be prepared to confront the issues as they arise in the relationship with clients or their support network.

Upon their first meeting, a case manager empathized with the client's tolerating a rapid turnover of case managers. She then explored with the client the similarities and differences between herself and the previous case managers. Laughing, the client blurted out, "You all are white."

Appearing embarrassed by his own candor, the client, despite prodding by the case manager, refused to elaborate. Instead, he became mute. The case manager, recognizing the social as well as the psychiatric issues impeding alliance between herself and the client, facilitated communication in the following ways. She made a conscious effort to respond, in body language and tone, that such observations were reasonable and permissible within the context of their relationship. She acknowledged the difference and noted that racial differences almost always represent some differences in life experiences and outlook. She noted that such differences were valuable, though usually not treated that way. She normalized the client's anxiety by commenting on how brave one has to be these days to face the issue of cultural difference. Then she inquired into the client's feelings. The client, appearing greatly relieved, became verbal, but again denied having any issue: "It really doesn't matter." The case manager then offered that there might be times in their relationship in which it would matter, that such occurrences would be okay to address as they came up.

They did come up again. In the beginning the statements were as oblique as the first. Each time the case manager would note it, and check in, the client denied any meaning, and the case manager accepted the claim while again reassuring the client. After several months the client began making deliberate statements about race and racism and how he saw its relation to his diagnosis of severe mental illness. He was able to acknowledge some curiosity and distrust of "some white therapists" and to relate painful experiences that shaped these feelings. His case manager actively listened to his concerns without defensiveness. She was wise in not quickly exploring the significance of his concerns to their relationship until she had succeeded in demonstrating to him that she heard and understood those concerns. While working with this case manager, the client decreased his ambivalence regarding medication compliance and increased his stability in the community.

Case managers must be prepared to respond to any potentially racialized dynamics in their clinical relationships by seeking appropriate consultation within their professional and, if possible, personal relationships. Unfortunately, this is typically an even greater challenge for most clinicians than broaching the issue with a client. In addition to all the reasons explained above, it has been extremely difficult to address these issues with co-workers because of fear that a bad outcome would create an unbearable strain in the working relationship. Such concerns need to be appreciated by agency management well enough to make airing them and building cultural competence a regular aspect of team building. Attention must be paid to maintaining open and honest communication in order to learn more about cross-cultural dynamics in relation to how they are manifested between client and clinician.

Development along this continuum is a prerequisite to providing good clinical care. Successful negotiation of the process makes the difference between adding cultural issues as a discrete component of care and being able to recognize their function in psychodynamic treatment. Once that is done, much of the understanding of how to use cultural issues in clinical work will be extrapolated from the clinical knowledge base. The following are examples of how to include a cultural perspective in assessment in treatment.

Culture as an Aspect of Assessment

Though it is necessary to educate oneself about the social history of a client population, it is unrealistic to expect to learn all there is to know about the client through self-education. The most fruitful method for this will be the questions presented to the client. There are an infinite number of examples. Perhaps the most common theme, however, is when and how the clients or their families migrated to their present communities. When did they or their families migrate to the region they are living in now? The more recent the migration and the more dramatic the move, the more significant the following questions would be. What prompted the move? Was it to escape oppression? Was their homeland destroyed by war? What was needed for them to effect their escape? Did it take years of sacrifice and suffering, and then weeks by boat in a perilous passage? What has been easiest and what has been most difficult for them to adjust to? Though the immigrant experiences are the most significant examples of trauma in migration, intranational migration can be traumatic as well. In a country as enormous, with a history as imperialistic, as the United States, it is not surprising that for many of its residents, their family's migration was a revolutionary event.

Another important area to explore is the persons consulted and the rituals used in problem solving and decision making. This can often reveal important, previously unknown links in the support network, such as spiritual leaders, and family matriarchs or patriarchs living in another region.

Summary

Ultimately, the goal is to understand culture as the process humans use to conduct their lives. Once this is understood, it becomes clear that developing a working knowledge of each client's unique manifestations of culture is crucial to developing a full therapeutic engagement. To the extent the therapist is successful in building an alliance, within the bounds of the relationship the therapist and client will develop their process or "culture" to facilitate the work. This will increase the menu of options in treatment. Once a true appreciation of the differences among people is reached, a person can perceive how much more similar people are than they ever are different. It is from a true realization of this fact that the clinician's best work is achieved.

References

Barbarin, O. (1984, Winter). Racial themes in psychotherapy with blacks: Effects of training on the attitudes of black and white psychiatrists. *American Journal of Social Psychiatry, 4*(1), 13-20.

Cross, T. (1988, Fall). The cultural competence continuum. *Focal Point, 3*(1).

Green, J. (1982). *Cultural awareness in the human services.* Englewood Cliffs, NJ: Prentice-Hall.

Hall, E. T. (1959). *The silent language.* Garden City, NY: Doubleday.

Hall, E. T. (1966). *The hidden dimension.* Garden City, NY: Doubleday.

Sager, C., Brayboy, T. L., & Waxenburg, B. M. (1970). *The black ghetto family in therapy.* New York: Grove.

Sue, D., & Sue, D. (1990). *Counseling the culturally different: Theory and practice* (2nd ed.). New York: John Wiley.

Sue, S. (1977). Community mental health services to minority groups: Some optimism, some pessimism. *American Psychologist, 32*, 616-624.

Thomas, A., & Sillen, S. (1972). *Racism and psychiatry.* New York: Brunner/Mazel.

4

Engaging Families and Natural Support Systems

SUSAN SCHEIDT

"Blood is thicker than water." "No matter what else, you've always got your family." "Families represent a fundamental system of support. They give us our first experience with interpersonal relationships and often provide our most lasting ties. Sometimes there are rifts, and family members sever their contact with one another. Yet even when there is no longer ongoing communication, early family experiences usually remain an influential factor in development.

Data collected by the National Institute of Mental Health (Goldman, 1982) reveal that there are between 800,000 and 1.5 million people in the United States who are chronically mentally ill. Estimates suggest that between 25% and 65% of people discharged from inpatient psychiatric units return to live with family members (Minkoff, 1978; Uzoka, 1979). Severely mentally ill individuals turn to relatives for support, as do those without psychiatric problems.

In addition to their relatives, people with psychiatric problems may be involved with an extensive network of others in their natural support systems. This may include anyone from long-lasting friends to a residential care home operator to a clerk at the corner grocery store. Some of these people may have close involvement with the client, and others may only be peripheral. Yet each of them can play a crucial role in the client's day-to-day survival in the community.

It would seem, then, that mental health professionals and families/ natural support systems would be logical allies in addressing the needs of people with mental illness. Unfortunately, this is not always the case, and each group often views the other with suspicion and animosity. Faced with the frustration that comes with not being able to meet all of the needs of their clients/relatives, professionals and family members end up blaming one another. This alienation is unfortunate, as treatment providers and family members usually have similar goals for the person with mental illness. Clinical case managers, who advocate for comprehensive care that includes psychological understanding, housing, income, rehabilitation opportunities, and socialization, are particularly similar to families in their goals for clients. This chapter addresses how case managers and family members can work together with the client to meet mutually shared goals and describes some of the difficulties in accomplishing this. It defines the concept of "family" to include natural support systems and discusses commonalities shared by case managers and family members. A brief history of the relationship between mental health professionals and families is reviewed, as well as the typical emotional experiences of families coming to terms with having a mentally ill relative. The heart of the chapter describes what families and case managers can learn from one another, why both groups often feel discouraged, and how to better engage families/natural support systems in treatment for the benefit of the client. The goal is to increase case managers' appreciation of the value of developing stronger ties with the support systems in their clients' lives.

Who Is "Family"?

In Chapter 1, family was defined as including "anyone that cares about the client." This definition, admittedly broad, is used to underscore the idea that all natural support systems need to be encouraged for severely ill clients who often have difficultly maintaining significant relationships. Much of this discussion is based on the experience of relatives, though the ideas apply to the broader definition of all those who are involved in the client's life.

Even the concept of "relatives" is broader than most people might assume. While this certainly includes parents, spouses, children, siblings, grandparents, aunts/uncles, and cousins, it also implies stepfamilies, half-siblings, and foster families. For some clients, there are family friends designated as "aunts," "uncles," and "cousins" who are not related by blood or marriage, but who have played a significant role in the client's life. One client frequently referred to her "Aunt Mary and Uncle Joe." When asked which of her parents they were related to, she said, "Both." Mary and Joe were long-time family friends who had been neighbors when the client was a baby and continued to be included in the family as a "play aunt" and "play uncle."

There may be other personal friends who are interested in being involved in the client's life. These may be people from the client's religious community, including a minister, priest, or rabbi, and other members of the church/temple. Other people may be a part of the client's natural support system by virtue of their occupation: residential care home operators, hotel managers, shelter personnel, conservators, payees, and staff at programs or clinics where the client is served. Other extended "family" members include personnel at grocery stores or restaurants that the client frequents, and members of any 12-Step programs the client may attend.

What Families and Case Managers Have in Common

Case managers and family members have several commonalities in terms of their roles in the lives of seriously mentally ill persons. These can be described as having a special bond with the client, having knowledge and skills that are valuable to the client, and experiencing similar limitations in achieving their desired goals.

Special Bond

Relatives often do experience the fact of blood relationships as being significant and lifelong. No matter where the client is, in whatever facility, in whatever state, they are still related. No matter how long between contacts, the relationship remains. This is similar to how many clinical case managers see themselves; their effectiveness depends on their ability to establish a relationship with their clients. Regardless of the treatment facility or programs the client is in, across various living situations, the case manager is committed to working with the client. Clients may exhibit disruptive behaviors that necessitate removal from a specific treatment program; but clinical case managers, like many family members, continue to support the client. This commitment to helping the client over time and situations helps to develop the special bond that clients may share with both clinical case managers and families/natural support systems. Both groups support the goal of the client's living as healthy and happy a life as possible. Even if their specific goals vary, their genuine concern is a common ideal.

In some cases, relatives may no longer be in contact with the client. This could be by the family's choice as they become overwhelmed or frustrated by the enormity of care that a severely mentally ill person requires. It may also be by the client's choice, having left the family due to paranoia, confusion, or unresolvable conflicts. In these situations, the case manager may become the closest relationship the client has. The definition of "family" may then become broader, encompassing other members of the natural support system as described above. Together all of these "family" members become important people in the client's life, regardless of whether the client is able to articulate the significance.

Knowledge/Skills

Family members and professionals each have areas of expertise regarding the client that they have gained through experience and training. Clinical case managers are usually trained mental health professionals. They have received an education in psychological principles and have learned about working with seriously mentally ill people from their colleagues and through professional experience. They know how to assess symptoms, identify signs of decompensation, and manage difficult behaviors. They also have practical knowledge about community resources and mental health treatment programs.

Family members vary in their knowledge and skills pertaining to mental illness. Some are sophisticated consumers, knowledgeable about the disease processes related to mental illnesses and possibly involved in local chapters of the Alliance for the Mentally Ill. Others, whose relative might be experiencing a first psychiatric decompensation, may feel quite confused and overwhelmed. Nonetheless, these relatives have a great deal of first-hand information about their impaired family member's functioning that professionals do not have. They can be a tremendous resource to professionals, contributing to the care of the client (Edwards, 1989).

Case managers and family members often have similar knowledge and skills about things that can be helpful to the client. Each may also have specific information that, when shared with the other group in a collaborative fashion, can have an impact on the client's recovery and rehabilitation.

Similar Limitations

Caring for severely mentally ill people is a challenging task. The clients often do not realize their need for assistance, and reject the help offered. Both family members and case managers face similar limitations in their work with mentally ill clients. Families often experience a great deal of stress related to their mentally ill relative, and when they do not feel supported they may become overwhelmed and "burned out." Case managers may also experience the sense of being stretched to their limits and having no more to give. Ultimately, case managers can terminate the relationship by transferring the client to another clinician, but families do not have that option. By better understanding the stressors, case managers and families alike can begin to address the issues and get support.

While people with mental illness can be interesting and enjoyable, those with a serious illness can be unstable and unpredictable, and ambivalent about maintaining relationships. This creates frustration for those who want so much to help, and indeed, do help the client. Repeated episodes of verbal or even physical abuse by the client can make it difficult to retain enthusiasm about the relationship. The client's needs may be so great, and both families and professionals are limited by time and resources to fill all of those needs. It becomes discouraging to see relapses despite all the best efforts to support the client.

Both groups discuss the challenge of the client's substance abuse to be especially frustrating where it exists. There are still extremely limited resources for those with dual diagnoses, and the seduction of street drugs remains great for many clients whose impulse control is compromised.

Case managers and family members sometimes share in a sense of isolation. Clients may be painfully aware of the social stigma of serious mental illness; families and clinical case managers can also be affected. Family members may feel a sense of shame to admit that their relative is in a psychiatric hospital. One residential care home operator told of how her friends "don't know why I want to take care of these mentals." Even within the mental health community, it is not fashionable to work with seriously mentally ill clients. Case managers may also experience embarrassment, such as being out in public with disheveled clients who are talking to themselves. For both professionals and people in the natural support system, the isolation may also coexist with a sense of mourning the dissolution of rescue fantasies, the belief that "if I try hard enough, I can save my client/relative from these problems."

Finally, both relatives and case managers are affected financially as a result of their commitments to the client. Families may spend much of their income or savings to try getting treatment for their relative; they often support the client fully or partially. Many parents counted on a time when their child would be able to help them financially, and they must accept that they will never be able to count on that because of their son or daughter's mental illness. While not nearly as extreme, clinical case managers also accept lower salaries by working in community mental health than they could make in private practice or other specializations within their field.

It is essential that both family members and case managers have arenas in which to discuss their stress and sense of being overwhelmed by the burden. To continue to support seriously mentally ill individuals, they need to be supported themselves. Their own friends, family, colleagues, supervisors, and support groups provide nurturance that allows people to continue giving. While case managers may help to support the families, families can also turn to self-help groups, such as the Alliance for the Mentally Ill. Case managers need to identify the problems and discuss them with peers on a regular basis to decrease the sense of isolation and retain enthusiasm for the work. Professionals and families both need to have interests and activities outside those related to the client.

History of the Families and Mental Health Professionals

Many family members are wary of contact with mental health professionals, fearing that they will be shamed or blamed for their relative's illness. Indeed, the history of professionals' relationships with the relatives of mentally ill people has been characterized by critical attitudes and implications of blame. As described by Terkelsen (1990), "The negative relationships now in evidence between relatives of the mentally ill as a group and mental health professionals as a group are an unrecognized legacy of three historically powerful forces in American social thought" (p. 4). He identifies the three significant social forces as: the asylum movement in the United States in the first half of the 19th century, the rise of psycho-analytic thought in the early to mid-1900s, and the deinstitutionalization movement that began in the 1950s and has continued to the present.

Asylum treatment alienated families in that it took the patients out of the family and community and placed them in large institutions. The idea was to provide the patients with a calm and peaceful environment in which to recover from the stresses of society that presumably caused the mental illness. Social conditions were seen as the causal factor, but families were indirectly blamed for not having protected their relative from the stress. As Terkelsen writes, "It is important to note that the family was not thought of as the germ, but rather as having allowed the germ to slip through" (p. 6). Families were generally discouraged from visiting their relatives in the asylums, thus supporting the view that the natural support system provided unfavorable influences.

The rise in psychoanalytic thought brought the explanation for mental illness out of society down to specific individuals. The family, especially the mother, was viewed as the "germ," the causal agent. It was the "schizophrenogenic" mother who was described as destroying her child by being cold and rejecting, overwhelming and intrusive, or just plain confusing. Early family therapy theories were just as condemning; families were seen as making patients "crazy" by giving them double messages that were impossible to follow, or by encouraging mental illness to deflect attention away from their own problems.

As Terkelsen reminds us, it is important to note that these were optimistic theories in their time. If the cause could be identified, interventions could be made to address the problem. It was easier to focus on individuals than the diffuse "societal stresses" as causal agents. However, the result was that families felt blamed and responsible for their relatives' mental illness, which left them feeling guilty and/or angry. In either case, these theories fostered alienation between mental health professionals and families.

Several factors contributed to the deinstitutionalization movement. The use of antipsychotic medications began with the introduction of chlorpromazine in 1953, and gave new hope to those who worked with the chronically mentally ill in asylums. There was suddenly the possibility of people who had lived much of their lives in an institution being able to live more normally in the community as a result of being "cured" with medications.

In 1963 President John F. Kennedy presented a "bold new approach," which included the humanitarian goal of preventing inappropriate hospitalizations and offering comprehensive treatment for mentally ill people near their homes. However, the Community Mental Health Act did not provide the appropriate mechanisms for integrating the community mental health movement and deinstitutionalization. Communities were not prepared to absorb the newly discharged patients into the community, either financially, programmatically, or ideologically. The readmission rate to psychiatric hospitals before deinstitutionalization was 25%; after it had begun in 1972, there was an increase of 65% in hospital readmission rates (Bassuk & Gearson, 1978).

When inadequate community care was provided, families were forced to take on more of the burden. After years of being estranged from both the patient and mental health professionals, family members were faced with responsibilities for which they were unprepared. They did not have the information to understand mental illness, know how to deal with difficult behaviors, or know how to locate needed resources. As Kreisman and Joy wrote in 1974, "It is surprising that the same investigators who provided ample demonstration of the career of the mental patient have so sadly neglected the reciprocal career of the patient's family." The families often experienced being overwhelmed by the task of caring for their mentally ill relative, becoming so exhausted and demoralized that they had no energy left for the patients or themselves.

Families' Emotional Experience: Stages of Acceptance

Families require education to meet their specific needs for increased information about mental illness, resources, and how to intervene with their family members. They also require considerable support and ways to cope with the emotional burden of having a mentally ill relative. There is a common pattern to the way most family members come to terms with the illness, although parents, siblings, spouses, children, and the extended natural support system may bring somewhat different perspectives. A family's cultural background and resources will also influence its reactions, but most family members and people close to a person with serious mental illness can relate to the following "stages of acceptance." Some families who have been hesitant to engage with treatment providers become much more involved when they feel understood in these ways.

Stages of Acceptance

1. Transition Period

The transition period is the earliest phase of decompensation, where family members begin to sense that something is wrong. Their relative is beginning to act somewhat differently from the past, and the family begins to feel uneasy. Parents may notice that their 20-year-old son is suddenly staying home in his room instead of going out with friends. A wife may notice that her husband is more irritable and yells at her without provocation. A young man may notice that his sister is using more marijuana and is starting to act "weird." A landlord may notice a tenant talking to herself when no one else is around.

2. Denial

The most common reaction to the transition period is a tendency to deny one's own perceptions. There is a strong pull to want to believe that there is really nothing wrong, that this will pass. The concept of denial is certainly not specific to mental illness; it is common to wish away many problems, including physical illnesses. Denial is sometimes used as something else for which to blame families, as if they are "bad" to be denying the mental illness. However, there are several logical reasons why people may deny mental illness in the early phases.

The Family's Naivete About Psychiatric Symptoms.   While relatives may begin to notice that something is wrong, they may not understand the significance of certain behaviors. For example, a father may notice his son is staying in his room, and call his son "lazy." A mental health professional might easily recognize the behavior as a symptom of a psychiatric decompensation. A minister or church members may not be able to distinguish hyperreligiosity from usual religious zeal.

The Patient's Fluctuating Behavior.   Especially in early stages of mental illness, a patient's behaviors can fluctuate dramatically. One day the person may be mumbling to herself and sounding quite odd; the next day, she may seem "like her old self" again. These "normal" periods may make it confusing for family members and friends, who want to believe that there is really nothing wrong.

Other People Sometimes Display "Odd" Behavior.   Many family members deny that their relative has a mental illness in the early phases by giving explanations that the person "doesn't seem that different." Parents may note that many teenagers are moody, or describe their daughter as "trying to be as crazy as her friends." A wife may interpret her husband's irritability as normal for someone in a job like his. A corner grocery clerk may think the client is only drunk and may not notice signs of decompensation. There is often difficulty distinguishing early symptoms from other individual personality characteristics.

3. Anxiety

Family members' anxiety is raised when they can no longer deny that there is a problem. The mild symptoms that seemed a bit "odd" have now developed into a full-blown syndrome that cannot be ignored. The son who had been staying in his room a bit more than usual has now barricaded the door and will not come out for meals. The 12-Step sponsor notices that a program member who was occasionally mumbling to herself at meetings is now talking and laughing loudly and speaking in odd, disjointed sentences. Family and friends recognize that there is a problem now, but they usually don't know what to do about it. The anxiety mounts as the sense of urgency increases.

4. Looking for Explanations

Most people are quite rational and believe that if they can just find the explanation for the problem, they can begin to solve it. At this phase families and friends are often quite desperate to identify one event that can explain the problem. "It must be because she fell off her bicycle in kindergarten." "I think its because he's been taking drugs." "I bet it's because his girlfriend broke up with him." "I guess it's because I always spoiled her—I should have been stricter." "I guess it's because I was too strict—I should have been more gentle." People in the natural support system may try to blame the family; the family may try to blame friends.

5. Changing Emotions

The emotions experienced by families and friends will very often extend across the wide range of human emotions. Naturally, individuals express their feelings in individual ways, and everyone will not react in precisely the same manner. Yet there are specific emotions that family members and friends describe repeatedly. These include fear, guilt, anger, shame/embarrassment, sadness, as well as hopefulness.

Fear. Families and friends experience fear of their loved one: not knowing what to expect, wondering if the client is dangerous, worrying that they will be in a situation and not know what to do. They also experience fear *for* their relative: What will happen to him if he doesn't take his medication? Will he be treated well in the hospital? Who will be able to take care of her after we're gone?

Guilt. As stated earlier in this chapter, guilt is often induced by professionals who either implicitly or explicitly blame the family. Yet even in the most supportive situations, family members often feel responsible for their relative's problems, asking themselves what they did wrong or should have done differently. While parents often voice this sense of guilt, it is not uncommon for spouses, children, and siblings to also feel responsible for the client's problems in some way. People in the natural support system can also feel that they could/should have done something differently to prevent a decompensation or the consequences of the client's inappropriate behavior. They may also feel a sense of guilt about complaining or getting angry at the client, knowing that the client often has little control over certain behaviors.

Anger. Families are often seen as angry by mental health professionals. Families have legitimate reasons to be angry. They often express anger at the mental health system for not including them in treatment, for pathologizing the family, for not providing the care their family member needs. They often express frustration about the legal system that discharges their relatives who need further treatment from hospitals, and the police who tell them "there's nothing we can do," even though their relative may have been behaving in a way that endangered herself or others. And sometimes family members and friends feel angry directly at the client, for seeming not to appreciate help, for refusing available treatments, or for troublesome behaviors.

Shame/Embarrassment. Family members, like the clients themselves, are greatly affected by the social stigma associated with mental illness. The shame is often deep and profound. Some people avoid telling others they have a relative with schizophrenia because their shame is so great. There is a sense of embarrassment about the illness itself, as well as embarrassment that may come from public reactions to their relative's odd behaviors. A residential care provider who accompanies a client to the clinic may feel embarrassed by the person's poor grooming as people stare at them on the bus.

Sadness. One of the most difficult emotions for family members to acknowledge is their sadness. There is often a profound sense of loss that the person they once knew is so changed and the relationship they had before is forever altered. Parents express sadness that many of the hopes and dreams they had for their child will not be realized; spouses grieve for the disappointments in the marital relationship. Some family or friends may actually develop a clinical depression as a result of this stress, but most experience ongoing feelings of sadness that come with seeing a loved one change as the result of a serious illness.

Hopefulness. Friends and relatives often discuss the sense of discouragement and hopelessness they experience when feeling overwhelmed by being close to someone with a mental illness. However, they often also have a great capacity for hope. As people who care about the client experience support, learn more about the illness and its treatment, and develop better coping skills, they often voice a sense of optimism that they have found some answers. A situation that looked totally bleak may begin to take on a new quality of hope that they will be able to deal with it, and no longer feel so alone.

6. Acceptance

Over time, the family often comes to terms with having a mentally ill relative in a way that affords them some serenity. Acceptance does not imply giving up, but moving ahead. Families and friends are able to see the situation for what it is, and to get the help they need. They may be ready to get involved in a support group, or find other ways to take care of themselves, so that they do not feel so burdened or overwhelmed. One mother stayed involved in the Alliance for the Mentally Ill long after her daughter was stable. "I know she is always at risk for another breakdown. Having this support for myself helps me to deal with my fear of that." A client's hotel manager said, "I don't mind having a person with a mental illness live here. I can accept that as long as I know I can call the clinic when he starts 'acting up.' "

What Families Want From Mental Health Professionals

Mental health professionals may assume that they understand the needs of families who have a mentally ill relative. But what do the families themselves say that they need? When surveyed, the families have expressed considerable dissatisfaction with their experiences with mental health providers and have made specific requests for what they need (Hatfield, 1983; Holden & Lewine, 1982; Johnson, 1990; Lefley, 1987; Scheidt, 1984).

Attitude Change

Family members are tired of being blamed for their relative's mental illness. They are particularly sensitive to covert expressions of blame, including the construct of "expressed emotion" (EE) (Hatfield, 1987). Early EE studies (Brown, Birley, & Wing, 1972; Brown, Monck, & Carstairs, 1962; Vaughn & Leff, 1976) suggested that relatives who scored high on measures of criticality and emotional involvement contributed to the relapse of their relatives with schizophrenia. More recent research (Kanter, Lamb, & Loeper, 1987) has found that there is no evidence that families' expressed emotion causes relapse, and others have suggested that high levels of EE may be an expected response to the illness and difficult situations faced by families (Miklowitz, Goldstein, & Falloon, 1983).

Families and friends of seriously mentally ill clients want genuine support from professionals. This includes sharing the burden of care with practical services, such as those offered by clinical case managers. It also includes an attitude of respect for family members and friends, recognizing the tremendous stress they are under and supporting their efforts to cope. They want to be acknowledged for the positive contributions they bring to the clients' lives.

Information/Practical Skills

When mental health professionals contact family members or people in the natural support system, it is often to obtain information about the client's developmental, psychiatric, and medical histories, and to ask about any family history of mental illness. Professionals often overlook the need that the client's friends and family have for information. Families and friends need to know about the disorder and its causes, medication and potential side effects, and signs of relapse. Myths about mental illness also need to be addressed, providing the most current information available. Some clinicians worry about not being knowledgeable enough to explain mental illness, or are concerned about the reactions they will receive. Yet most relatives and support people in a client's life appreciate an honest, straightforward assessment of the problem as seen by the clinician.

People who are involved with the client also want specific coping strategies to address the client's difficult behaviors. They want to know how to respond to the client's delusions, how to increase the client's motivation to be more active, and how to deal with such emergencies as suicidal or assaultive threats and behaviors. Specific psychoeducational programs

have been developed to provide information as well as improve communication and problem-solving skills (Anderson, Hogarty, & Reiss, 1980;
Falloon, Boyd, & McGill, 1984; National Institute of Mental Health
[NIMH], 1985). Yet individual clinicians need to help families and friends
in these areas as well. Case managers may be available by phone to
families, serve as a liaison to the police in emergencies, and help the people
in the client's support network with stress management strategies.

Resources

Families and friends of mentally ill persons are very clear about one
thing: While they need and appreciate support and information, they require
practical resources to help their loved ones. While these are difficult economic times in mental health, there are existing resources that may be
very difficult for families to access without professional help. Obtaining
financial entitlements for clients can be an awesome task for the most
skilled of case managers; individual clients and people in their support
system may find it unsurmountable to accomplish alone. Families need
help in finding housing for their relatives, and may need occasional respite
care if the client lives at home with the family. Those who are concerned
about the client want meaningful activities for their loved ones, including
treatment programs and vocational rehabilitation. Access to health care,
money management assistance for the client, and outreach programs that
can reach to the family home are also basic services that can help to ease
the family burden. The case manager may also assist by helping relatives
obtain health and support services for themselves. By helping families
and friends obtain practical resources for clients as well as themselves,
the clinician can also support them in finding time for more rest, a possible
vacation, or ways to enjoy their lives more fully.

What Families/Friends Can Offer Professionals

Understanding the Clients

Families and the extended support network can provide a wealth of
information about clients. As discussed earlier, families and friends can
tell professionals about the client's developmental, social, psychiatric,
and medical histories, and are usually willing to if asked respectfully and
given information in return. The clinician should ask about more than the

client's deficits and problems, also exploring the client's strengths, special talents, dreams and ambitions, as understood by the people who know the client best. Mental health professionals often have a narrow view of the client's functioning, and yet make assumptions that they know the client well. Family members and friends must be acknowledged as having a longitudinal perspective on the client that is invaluable in providing comprehensive care.

Ongoing Monitoring

Professionals can help educate people in the client's support network about mental illness, and can give friends and relatives the language to describe the client's behaviors. At the same time, professionals must acknowledge how much the family and support system can contribute to care by their ongoing monitoring of the client. Family and friends help to assess the effects of medications, note side effects, and report early signs of relapse. They can also report signs of improvement and higher functioning that let the treatment team know that the interventions are working.

Coping Skills

While families and friends may benefit from communication and problem-solving skills training, they can also teach professionals practical solutions they have developed for addressing the client's daily routine, difficult behaviors, social stigmatization, and the ongoing stress of caring about someone with a mental illness. By necessity, families and friends have often developed creative solutions for problems that perplex professionals.

Collaborative Case Management With Families
and Natural Support Systems: Recommendations

This chapter has described what families and the clients' natural support systems have in common with mental health professionals, and what each of the groups needs and can learn from the other. How is this translated into a practical collaboration that will support each group and, most important, benefit the client?

1. Identify the Client's Support Network. To include families and support systems in treatment, the case manager must work with the client to identify who the important people are in the client's life. The clinician can ask the client about family of origin, taking care to elicit information about stepfamilies, extended family members, foster families. It may be important to note who was in the family household at different points in the client's development. One useful way to obtain this information can be by drawing a genogram, or family tree (McGoldrick & Gerson, 1985). Clients who have difficulty thinking abstractly or who become threatened discussing their family often respond well to a neutral gathering of the information in a concrete, graphic way. Asking the client questions such as, "Who are you closest to in your family?" "Which family member would you call if you were in trouble?" and "Who comes to Thanksgiving dinner?" may be helpful in identifying key family members who might be involved in treatment.

A similar strategy is useful in identifying people in the clients' extended support system. Questions such as, "Who do you talk to each day?" "If you were locked out of your hotel room, who would you go to for help?" "Is there anyone you can borrow money from when you're broke?" can help to identify key people in the client's network. Some people may be very isolated and feel that they have no other support except the case manager. It is still important to try identifying anyone with whom they might have contact, such as a grocery store clerk or bank teller who might take a special interest in them and who represents some kind of support. Some clients will also be involved in a church or synagogue; others may attend 12-Step meetings. Others will describe their primary contact as their "drinking buddies" who hang out on the corner, or other residents at their hotel. Many people in the client's support system may not be willing/able to actively participate in treatment, but it is important to identify them to help the client make better use of the available supports.

2. Decide Who to Include in the Treatment. The process of deciding who to include in treatment is likely to extend throughout the case manager's involvement with a client. Certain key family members and friends may be natural choices; other people who seem more remote or peripheral may emerge as central later in the client's care. It is useful to work with clients to identify people they want to have involved; at other times, clients may initially resist having certain family members contacted, but will eventually respond well to encouragement to involve them.

However, the case manager should listen carefully to the client's concerns about who to involve or not involve. As with people in the general population, clients may have very legitimate reasons for not wanting to include certain people in treatment. Some families and friends are indeed dysfunctional, with past or current substance abuse and histories of physical abuse or sexual abuse toward the client. Contact with these significant others may be healing if some of the issues can be confronted and worked through, but it can also be healthy for the client to decide to separate from destructive influences. The effects of abuse and other dysfunctional family patterns can be devastating to clients; they can be helped by listening to their stories, validating them through their emotional responses from sadness to rage, supporting their efforts to change harmful patterns, and helping them connect with support groups where others share their experiences.

3. Engage the Significant Others in Treatment. Some family members and people in the client's natural support system are eager to be involved in treatment. They may call to get information or provide history and details of the client's life. While confidentiality laws must be recognized, the majority of clients will eventually allow contact with the important people in their lives if the case manager sets this as a priority. However, family members and friends are often reluctant to engage in treatment. They may feel discouraged by the chronicity and severity of their relative's illness, or they may be alienated from the mental health system because of experiencing shame, blame, and disrespect in the past. These friends and family may require special efforts from the case manager to engage in treatment.

As is the case with seriously mentally ill clients, their significant others may have difficulty with scheduled appointments at a clinic. If it is possible to meet them in their natural environment, the clinician should try to meet them at their home on "their turf." They may be apprehensive as to why this "social worker" is coming to visit, many having had negative experiences with government employees or workers from Child Protective Services coming to their homes. These families will need considerable support and reassurance. They should be praised for their willingness to help the client, and given an opportunity to express the range of emotions they have experienced as a result of being close to someone with a major mental disorder. The clinician's awareness of the stages of acceptance described earlier can help to identify the particular issues to address.

It is important that the clinician be respectful of the family environment. If coffee or food is offered, the case manager should acknowledge the gesture by accepting, if possible, or by graciously refusing while still expressing appreciation. It is within these informal settings that relationships are often established with the client and the extended support system. If appointments are made for the clinic, phone calls and letters to remind family and friends are often useful. Occasionally, calls or notes to acknowledge a meeting after the visit can help to establish rapport. While it may not be customary to serve clients refreshments at the clinic, offers of coffee or tea, when possible, can go a long way in creating a welcoming atmosphere.

People in the client's support network can make a tremendous impact on treatment if allowed to participate more fully with the treatment team. They should be encouraged to keep some sort of record or journal that describes the client's history of inpatient and outpatient treatment, medications, response to treatment, side effects of medication, and names of treatment providers. Another idea is to consider inviting the family or friends to treatment team meetings, where they can get an idea of how the case manager collaborates with team members, and allowing the significant others to actively participate in decision making as it relates to the client.

4. Provide Education. As stated earlier, it is essential that families are given information about mental illness and its impact on the clients, and medications and side effects. How the information is given can make an enormous difference as to how the family receives it. Well-meaning clinicians, attempting to educate clients and family members, may give complicated written information, or quickly explain the illness in medical terms difficult for a layperson to comprehend. When providing psychoeducation, it is important for the clinicians to remember their psychological training. It is helpful to assess the family members' concept of the problem, ask about their beliefs about causality, and consider the cultural context of their understanding. Some people in the client's support network may blame the client for being "lazy," or attribute all of the problems to substance abuse when it is not appropriate. One family that was highly religious attributed their relative's schizophrenia to demon possession and could not understand how the medications could help. The clinician accepted their faith while emphasizing that she had seen others recover with medication and therapy. On occasion, members of the clergy can be engaged to support treatment if they are willing.

As information is given to family members, it is important to watch for their reactions and discuss the impact that hearing about mental illness is having on them. The clinician should pace the delivery of information on the family's ability to process it. Mental health professionals should not assume that all clients and relatives can read and write, and must adapt educational interventions to the specific family's needs.

   5. *Encourage Positive Communication and Specific Problem Solving.* Family and friends in the client's extended support system often feel quite overwhelmed by the magnitude of the client's problems. They may be so focused on finding a solution to the problems that they forget to acknowledge the client's strengths and efforts in a positive way. Tension may also arise between family members as they struggle with the stresses that mental illness can bring to a system. The case manager can model good communication and acknowledgment for specific behaviors when working with the client and people in the support network. "I really appreciate your making the effort to be here today," "I like the way you have been asking about your medication," "I'm impressed by your willingness to take your friend to day treatment" are examples of clear praise for specific acts. The clinician can work with family and friends to teach them to use similarly positive comments with the client and each other, and to praise all people in the support system for making efforts to do so.

   Families and friends often report feeling confused by the complexity of decisions they need to make regarding their relative's illness. One way to help them cope better is to teach them a specific six-step problem-solving model. With the help of an experienced case manager, family members can learn to identify the problem, generate as many solutions as possible, evaluate the pros and cons of each solution, choose the best alternative, implement the solution, and evaluate its effectiveness. While some clients and their families may reject such a systematized approach, it can help to structure their problem solving and broaden their scope by learning to generate alternative solutions.

   6. *Teach Family and Friends to Help With Practical Supports.* As has been described elsewhere in this book, clinical case management is a comprehensive intervention that requires considerable skill and training. Yet a negative stereotype has persisted that implies that case management consists of making phone calls and obtaining financial entitlements. These are necessary, but not sufficient, tasks of the case manager. And it is these tasks with which people in the natural support system are often willing to help, if they can be given some instruction and support in how to proceed. An apprenticeship model is useful in working with families and friends: By accompanying them to a program/office and modeling the task, the case manager can often help the supportive person gain the information

and develop the skills necessary to assist the client alone the next time. This not only frees the time of the case manager, but also contributes to a sense of efficacy that the significant other can experience in accomplishing concrete goals. It can also provide an opportunity for the relatives and clients to develop their relationship as they both participate in achieving a minor victory in obtaining resources. Families are also very often interested in learning more about potential living situations for their relatives. They can better help to find the client housing if they understand the system of acute hospitalization, halfway houses, residential care homes, and supported independent living resources.

7. Encourage Political Advocacy. Family members and friends of the client should also be encouraged to become more politically active in issues pertaining to severely mentally ill clients. Many of the problems that they face can be improved through legislative action. As lawmakers restrict funds for mental health programs, it is important for advocates of mentally ill individuals to make them aware of the effects of budget acts on the lives of the clients, their families, and society. Families and other lay people close to the client can advocate for better services as well as for laws that impact on mental health care; their testimony can often be more powerful than that of professionals.

Families can also make recommendations for the education and professional training that students in mental health disciplines receive. It is not uncommon for social work and psychology students to still be taught that family members are largely responsible for causing severe mental illness. While their textbooks may describe biological contributions, biases of teachers and mentors may continue to promote the idea that it is "bad" families that make people "crazy." Conversely, in psychiatry training, the biological model of mental illness may be so prominent that the family members are ignored altogether. The patient may be seen as a disease and not a person. Family members need to organize and speak out against such one-dimensional models of human experience. Case managers who maintain a more inclusive biopsychosocial model of mental illness can work together with the client's support network to advocate for more balanced curricula in mental health training programs.

8. Recognize That Clients, Family Members, Significant Others, and Professionals All Need Nurturance. Coping with serious mental illness is hard work, whether it be the those with the illness, their families, or the other people trying to help. Mental illness takes its toll, and any of those affected by it can become so consumed by its effects that they do not take enough breaks to nurture themselves. Family members and friends can be encouraged to become involved in support groups that help them realize they are not so alone. They may share the burden with other members of the group and develop a sense of hope as they see other people coping with similar problems. They may also need permission to be involved in activities that have nothing to do with mental illness. Relatives have expressed a sense of relief to know that it is acceptable to develop their own personal hobbies, or to take a vacation that does not include the client. Their guilt about their relative's illness is often so great that they do not feel that they deserve a break. When they do allow themselves to take care of themselves, they often find they are freed from resentment they have carried and are better able to be available to the client.

Similarly, case managers also need to recognize their limits and be able to take care of themselves. The concept of codependence has recently become more prominent in the literature, and many people in the helping professions have recognized that they often put others' needs before their own, at their own expense. While case managers may be trying to help family members pull back from their mentally ill relative and pay attention to their own needs, case managers may overextend themselves. They may work many additional hours without pay, put themselves in potentially dangerous situations to help their clients, or find themselves preoccupied with their clients even when not working. Like family members, mental health professionals may develop unhealthy coping mechanisms to deal with their stress. Case managers also need to take care of themselves, using supervision, support groups, or personal therapy and meaningful activities to get their needs met. Otherwise the potential for getting their needs met through clients is a risk. Like people in the client's natural support system, case managers must come to accept their limitations in helping the mentally ill client, even though acknowledging that is often painful. Once limitations are recognized, it frees the family and friends, as well as the professional, to focus energies where they can be most effective.

Summary

Serious mental illness involves a complex set of challenges that affect the person with the illness, the people in the client's life, and the professionals who want to help. The history of families and mental health treatment providers has often placed the two groups in opposition, blaming one another for the frustrations inherent in addressing all the needs of mentally ill clients. This chapter has illustrated that families, friends, and clinical case managers working with severely mentally ill individuals have much in common, foremost of which is their desire to create a more satisfying and meaningful life for the person who suffers from mental illness. By becoming allies instead of adversaries, case managers and the people in the client's natural support system can unite forces to improve care and help mentally ill individuals achieve a safe place to live, money for food and clothing, quality health care, a sense of relatedness, and productive activities. These are the basic requirements needed for human survival.

Seriously mentally ill clients deserve to be treated as people and not as problems. Clinical case managers can be instrumental in helping clients, families, people in support systems, and other professionals coordinate care. Finding ways to support the needs and goals of the client, while respecting those of their friends and families, will maximize the likelihood that their relationships will endure. Relationships are the cornerstone of leading meaningful lives.

References

Anderson, C. M., Hogarty, G. E., & Reiss, D. J. (1980). Family treatment of adult schizophrenic patients: A psycho-educational approach. *Schizophrenia Bulletin, 6,* 440-505.

Bassuk, E., & Gearson, S. (1978). Deinstitutionalization and mental health services. *Scientific American, 238,* 2-10.

Brown, G. W., Birley, J. L., & Wing, J. K. (1972). Influence of family life on the course of schizophrenic disorders: A replication. *British Journal of Psychiatry, 121,* 241-258.

Brown, G. W., Monck, E. M., & Carstairs, G. M. (1962). Influence of family life on the course of schizophrenic illness. *British Journal of Preventative and Social Medicine, 16,* 55-68.

Edwards, V. (1989, April). *Helping with multiple stressors affecting families of minority clients.* Paper presented at the meeting of the American Orthopsychiatric Association Conference, New York.

Falloon, I.R.H., Boyd, J. L., & McGill, C. W. (1984). *Family care of schizophrenia.* New York: Guilford.

Goldman, H. H. (1982). Mental illness and family burden: A public health perspective. *Hospital and Community Psychiatry, 33,* 557-559.

Hatfield, A. B. (1983). What families want of family therapists. In W. McFarlane (Ed.), *Family therapy in schizophrenia* (pp. 41-65). New York: Guilford.

Hatfield, A. B. (1987). The expressed emotion theory: Why families object. *Hospital and Community Psychiatry, 38,* 341.

Holden, D. F., & Lewine, R. J. (1982). How families evaluate mental health professionals, resources, and effects of illness. *Schizophrenia Bulletin, 8*, 626-633.

Johnson, D. L. (1990). The family's experience of living with mental illness. In H. P. Lefley & D. L. Johnson (Eds.), *Families as allies in treatment of the mentally ill* (pp. 31-63). Washington, DC: American Psychiatric Press.

Kanter, J., Lamb, H. R., & Loeper, C. (1987). Expressed emotion in families: A critical review. *Hospital and Community Psychiatry, 38*, 374-380.

Kreisman, D. E., & Joy, V. D. (1974). Family response to the mental illness of a relative: A review of the literature. *Schizophrenia Bulletin, 10*, 34-57.

Lefley, H. P. (1987). The family's response to the mental illness of a relative. In A. B. Hatfield (Ed.), *Families of the mentally ill: Meeting the challenges* (pp. 3-21). San Francisco: Jossey-Bass.

McGoldrick, M., & Gerson, R. (1985). *Genograms in family assessment.* New York: Norton.

Miklowitz, D. J., Goldstein, M. J., & Falloon, I.R.H. (1983). Premorbid and symptomatic characteristics of schizophrenics from families with high and low levels of expressed emotion. *Journal of Abnormal Psychology, 92*, 359-367.

Minkoff, K. (1978). A map of chronic mental patients. In J. A. Talbott (Ed.), *The chronic mental patient* (pp. 11-37). Washington, DC: American Psychiatric Press.

National Institute of Mental Health (NIMH). (1985). *Treatment strategies in schizophrenia manual.* Unpublished manuscript.

Scheidt, S. D. (1984). *SUPPORT: A psycho-educational program for families of schizophrenic patients.* Unpublished doctoral dissertation, Rutgers University, New Brunswick, NJ.

Terkelsen, K. G. (1990). A historical perspective on family-provider relationships. In H. P. Lefley & D. L. Johnson (Eds.), *Families as allies in the treatment of the mentally ill* (pp. 3-21). Washington, DC: American Psychiatric Press.

Uzoka, A. (1979). The myth of the nuclear family: Historical background and implications. *American Psychologist, 34*, 1095-1106.

Vaughn, C. E., & Leff, J. P. (1976). The measurement of expressed emotion in the families of psychiatric patients. *British Journal of Social and Clinical Psychology, 15*, 157-165.

PART II

Clinical Case Management Activities

5

Comprehensive Assessment
and Treatment Planning

ALLAN F. LEUNG

Like the proverbial blind men who had erroneously concluded the elephant's true nature, so too can the clinician's assessment, and the treatment plan that develops with it, provide misinformation about the client's clinical status if they do not consider all aspects of functioning. Comprehensive assessment minimizes this possibility by obtaining information that evaluates all areas of the client's life.

Comprehensive assessment is critical when working with severely mentally ill individuals who often experience multiple problems and needs. As noted in Chapter 1, a treatment approach is comprehensive when all areas of possible benefit are addressed. To do this, comprehensive assessment evaluates four domains of functioning. On a conceptual level, they are the psychological or intrapsychic, the biological, the social, and the environmental. By developing a formulation of clients' functioning in these domains, clinicians address each client's unique blending of strengths, symptoms, levels of disability, and needs.

Comprehensive assessment occurs in multiple settings. Conventionally, assessment has occurred in the office, relying on what clients, and sometimes third parties, report. While valuable, this information can be misleading. For example, clients may be only minimally in touch with reality, or may be suspicious or mistrustful, and thus provide either little or incorrect information. By observing and interacting with clients across their habitats as true participant observers, clinicians draw on their observational skills and expertise to obtain firsthand knowledge of clients' psychological and social functioning. Comprehensive assessment is only one aspect of an intertwined process. Treatment planning is the other. Planning occurs simultaneously and represents clinicians' attempts to identify and prioritize their clients' needs, in an effort to develop strategies to resolve clients' psychological and practical problems and pursue their goals. The assessment and planning processes are not static. Clinicians modify their initial assessment over time as more is learned about clients' psychological states, character traits, and environmental needs. For clients who have long histories of severe psychological disturbance, comprehensive assessment and treatment planning are long-term processes. Therefore, clinical case management must be an intensive and continuous treatment approach in order to meet clients' total needs.

Because of the interrelationship between these two concepts, treatment planning is incorporated into the discussion of comprehensive assessment by describing plans and interventions within the case examples that are presented. Treatment planning issues, including client participation and prioritization, will follow.

Comprehensive Assessment

To understand clients' experiences and patterns of behavior in the four domains of psychological or intrapsychic, biological, social, and environmental functioning, clinicians obtain clinical data from three interrelated areas: history and present status, social support network, and the resources available in the community. By understanding these areas and their interrelationships, clinicians obtain a clinical picture of their clients' psychological adequacy in maintaining themselves in their social and physical environments.

Assessment of the Individual's History and Present Status

A model developed by Ossorio[1] is adapted here to provide a conceptual framework for client assessment. In this model, several parameters are considered to determine patterns of behavior. These patterns are viewed as successful when they lead to the accomplishment (i.e., achievement) of one's goals through one's actions (i.e., performance). This framework can be schematically represented as follows:

$$B = I + M + K + KH \rightarrow P, A,$$

where B refers to the Behavior (or behavior pattern) in question; I represents clients' Identity; M, their Motivations; K, Knowledge of themselves, of others, and of the world; KH, Know-how or their abilities and skills; and P, the actions (Performance) clients employ in order to accomplish their goals, A, or Achievement.

Identity. This parameter acknowledges that every individual's expression of life is a unique one that has developed as a result of personal life experiences. This implies that clinicians need to not only consider clients' strengths and weaknesses, but must also understand their dynamic interrelationships. This is required in order to learn what factors have advanced or hindered clients' efforts toward meeting their psychological and practical needs.

The areas of assessment within this parameter include premorbid characteristics, health, the mental illness, self-protective coping abilities, social skills, substance use history, developmental history, and ethnic and cultural background.

The clients' premorbid characteristics to be examined are cognitive and intellectual development, as well as their level of intelligence, their status with regards to information processing, and their learning style. Through this assessment, clinicians determine what form their interventions will take.

For example, a 30-year-old Chinese-American man, E.N., was referred for clinical case management services following four acute hospitalizations in a one-year period. Each of his hospitalizations was precipitated by preoccupying intrusive suicidal thoughts. These intensified with the client's perception that he was unable to control his destructive impulses. Assisting him to develop constructive coping strategies and "no-suicide" agreements were minimally effective. Psychological testing revealed that E.N.'s intellectual ability was in the borderline range (IQ: 71) and that he had significant recent memory impairment. Knowing this, the clinician's treatment plan included developing interventions that were more concrete. To help the client be more aware of the nature of the progress he was making (albeit slowly) and to accommodate to his memory impairment, the clinician had the client walk across his office, taking "two steps forward and one step back" while verbally repeating this phrase aloud. This simple and concrete approach instilled hope and reduced the suicidal thinking.

Clients' current health status and physical limitations are also important to consider. These become particularly important when they interact with clients' psychiatric disturbance.

54-year-old C.V. was recently diagnosed with near-end-state Chronic Obstructive Pulmonary Disease (COPD), requiring her to be on home oxygen. Her physician told the clinician that C.V. was ambulatory and, in fact, it was "good for her to get out." Despite coaxing and encouragement, C.V. would refuse the clinician's attempts to take her for short walks. Initially, the clinician thought this was a manifestation of her delusional disorder; she was unrealistically fearful that there were men outside her door who wanted to harm her. Even when this belief remitted with medications, C.V. refused to go out. Eventually, the clinician realized that, psychologically, C.V. was minimizing her illness, viewing it as if it were a cold from which she would recover. Her refusal to venture out was primarily a result of her unconscious response to her recently diagnosed medical condition. The clinician revised the plan and addressed the client's denial of the seriousness of her medical illness, using psychoeducational and, later, more psychologically oriented interventions.

Clients' medical histories also provide information about physical conditions that affect their psychological functioning. A thorough medical history is helpful. For instance, neurological deficits such as significant memory loss may be due to various factors like chronic alcohol dependence, learning disabilities, mental retardation, or HIV infection.

Clients' capacity to protect themselves is another area of assessment, particularly when clients are impoverished. Clients often live in the inner city or other areas where exploitation is high. Psychological vulnerability also occurs for those living in marginal environments. Coping with the stress of these living situations depends, in part, on clients' abilities to protect themselves. It is critical to obtain information about the precautions clients take and what they do to protect themselves. Do they take preventive measures to avoid danger? Do they have the psychological capacity to protect themselves, or are they exploited or often injured?

For example, one client told her clinician that she carried a big hunting knife for protection when she ventured out into the community. When asked whether she had ever used such a weapon, she said she had not, but had learned by watching television. The clinician recognized that the client's desire to protect herself was appropriate, but the means were questionable. After further discussion, the client agreed to attend a self-defense class where she would learn more effective, and hopefully less dangerous, means of self-protection. An added benefit of this intervention was the social contacts that the client was exposed to, which responded to another aspect of the treatment plan.

Social skills are critical to community living. Case managers must assess clients' social abilities and why they may be lacking. If these skills are minimal, does this reflect recent deterioration, suggesting an intervention to facilitate clients' use of preexisting abilities? Or have the levels of social adjustment been chronically poor, suggesting interventions to develop these skills?

Obtaining histories of the mental illnesses enables clinicians to learn about the impact of long-term psychiatric disturbance on their clients' current functioning. This, with other information, allows clinicians to develop a deeper understanding of their clients' inner world and its unique expression.

The following vignette illustrates this. M.N.'s intrapsychic world consisted of a "rock-and-roll universe" populated by well-known bands. He identified with particular rock stars because he felt they had similar life experiences. The clinician assessed that M.N.'s beliefs were not of delusional proportions and tentatively concluded that "differentness" between self and others was threatening for M.N. This led to M.N.'s withdrawal from others and social isolation. He felt profoundly inadequate and psychologically damaged. Identifying with rock stars was the client's way of maintaining a semblance of psychological integrity, by residing in a world that offered safety, connections with "others," and wholeness. Taking this into planning considerations, the clinician arranged for M.N. to attend a small medications group composed of clients who engaged in few interactions with one another. This exposed M.N. to others with minimal psychological threat while simultaneously meeting the need for medications, another critical aspect of the treatment plan. In one-on-one meetings, the clinician and the client spoke about the latter's participation in the group, basing the discussion on input from the group facilitators.

Clients' psychiatric histories also help clinicians identify individual patterns of symptom exacerbation. R.A., a 32-year-old man, was referred for crisis-prone behaviors, including suicidal impulses. These experiences even occurred when he was worried about a minor situation, despite his having acted on a constructive alternative. As a result, he presented as often as weekly at the Psychiatric Emergency Service.

The treatment plan involved the clinician helping R.A. not only to identify this pattern but also to understand the relationship between his moderate dysphoric impulses and his behavior. R.A. was able to learn to manage his impulses by "delaying" long enough to use a more constructive strategy: calling the clinician.

Because mentally ill clients often use substances, it is important to obtain detailed histories of their use, including current usage. The quantity, pattern of use, and the circumstances under which it occurs provide clinicians opportunities to assist clients in identifying the meaning behind the substance use. For example, use may serve to deny past painful experiences or to fill long, empty, aimless days. Assessing the meaning of substance use helps determine the extent to which substance abuse treatment will be pursued. If use interferes with a client's ability to function and/or presents a significant health problem, the clinician might target the abuse as a priority in the treatment plan. This decision may involve making appointments or actually accompanying clients to facilities for treatment.

Taking a developmental history provides information about clients' highest levels of social and emotional functioning. Psychosocial developmental milestones are noted for their levels of accomplishment. Clinicians' understanding of these will enable them to compare these capacities or baselines to clients' current levels of functioning. Moreover, clients' psychodynamics are elucidated.

Cultural values and norms are operative throughout clients' development and they are eventually internalized, becoming cultural traits. Clients' cultural values and their meanings are important areas for clinicians to assess. As Chapter 3 notes, culture is a resource to be used in developing treatment plans. This consideration enables clinicians to both appreciate and utilize strengths that are derived from ethnocultural sources. For example, clinicians may become more attuned to culturally relevant formal and informal support networks that are available, to culturally syntonic manifestations of emotional expressiveness, to responses to authority, to the normative expression of verbal communications, and to the cultural meaning of autonomy. An understanding of culture is required for an adequate assessment, and leads to appropriate planning for effective interventions.

Motivation.   Understanding motivation enables clinicians to answer the question, "What does the client want?" This perspective, rather than a purely psychopathological one, allows them to support clients' often latent desires for change and to inspire their clients to adopt proactive stances to their problems and goals.

Clients are motivated by different needs. Motivations may be aroused by survival and physical needs, by affiliative needs such as satisfying social relationships, by the desire for autonomy, by the need to work or contribute to others, or by transcending previous limitations through expressing ethical, moral, and spiritual values.

Clients may be aware of their motivations, or they may need a process whereby a clinician empathically facilitates identification of them. Awareness of motivations may be prevented by a greater need to reduce tension and anxiety. The established, often automatic, ways in which clients have learned to do this often prevent them from understanding their problems and reaching their goals. Clinicians are alert to these maladaptive patterns of behavior by which clients inadvertently create obstacles to their efforts to actualize adaptive motivations.

Affiliative motivations are assessed with information from the client's history, from observations by the clinician, and, most important, from the client's expressed desire for love and affection, to be cared for, and to care for others (Kanter, 1985).

R.A. would incessantly talk about his desire for love from a woman. The clinician eventually understood that this love R.A. spoke about was really an amalgam of his longing for companionship because he was desperately lonely and isolated, as well as for the gratification of his sexual urges.

Despite R.A.'s outgoing, engaging, and personable demeanor, and his ability to engage in activities, he never followed through on plans developed with his clinician. Plans to attend church social activities or group recreational activities would fall by the wayside.

Eventually, the clinician learned that R.A. experienced himself as damaged, having as a child suffered severe burns and widespread scarring over much of his upper body. This disfigurement hindered his ability to maintain a positive sense of self-esteem. Learning this, the clinician surmised that the client's desire to protect himself from emotional injury outweighed his desire to satisfy affiliative needs. Instead of continuing to encourage R.A. to find social activities, the clinician decided to help him explore and resolve his apparent conflicting motivations.

Clinicians must also examine their clients' motivations for independence and autonomy. This can involve assessing their clients' capacity to maintain self-esteem, particularly when faced with disappointment; to experience a sense of mastery and accomplishment; and to experience pleasure derived from recreation and sexual satisfaction.

As R.A. illustrates, clients have multiple motivations that can be in conflict with one another. Understanding the meanings behind clients' motivations often provide clues to unravel their unconscious conflicts or expressions of concerns, which may only manifest as behaviors without apparent awareness (Kanter, 1985).

Clinicians also evaluate their clients' capacity and ability to go beyond or rise above their limitations. This requires understanding what seeds exist deep within the clients that may eventually germinate and inspire them to go beyond their perceived and real deficits.

A.A., a 45-year-old woman diagnosed with paranoid schizophrenia, had a cancerous tumor on her cervix. She had been working with her case manager for several years (more details of this earlier period of treatment follow) when she learned of this. It was urgent that she have a biopsy as soon as possible to determine the severity of the disease. Because A.A. wanted to have more children, motivated by unrealistic fantasies of remaking the past, she initially refused to have this procedure despite the urgency that it be performed. Eventually, she agreed, and on the day of the surgery, the case manager (who was there to give support at A.A.'s request) and the client's aunt waited several hours with her before the operation. Initially, A.A. was "scared." She emphasized this point by reminding the clinician how, on several previous nights, she had been incontinent while sleeping. As the aunt and the client waited, the case manager observed their relationship and interactions. As time passed, the clinician heard A.A. say several times, "I'm gonna be strong," as she spoke with her aunt and reminisced and chuckled about times when they both lived in another part of the country. Her aunt comforted A.A., assuring her she would feel no pain. She became more relaxed, but the most striking change was her facial expression: She appeared tranquil and at peace. By the time she was wheeled into the operating room, A.A. told the case manager that she was no longer scared. The clinician thought to himself that he had witnessed a transformation and, indeed, A.A. had transcended her limitations.

Knowledge. Assessing clients' fund of knowledge means learning about the information they possess and can potentially act on in order to bring about constructive changes. This information includes clients' views of themselves, others, and the world in which they live. Clinicians must also assess the accuracy and breadth of the knowledge clients have in order to correct inaccurate or distorted information or misunderstandings.

For example, E.N., the 30-year-old man who had borderline intellectual ability, would become very quiet whenever the clinician inquired about his activities during the week. This was particularly true when E.N. had episodes of suicidal thinking and impulses. Eventually, the clinician learned that for E.N., suicidal thinking meant he was unlike others and therefore an aberration. Compounding this negative view was an accurate one—that his "learning disabilities" imposed limitations on his prospects for gainful employment, which he greatly desired. He also believed others thought as negatively of him as he did about himself.

The clinician implemented a plan in which E.N. volunteered at the Salvation Army. Working there demonstrated to the client a greater range of knowledge (and skills) than he previously thought he possessed. By acquiring new information about his abilities, E.N. began to develop a new view of himself.

Know-How. Clinicians systematically assess their clients' know-how, or abilities and skills, in a variety of areas. These include psychological, social, and practical abilities.

The various strategies and skills that clients possess have both quantitative and qualitative aspects. For example, in assessing job-hunting abilities, clients may indicate one or more ways (e.g., newspaper ads, unemployment office, word-of-mouth) to pursue work. The more ways clients have to accomplish something, the more likely they are to succeed.

In the above example, the clinician may determine that despite the possession of a number of job-hunting skills, the client does not present job qualifications in the best light, or is not able to follow up on want ads. These are qualitative aspects of the client's abilities.

A client's functional history is an important source of information on the client's abilities. Previous educational and vocational functioning indicate the likelihood of future success. For example, clients have often met with despairing disappointment and failure when they have attempted to work. In supporting clients' efforts to work, clinicians consider vocational and educational histories to avoid setting goals too high, which can reinforce a history of failure, or too low, which may be experienced as condescending or infantilizing.

Know-how involves psychological considerations. Clinicians not only address behavioral issues in, for example, vocational endeavors, but also pay attention to anxiety and other symptoms that arise in these contexts. Other psychological variables to be considered are clients' abilities to control their impulses, to delay gratification, and to concentrate on complex tasks.

Social skills also require close attention. A history of previous relationships, including those with family and friends as well as romantic involvements in the past and in the present, is most helpful.

Moreover, the concepts embodied in object relations theory and self-psychology prove very useful in identifying the underlying, intrapsychic layer and the psychodynamics that will influence clients' social behaviors and emotional functioning. Establishing that clients experience others as part-objects, for instance, enables clinicians to develop treatment plans that will assist them toward greater psychological differentiation. When progress has been made in this area, clients are better able to modulate their affect when they relate to others as psychologically separate individuals.

Performance and Achievement. The performance and achievement parameters have been alluded to in the discussions of identity, motivation, knowledge, and know-how. Performance and achievement can be thought of as the confluence of these parameters, giving rise to some action (performance) that is intended to accomplish a particular purpose (achievement). They refer to clients' fund of personal power that they can bring to bear in resolving their problems, which results from their practical, psychological, and social functioning.

When there is significant incongruence between clients' performance and *successful* achievement, a psychological, social, and/or environmental factor may be interfering. Determining what particular factors are operating enables clinicians and clients to develop relevant treatment plans. For example, if inadequate skills lead to poor performance on a particular job, the plan may include vocational training or volunteer work. If the poor performance is related to environmental obstacles, such as poor transportation that causes the client to arrive late to work, a very different intervention is called for.

Incongruence between performance and achievement may result from unconscious motivations and conflicts. For instance, clients' beliefs about themselves may be so negative that they result in paralyzing indecisiveness in spite of their motivations and skills to involve themselves in the work world. Work on the psychological issues may need to proceed, or occur along with, more practical interventions.

A.A. (who was presented earlier) is a single, 45-year-old, African-American mother of three children with a diagnosis of chronic paranoid schizophrenia. Her children were removed from her custody following a psychotic episode, in which she held one of the children out a second-story window, threatening to drop her. This incident led to one of 10 hospitalizations that occurred over recent years.

As in the past, A.A.'s relatives agreed to care for her children while she recovered. A.A. reluctantly agreed to this because the only other alternative was foster care. The children, however, were very happy with this arrangement.

Her ambivalence stemmed from both reality-oriented and psychotic sources. A.A. indicated that one relative's husband had made sexual advances toward her, which frightened her and stimulated emotionally loaded memories of the violence she had been subjected to at the hands of her ex-husband. These recent sexual advances motivated A.A. to avoid some family members, which ensured emotional safety for herself. Her psychotic thinking, however, led to delusional beliefs that her extended family was the cause of her children's poor academic grades (her children were, in fact, getting passing grades), of her son's drug usage (her son did not use street drugs), and of her children's friendships with "undesirable" children. Psychologically, A.A. sought to put distance between herself and parts of her family.

Yet A.A. was grateful to her family. She recognized that they were instrumental in caring for her children and had always "been there" when she was hospitalized.

One of A.A.'s goals was the reunification of the family. She agreed to a course of treatment that included her participation in residential and day treatment programs while continuing her contacts with the clinical case manager. This plan increased the likelihood of successful reunification. A peer case manager assisted A.A. in meeting practical needs. As her clinical status improved, she attended parenting classes and, as reunification approached—2 years after A.A. began treatment—she and her children began family therapy.

In terms of the conceptual model used in this chapter, A.A.'s desire to distance herself from her family, motivated by her need for psychological safety and consequent use of projective mechanisms to achieve this, led her to a solution, sometimes psychotic in nature, that satisfied this need. However, it simultaneously severed the family support she required to maintain family cohesiveness and functioning. A psychological conflict interfered with her performance and this hindered the achievement of her goal.

Family therapy was a component of the treatment plan that responded to two purposes: first, to assist the family through the reunification process, and second, as a forum to help A.A. and the rest of the family maintain the positive emotional ties that existed between them and the children.

When clinicians use the conceptual model presented here, it is important to remember that the information they learn about the client's functioning in each of these parameters has to be integrated. Clinicians need to consider all the parameters collectively in order to understand their clients as whole persons.

Assessment of Social Support Networks

As noted above, social support is critical to successful functioning. McGill and Surber (1989) consider any individual who plays a supportive role in a client's life as a useful source of information. Clinicians must determine what family, friends, and acquaintances clients have, and the nature of their relationships.

Family members may be an important source of support for clients as well as a rich source of information for the case manager. It is necessary to assess family members' understanding of and attitudes toward their relative's psychiatric illness. Attention must also be paid to the family's burden in caring for their relative; the family's expectations, goals, and aspirations; and the strength and resources they can bring to bear in caring for the client.

Kanter (1985) notes that family relationships are often the context in which clients' serious deficits in social functioning manifest themselves. Opportunities to observe clients interacting with family members provide valuable information with regard to this.

In one case, the clinician observed the client, a 25-year-old man, accost his mother verbally because she loved her other adult children more than she did him. He angrily demanded that she include his name on the deed to the family home as proof of her love for him. The mother became so frightened that she fled to her bedroom, with the client trailing close behind. The clinician, who had witnessed similar behaviors by the client with others, but in milder forms, now had a much better understanding of the client's significant social (and psychological and emotional) limitations. The treatment plan prioritized safety and socialization as immediate issues to be addressed. Interventions included psychological counseling to assist the client in modulating and managing his aggressive impulses, and family meetings to assist the family in dealing with the client's frightening and inappropriate behaviors.

Friendships and acquaintances may be important sources of support. For instance, a particular friend may have always provided support when the client was decompensating. Or a client and a particular friend protected each other in an inner-city hotel. On the other hand, some friends may exert negative influences because they coax clients into abusing drugs or financially exploit them.

Community members such as a sympathetic merchant may provide groceries and "run a tab." Another store owner may fulfill the role of a money manager by agreeing to cash the client's checks and disburse a daily "allowance." Staff of other human service programs, such as a social worker in the department of social services or a medical practitioner, can also provide significant supports for clients. It is necessary for the clinician to assess the depth and breadth of the client's support system. Clinicians have an important role with regard to the individuals who can play critical supportive roles in clients' lives. If case managers provide education, support, and realistic hope to those in the client's support system (with the client's permission), these individuals can greatly enhance the clinician's treatment plan.

A.A., the 45-year-old, African-American mother of three who was introduced above, experienced ambivalent feelings toward her extended family. During the later course of treatment, she was encouraged to take her children on weekend outings to get reacquainted. During this period, A.A.'s 14-year-old daughter reported that she was abused by an adult cousin.

Child Protective Services (CPS) concluded that the allegations were unfounded. The CPS worker believed that the allegations were an active bid to reunite with her mother. The case manager hypothesized that the mother's desire to reunite with her family was played out by her daughter. In addition, the incident occurred during a period of time when the client manifested heightened suspicions about the extended family's adverse influence on her children. Unfortunately, this incident angered the relative with whom the children lived, and she threatened to place A.A.'s children in foster care.

This incident not only needed to be explored with A.A. for its psychological significance, but also required interventions that would maintain the practical and emotional support of the extended family. To repair the rupture in the family system and to support family reunification, the case manager helped the family understand the client's behavior and acknowledge the vital role the relative had played in raising A.A.'s children. This rejuvenated the relative's hopes and determination to continue providing care.

Another aspect of this case involved the clinician's recognition of the emotional support the client's care providers, including mental health consumers, gave the client. Periodic conferences with these treatment providers, which sometimes included the client, served to both develop common goals and coordinate the treatment plan. More significantly, they motivated all of the care providers to support the client's efforts over several years.

Another way of assessing clients' social support network is to learn about their daily activities. Clinicians learn to what extent their clients' lives are peopled, as well as the nature and extent of their daily activities.

If their clients have few or no social contacts, treatment planning will involve efforts to develop social relationships. Examples include referrals to a day treatment program, a client-run socialization program, or a substance abuse meeting. Other socially oriented activities may include family get-togethers, volunteer activities, church social activities, and shopping trips with friends.

Assessment of Community Resources

Here, clinicians not only determine what resources are available, but also consider these in light of their clients' individual attributes (identity), motivations, knowledge, know-how, performance, and achievement. This means that case managers match their clients to appropriate existing community resources.

For instance, day treatment programs vary, according to the nature and scope of the services they provide as well as to the therapeutic milieu they create. A particular client may require a program that makes few demands with regard to attendance requirements and activities schedules, rather than a relatively stringent one. Another client may require interventions that focus on vocational training, while another may best benefit from a program that offers more socialization activities. Some clients may benefit more from individual therapy, and others from group therapy. Thus, clinicians consider clients' functional levels when they assess community resources.

Moreover, clinicians assess community resources' responses to their clients' needs (Kanter, 1985). They evaluate social barriers that hinder clients' receiving necessary services. For example, C.V., the client who had been diagnosed with near-end-state Chronic Obstructive Pulmonary Disease, would not leave her hotel room because she feared she would have an "attack." The clinician decided that her medical condition warranted immediate attention. Securing medical assistance was only partially successful when the public health nurse agreed to make home visits until a physician was found. Several weeks had passed before the clinician was able to find a physician who made house calls.

This was a very frustrating and potentially catastrophic situation. In a sense, it pitted the clinician against professional norms that limited physicians' ability to make house calls, which inadvertently created barriers to the adequate care of mentally ill (and other) clients.

In C.V.'s case, the problem of finding a physician stood in stark contrast to the ease with which C.V.'s psychiatric needs were met. The program for which the clinician worked had psychiatrists and psychiatric technicians who readily agreed to accompany the clinician to C.V.'s room, monitor her mental status, and follow her psychiatric medication regimen. Clinicians' efforts to identify resources to meet their clients' needs may lead to the discovery that no services exist to address these needs. In this age of budget cuts, clinicians must use existing resources creatively. Assessing these requires clinicians to expand their inquiries beyond mental health, social service, educational, and vocational services provided by the community (Kanter, 1985).

For example, religious organizations may offer a rich variety of social services, and social and recreational activities. Case managers may contact various churches to determine what resources are available and whether they meet clients' needs. The writer has found these organizations very helpful in providing furniture and appliances to help clients establish a household and in offering social activities (e.g., choirs and outings). Assessing community resources considers factors such as how responsive they are to client needs (immediate versus long-term), the nature of their referral process (ease versus complexity), and the quality of their personnel (accepting and tolerant versus rigid and insensitive). It is also very important to evaluate the organization's attitudes toward mentally ill clients.

Family, friends, and other interested individuals are also assessed for their abilities to assist clients. As noted in the section concerning sources of social support, these parties are potentially rich suppliers of assistance to the client. They are assessed for their understanding of the client's psychiatric condition and its behavioral and emotional correlates, and their capacities to provide practical assistance. Clinicians assess whether significant others can accurately observe for side effects of medications, as well as help in medication management. In conjunction with this, psychoeducation may be considered for inclusion in the treatment plan. For those clients who have difficulties in budgeting their money, family and friends may serve as money managers, helping clients budget. Or they may become clients' "big brothers" and "big sisters," accompanying clients on errands and outings.

To determine whether significant others can help the client in these and other ways, case managers also assess for the interpersonal dynamics that exist, noting adaptive and maladaptive ones. They also consider family dynamics from the perspective of clients' psychosocial and developmental histories. Family and friends who would contribute to clients' difficulties may be excluded from the treatment plan. Maladaptive family dynamics that adversely affect clients' current functioning may be addressed through family meetings or family therapy.

Treatment Planning

As noted earlier, comprehensive assessment and treatment planning are actually reciprocal processes. Each aspect of a client's functioning provides the context in which clinicians determine the extent to which potential sources of emotional and practical support can genuinely assist clients. In other words, clients' willingness and readiness to psychologically avail themselves of supports can be understood only with accurate clinical pictures of their functioning. This must be translated into viable treatment plans. Once formulated, plans provide the context in which their adequacy and accuracy reflect clinicians' understanding of their clients. This reciprocal and overarching process becomes the basis for continued refinement of the assessment and plan as more information is learned during the course of treatment.

Coordination of Treatment

Treatment planning serves as the basis for the coordination of services at the systems level, thus facilitating an integrative function (Harris & Bergman, 1987). In the case of E.N., the 30-year-old man who possessed borderline intellectual ability, the clinician's tasks included arranging for the client to visit the Salvation Army's facilities, to learn about his responsibilities and duties, and to meet the individual who would be supervising him. Prior to this visit, the clinician discussed with the prospective supervisor the general intent of the treatment plan and the logistics that would be involved. Because of these efforts, the clinician was also able to effectively engage the client in doing something "real" while exploring his thoughts and feelings about doing volunteer work in office meetings.

Exploring E.N.'s thoughts and feelings illustrates another principle of treatment planning. It is enhanced when it "is done with the client, rather than for the client" (McGill & Surber, 1989). This allows clinicians to continue to individualize treatment. The plan comes to reflect the subtleties of the clients' wishes, needs, knowledge, skills, and conflicts in operational terms that have meaning for them. By involving clients, the ultimate goals of treatment planning—the maintenance and eventual enhancement of clients' psychological and social functioning while meeting their environmental needs in the community—stand a greater likelihood of success.

While this is a collaborative process, there are times when clinicians might exercise their role as an expert or authority. This is particularly true when they determine that their clients' functional levels are sufficiently compromised to engage in effective actions, warranting a more directive approach in order for them to live independently in the community (Harris & Bergman, 1987). In one case, D.L. professed a strong desire to enter a drug treatment program. With the case manager's encouragement, he called several programs to learn about their services and referral processes. Unfortunately, D.L. never made it to the intake appointments for his chosen programs because his substance usage would typically increase and he would invariably report to the clinician his stuporous state, which prevented his following through on the treatment plan. His substance abuse was becoming increasingly frequent and dangerous, because it was during these periods that D.L. would become suicidally impulsive, heightening the possibility of psychiatric hospitalization. With D.L.'s agreement, the clinician decided to not only accompany D.L. to his appointments, but also directed the client to meet with the case manager the 3 days preceding them, to provide more support.

Priorities of Treatment Planning

It is suggested that there are several priorities for implementing the treatment plan. These are (a) safety, (b) survival needs, (c) treatment or response to problems that cause deterioration if unattended, and (d) interventions that foster growth and development.

Safety. From this perspective, the safety of clients and the community becomes a first priority (McGill & Surber, 1989). When clients decompensate to a point where they endanger themselves or others, or are gravely disabled, a structured setting and additional support are necessary; and the clinician may decide to hospitalize the client or increase structure in the community by mobilizing supports.

Survival Needs. These are the second priority and include shelter, food, and clothing (McGill & Surber). The treatment plan must include an immediate response to these needs, and a long-term, overall strategy to assure that clients have an income and the means to manage the plan. Accordingly, the treatment plan might include applications for short-term monetary assistance and long-term disability benefits.

For example, R.G., a 38-year-old man, was fond of the San Francisco Giants; and on a particular spring day, he impulsively decided to live in San Francisco. He had suddenly disappeared from his residential care home, located several hours from San Francisco, without informing anyone. He told the clinician that he had definitely decided to live here but had no money for food or housing. Since his arrival, R.G. had been living on the streets and eating at a local church. He indicated that he received SSI benefits, but that his case manager in the other city was his payee. He refused several attempts to convince him to return to his home city.

The clinician arranged for R.G. to stay at a hotel, contacted his former case manager to forward funds, referred R.G. to a psychiatrist for medication evaluation, and met with R.G. several times during the week to provide emotional and practical support. The latter was considered necessary because R.G.'s thinking was mildly disorganized, he was easily agitated, and his speech was pressured. Given these signs, the clinician attempted to utilize psychological interventions, supported by environmental manipulation, to meet R.G.'s immediate needs.

Treatment or Response to Unattended Problems. These are the third priority that clinicians attend to in planning. As noted in the preceding example, clinicians assure that medications are available for their clients. It is not unlikely that clinicians will work with clients who refuse medications, often leading to serious consequences. These situations should include strategies that encourage them to participate in this aspect of treatment.

Clients' needs for medical attention are yet another area that clinicians assess and plan for. This is especially important if a medical condition significantly influences a client's psychological functioning or interferes with the client's achieving goals. Signs and symptoms of hyperthyroidism, for example, include anxiety, irritability, tension, and a certain emotional fragility that is characterized by episodes of prominent emotional expressions, such as crying or laughing without provocation.

The need for substance abuse treatment and assistance in dealing with legal problems is also included in the treatment plan. Ongoing substance abuse and/or dependence affects clients' psychiatric symptoms, often leading to crisis and decompensation. Engaging in this and other illegal activities exposes clients to incarceration, or they may be already involved in the criminal justice system. Thus, planning might include the clinician's advising the court of the client's mental illness, recommending psychiatric treatment, or securing legal services for the client, as well as either referring the client for or providing substance abuse services.

Growth and Development. The fourth priority includes activities that clinicians and their clients agree are important for development and growth. To facilitate these, clinicians must pay particular attention to their clients' psychotherapeutic needs. "The case manager must build a relationship, respect defenses, explore relevant issues, and consider what sort of reflective, clarifying, or interpretive comments are most appropriate" (Kanter, 1989, p. 365).

Development and growth are also facilitated when clinicians plan interventions that lead clients to greater understanding, self-management, and acceptance of their mental illness. Psychoeducation may be the appropriate intervention when clients can tolerate direct discussion of their psychiatric impairments (Kanter, 1989; McGill & Surber, 1989).

Clinicians' knowledge of their clients, their social support network, and environmental circumstances place them in an advantageous position to intervene when changes in these circumstances predispose subtle changes in clients' clinical statuses. This position allows case managers to utilize these changes as vehicles for growth. Being able to point to previous similar circumstances, in which the client responded in a particular manner, may serve as a starting point for exploring different, more adaptive, ways of handling a current situation. Crisis situations offer particularly fertile opportunities for growth enhancement.

Monitoring

The treatment plan provides clinicians the tool to evaluate the accuracy of their assessment and the progress made by clients. Monitoring is the means by which these are accomplished. As Lamb notes, it refers "to the continuous evaluation of progress during treatment" (Lamb, 1980, p. 763). Because mentally ill individuals often participate in clinical case management services for long periods, monitoring also serves to ensure that treatment priorities are reviewed, as well as to assure that systems coordination continues to be responsive to the client's needs.

Summary

Comprehensive assessment leads to the development of treatment plans for serious mentally ill individuals that span four conceptual domains: the psychological, biological, social, and environmental. The assessment of these domains involves the clinician's gaining knowledge and understanding of clients' history and present status, their social support network, and the availability of community resources to provide an understanding of their unique constellation of needs, knowledge, skill, competencies, accomplishments, symptoms, conflicts, disabilities, and resources.

Treatment planning is inextricably intertwined with the assessment process. It is done with clients and is implemented in response to a priority of needs. These priorities are safety, survival needs, treatment or resolution for serious conditions or problems, and services that foster development and growth. When the plan is implemented, the clinical case manager provides and coordinates interventions with other care providers and services, and uses the plan to monitor the client's progress.

Note

1. Peter Ossorio's conceptual model served as the basis for clinical consultation that occurred between Dan Popov, Ph.D., and the author between 1976 and 1979. The model is a part of a broader one that Dr. Ossorio called Descriptive Psychology. Dr. Ossorio is a psychologist and a faculty member at the University of Colorado, Boulder. Dr. Popov is a psychologist who formerly practiced in Monterey, California.

References

Harris, H., & Bergman, H. C. (1987). Case management with the chronically mentally ill: A clinical perspective. *American Journal of Orthopsychiatry, 57*(2), 296-302.

Kanter, J. S. (1985). Psychosocial assessment in community treatment. In J. S. Kanter (Ed.), *New directions for mental health services* (Vol. 27, pp. 63-75). San Francisco: Jossey-Bass.

Kanter, J. S. (1989). Clinical case management: Definition, principles, components. *Hospital and Community Psychiatry, 40*(4), 361-368.

Lamb, H. R. (1980). Therapist-case managers: More than brokers of services. *Hospital and Community Psychiatry, 31*(11), 762-764.

McGill, C. W., & Surber, R. W. (1989). Case management. In A. S. Bellack (Ed.), *Clinical guide for the treatment of schizophrenia* (pp. 77-99). New York: Plenum.

6

Linkage and Monitoring

ROBERT W. SURBER

It follows from the broad definition of what is therapeutic, described in Chapter 1, that linking clients to community resources is an important mental health treatment role. Even when a case management program provides relatively comprehensive care, there are many needs that a client may have that must be provided by resources outside the program. The resources to which clients need to be linked go well beyond the formal human service system and include all of the human and physical resources of the community.

Monitoring derives from the concept of continuity of care. Seriously mentally ill clients usually suffer from chronic disorders that require ongoing treatment and support. However, clients frequently make dramatic changes over time. These include changes in symptoms, behaviors, and needs, which require various interventions. To be able to identify and respond to changing needs, the case manager keeps in touch with clients through monitoring.

This chapter will describe the processes of linkage and monitoring in detail.

Linkage

Linkage is defined as the process by which the client obtains the benefit of available resources. Therefore, it goes well beyond merely making a referral, or getting a client to or through an intake process. The linkage process may continue throughout the time that a client utilizes a particular resource. `

By this definition linkage can be one of the most challenging aspects of the case management role. This is because there frequently are obstacles that exist within the clients, and also obstacles within the community resources that conspire to defeat the linkage process. The case manager is expected to develop strategies to overcome these obstacles so that the client does make use of needed resources.

Finally, it is also suggested that due to the complexities of linking clients to resources, linkage requires a high degree of skill.

Premises of Linkage

A first premise is that clients are to be involved in the linkage process. Involvement, of course, includes clients determining what services and resources they need and choosing between the available alternatives. However, it also means that clients must participate in making use of resources. Linkage is a process that should not only support client strengths and abilities, but also utilize client resources.

A second premise is that all available community resources are to be utilized to support client needs. Indeed, clients are likely to be ill served if they rely completely on the formal human service system, which often has too few resources for too many clients. Therefore, it is incumbent on case managers to help clients mobilize all of the available resources in the community in support of the care plan. In terms of human resources this includes medical and social service staff, family and friends, landlords and hotel managers, clergy and mental health consumers, local store owners and employers, and so forth. There are also a variety of concrete resources available in communities that can be used to the clients' benefit, such as parks, libraries, tourist attractions, educational programs, theaters, restaurants, transportation systems, museums, and the like.

Obstacles to Linkage

The difficulties in the linkage process result in obstacles that are presented both by the clients and by the community resources.

Obstacles Within the Clients

There are a number of difficulties experienced by clients that can impede effective linkage. These include the symptoms of mental illness, skill deficits, psychological issues, and inadequate resources.

The symptoms of mental illnesses can interfere with functioning in a number of ways. For instance, the positive symptoms of schizophrenia, such as hallucinations, delusions, and disordered thinking, can interfere with the individuals' ability to organize themselves so that they can use resources that might be available. The negative symptoms of schizophrenia, such as apathy, anergia, and anhedonia, also limit the clients' capacity. The symptoms of mania and depression can be similarly debilitating.

The medications prescribed to ameliorate symptoms can induce side effects, such as lethargy, tremors, and sexual dysfunctions, which can also interfere with relationships and functioning, and detract from clients' ability to take advantage of available resources.

Mental illness can also interfere with skill development. A major skill deficit for many clients is the inability to develop and maintain interdependent relationships. This lack may dramatically interfere with clients' ability to meet their needs.

Many clients have limitations in daily living skills, in such areas as personal hygiene, use of transportation, cooking, money management, maintaining housing, and solving problems. Finally, a large number of clients lack rudimentary prevocational skills and work experience.

There is also a variety of psychological issues that create obstacles to linkage. One that can cause considerable frustration for case managers, if not understood, is ambivalence about competing needs. Ambivalence can express itself in many ways, such as the need for autonomy and genuine dependency needs, or the need to be loved and fear of intimacy, or the need to work and fear of failure.

Many clients also suffer from low self-esteem and feelings of despair and hopelessness. These feelings can lead to goals and aspirations that are understated out of fear, or overstated in an attempt to compensate for them.

Life experiences in general, and specifically experiences with mental health providers, cause some clients to be mistrustful and not interested in accepting help from others in general, and mental health practitioners in particular. This inability to trust interferes with access to many resources that could help with both survival and growth.

Because mental illness tends to strike in late adolescence and young adulthood, it often interferes with normal developmental processes. This can impede the development of relationships, which can greatly limit a client's access to many resources.

Finally, a very large number of mentally ill individuals are poor, and many are very poor. This poverty is not only of financial resources, but also often of social supports. This has been described as a lack of social margin, which means that there are few social supports during times of crisis and high need (Segal & Baumohl, 1980). Mentally ill individuals are more likely than most people to have times of crisis and high need, and are also more likely to have fewer resources to respond to them. Therefore, their poverty is likely to grow deeper, which will further diminish access to community resources.

Obstacles Within Community Resources

Difficulties with linkage occur not only within the clients, but also within the community resources. Unless these obstacles are understood and responded to, linkage efforts may fail.

A major obstacle is the unwillingness of many agencies and individuals to respond to the needs of those with mental illness. This can be a result of stigma and fear, prior poor experience with mentally ill individuals, inflexible and highly demanding expectations that cannot be met by clients, or rules and regulations that inadvertently exclude those with mental health needs. Examples include the landlord or employer who will not rent to or hire anyone whom they know has been psychiatrically hospitalized. Some human service programs also exclude mentally ill persons—such as the alcohol treatment program for women that told a case manager they did not do well with people with schizophrenia, and refused a referral. In fact, many substance abuse treatment programs exclude mentally ill clients, sometimes because the clients are taking medications prescribed to treat the mental illness.

Even some mental health programs exclude a number of highly disabled mentally ill clients because of behaviors that stem from the symptoms of their illnesses, such as hostile outbursts, poor hygiene, and amotivation. Mentally ill clients are also excluded from mental health treatment programs because of having substance abuse disorders or histories of violent behavior.

Historically, departments of rehabilitation have been charged with the responsibility of getting their clients into full-time productive employment. They have frequently not been interested in working with populations, like those with mental illness, who may be able to achieve only limited goals.

Many community resources may not be readily accessible to the mentally ill clients who could benefit from them. Some are financially inaccessible because poor people cannot afford them. Others are geographically inaccessible to individuals who depend on public transportation.

Finally, some services are linguistically or culturally inaccessible because they cannot provide care in the language the client speaks, or is comfortable speaking, or cannot engage the client and provide appropriate care because they lack expertise with the client's culture.

A lack of community resources also impedes mentally ill clients from meeting their needs. This lack may result in priorities being placed on other populations. It might result in staff who are overwhelmed and sometimes hostile to clients who have unique and time-consuming needs. It often means that certain services are unavailable.

Strategies for Linkage

The case manager is expected to develop strategies to overcome the difficulties of linkage. Although strategies will be described separately, for responding to the obstacles induced by clients and those created by community resources, these strategies must be implemented concurrently.

Being Resourceful

The first strategy of linkage is to identify resources that clients could use. All of the many ways to locate resources should be used. The more familiar case managers are with the community, the more successful they will be at finding resources that can be useful for their clients.

Some organizations compile resource directories for formal human services, and these do have some value as a starting point. Another excellent directory that is available in every community is the telephone book.

Fellow case managers are not only usually knowledgeable about what resources are available, they may also know how particular services respond to different types of clients, and can provide information about who to contact and tips on what approach to take. Other colleagues in other agencies can be similarly helpful.

A case manager's own social contacts, such as family, friends, fellow church and social organization members, neighbors, and personal service providers, have a wealth of knowledge about local resources that they are usually willing to share if asked.

One benefit of working in community settings, rather than only in an office, is that the case manager has many opportunities to discover resources in and on the way to the neighborhoods visited. One might discover the "Help Wanted" sign of a local retailer, or a neighborhood park, or a coffee shop where chess is played, or a poster for a free concert, or a dentist who accepts Medicaid, or a notice for a garage sale, or an announcement for a neighborhood fair or church social event, or even a bakery that sells the case manager's favorite pastry. As discussed in Chapter 1, it has been suggested that communities should be viewed as oases of resources (Rapp, 1992). This can be so if case managers are observant and resourceful.

One case manager's client was working on issues of personal hygiene and appearance in order to pursue the goal of working as a receptionist. One of the obstacles was that the client was very tall and could not find inexpensive clothing that would fit him. In a group supervision session one of the case manager's colleagues mentioned a church that had clothes donated to it by a basketball team. This resource would have never been discovered without either the case manager's efforts at pursuing resources or the help of colleagues.

Strategies for Working With Clients

Overcoming the obstacles that clients bring to the linkage process includes understanding both what a client wants and what a client can do. It also includes finding ways to motivate clients and to utilize family and support system resources.

Understanding What Clients Want

Understanding a client's wishes is one key to successful linkage. No linkage can be successful without some degree of participation by the client in the process. Obviously, clients are more likely to participate in obtaining a resource that they want than they will ones they do not see as useful.

Because engagement to the case management program is the first expectation of the case manager, it is often helpful to offer assistance in gaining concrete resources that the client wants. This might include help in obtaining financial resources, housing, or clothing; or interceding with angry family members; or obtaining a low-cost bus pass; or checking on the well-being of a pet; or explaining what the client has to do to get out of the hospital; or providing hope that the client can get better. At this juncture it is necessary to determine both what the client most wants and what the case manager can realistically provide. If the case manager can provide useful interventions that respond to expressed wishes, the client will more likely be invested in continuing the relationship.

Although the focus might be on concrete interventions rather than psychological interventions, this notion of providing something the client wants is a part of all psychotherapeutic treatment. It has been suggested that all clients return to the second psychotherapy session only if they believe that the therapist has something to offer them (Fariello, 1991). What clients say they want is not always what they want. This is not usually out of any attempt at deception, but may result from ambivalence. For instance, one client indicated for several years, with complete sincerity, that he wanted to have a girlfriend. Yet, despite success in many other areas, all of the case manager's efforts to support the client in achieving this goal were met by the client's either having many excuses for not acting or changing the subject. Eventually, the case manager came to realize that the symptoms worsened considerably when the client experienced strong feelings, and that he might be fearful of the intimacy of a close relationship. Both the client's wish for a girlfriend and the fear of intimacy were genuine, but the client could verbalize only the wish. The case manager needed to understand and work with both.

Many major decisions in life are fraught with ambivalence. It is frequently necessary to help clients acknowledge and work with the ambivalence before moving ahead too quickly to respond to stated goals (Nickens, 1989). This can often be the case when clients express the wish to live more independently, or begin work, or move out of the area.

It must be stated that this does not mean that a case manager should be discouraging of a client's stated goals. Goals provide both meaning for the client and useful information for those who provide care. This is so even if the goals might be considered unrealistic or grandiose. It is counterproductive to try talking clients out of goals that seem unattainable. It is usually more helpful to try directing the client toward attainable ends. A manager of a crisis residential treatment program has reported that one of his homeless client's stated goals was to become a brain surgeon. Instead of being disparaging of the client's goal, he suggested that the first step toward becoming a brain surgeon was to find permanent housing. The client joined him in working on this goal (Nickens, 1989).

Understanding What Clients Can Do

Understanding what a client is able to do is as important as understanding what the client wants to do (Kanter, 1985). Clients must be able to participate effectively with the resources they are linked to. The linkage process will not only fail but may also have deleterious effects, if clients are referred to resources with which they cannot cope. This requires a careful and comprehensive assessment of the client's ability to perform in a particular setting. Factors to consider include psychiatric stability, interpersonal and daily living skills, psychological preparedness, motivation, and support.

A case manager does not want to set the client up for repeated failures that could cause lower self-esteem, hopelessness, and the desire to withdraw. On the other hand a case manager does want to encourage clients to grow and develop to the maximum. A fear of failure on either the case manager's or the client's part can result in overprotectiveness and stagnation.

The only way to resolve the conflict between pushing a client too far and not pushing a client far enough is to take risks. This is because the only way to truly assess a client's abilities is to test them. And this requires supporting clients in situations where they can either succeed or fail. With proper support and understanding, failure can be used by both the case manager and the client to learn about the client's abilities, motivation, and determination.

Because of the need to take risks, it is frequently a poor strategy to discourage clients from trying to do things they want to do, which the case manager or others feel are beyond their capacity. It is only by doing and succeeding, or failing, that clients learn to know and accept their abilities and limitations. The only positive effect that can come from discouraging clients from doing what they are determined to try is to create the desire in some of them to prove the case manager wrong.

One of the ways to assess what clients can do is to do things with them. Accompanying clients while shopping, or taking the bus, or applying for Social Security, or visiting their family is the best way to directly observe their ability to perform and cope with new and difficult situations. Case managers frequently report surprise at how highly disabled clients are able to function in relatively complex activities when pursuing their own goals. For example, one clinician described a man with schizophrenia, who seemed highly disabled when being assessed in the clinic or at home because he appeared to be thoroughly disorganized and talked to himself incessantly in a very loud voice. However, on a shopping trip to buy music tapes, the client was able to negotiate public transportation, find and purchase the music he wanted, and do so without calling undue attention to himself.

Assessing clients' abilities can usually be done accurately only in community settings. It is only in the community that one can observe how clients relate to the environment and to other people in the settings where they are expected to function. Attempting to assess a client's abilities in treatment environments can produce very misleading results. The staff of one acute inpatient unit had carefully assessed a woman with schizoaffective disorder to determine whether she should be discharged back to her hotel room, or whether she needed longer-term hospitalization. From her functioning in a variety of activities in the hospital, it was concluded that her independent living skills had deteriorated to the point that she needed a more protective and more supportive setting. This conclusion was reconsidered when the woman's case manager brought some personal belongings to the hospital. The case manager reported that the client's room was found to be neat and orderly and well stocked with food. It was also reported that her clothes were clean and placed neatly in her drawers. The client had paid her rent before being hospitalized, and made a point of asking her case manager to bring her automatic teller machine card to the hospital.

Developing Motivation Through Education and Support

The need to motivate clients to utilize resources that they need, to strive toward their goals, and to continue to make gains toward personal growth clearly demonstrates that linkage requires sophisticated clinical skills. This is because motivation is a psychological process that is developed through the relationship between clinician and client.

The importance of client goals has been emphasized throughout this book. Goals are primary motivators. Therefore, when encouraging clients to utilize resources, or when supporting clients' efforts, it is always helpful to be mindful of the clients' expressed goals and wishes.

One strategy for developing motivation is to provide education. At the most basic level, a case manager can educate clients about what resources are available and how they might be helpful. In a similar vein, information about the intake process, admission criteria, the workings of the program, and what is expected of the client can all demystify the process, reduce anxiety, and make clients more comfortable in pursuing services that they need.

Another aspect of education is helping clients see how participating with some services or activities can help them achieve their goals. For instance, the case manager of a young man with schizophrenia, who was resistant to taking medication, noticed that he became very anxious in even limited social situations. As the client's goal was to make more friends, the case manager was able to help him see not only that his social skills improved when he was less anxious, but also that his medications reduced his anxiety.

By contrast, helping clients see the negative consequences of not utilizing available resources or treatment is an alternate strategy. The mother of a man with schizophrenia made it very clear to her son that she could not tolerate his paranoid and threatening behavior, which occurred when he stopped taking medications. She told him that he and his family could not continue to live in her house unless he continued to take medications. The client was able to later acknowledge to his mother and case manager that his feelings and behaviors when not taking medications threatened not only his housing, but also his relationship with his wife and his ability to care for his infant son.

Pointing out negative consequences seldom has value in the abstract or as a supposition. It is counterproductive if used in a way that makes the clients feel threatened. Clients can best come to see the link between their behavior and the negative consequences when they are actually experiencing negative consequences.

Providing support is a critical aspect of helping to motivate clients. One component is emotional support. Many clients have little confidence in the possibility of improving their lives. This may be because of low self-esteem or lack of confidence due to previous poor experiences. Motivating these clients involves providing encouragement, faith, and hope. Obviously, this must be done in a manner that is genuine, honest, and realistic. Nevertheless, clients do often respond to encouragement to do something, just because a person they trust believes that they can do it. Standing by clients during times of failure can minimize the negative impact. Celebrating their successes can support self-confidence. One success may lead to an attempt for another. Similarly, clients can accept help only from clinicians who have hope that they can get better and improve their situation, even though the clients, themselves, may feel hopeless about their plight (Lovejoy, 1982).

Support often can be provided more concretely. Direct support may include activities from helping clients problem solve, to accompanying clients and actively assisting them in obtaining resources, to providing services directly to clients. There is considerable value in providing direct and active support. The primary reason is that there are some things that clients cannot do for themselves.

The disabilities of mental illness can dramatically reduce clients' ability to function in many areas, which creates genuine dependency needs. Therefore, it is often necessary to do many things for clients, or arrange to have things done for them, that they cannot do for themselves. This can include obtaining housing and entitlements or money management services, helping clients move, working through poor family relationships, assisting with transportation, or shopping for and preparing food. Obviously, it would be unethical not to assist clients with these basic needs if they are incapable of meeting them on their own.

As noted above, there are times, particularly early in the development of the case management relationship, when it can be useful to actively provide support. Due to both the symptoms of mental illness and previous negative experiences with mental health services, many clients do not trust that it will be of value to utilize the services of a case manager. Since clients must participate with case management services for them to be useful, case managers must show clients how they can be helpful. A useful strategy for demonstrating the value of the case management program is to do something or provide something that the client wants.

On the other hand, there are many times when it is more valuable to *not* do things for clients. Indeed, doing things for clients that they can do for themselves is not only not supportive but also will often have negative consequences.

The intent of any clinical intervention is to support clients' strengths. If case managers take over functions and activities that clients can do for themselves, it will not allow clients to build on their own strengths. Some clients will be satisfied to have a case manager or others do for them what they can do for themselves. Doing things for these clients can lead to regressed behavior and unnecessary dependence. Therefore, it is important to provide active support only when there is a clear clinical justification for it.

It is not always easy to assess what clients can do for themselves and what must be done for them. Therefore, even when accompanying clients in various activities, one must be mindful to take over for the client as little as possible. For instance, on a visit to an entitlement office the case manager might first ask if the client knows the way on public transportation and then allow the client to lead the way. Once at the office the case manager can begin by allowing the client to relate to the staff and complete the forms independently. By waiting to see what the client can do, rather than taking over immediately, the case manager can assess the client's capabilities and build self-esteem by supporting the client's successes. At the same time the case manager can step in and provide active support when the client cannot cope alone.

There are times when a client can be overwhelmed by a problem and will ask the case manager to take over. Rather than accepting total responsibility, the case manager can be more effective by helping the client partialize the problem to see what can be done by the client and how help might be needed.

There are frequently times when case managers are tempted to intervene directly because it is faster and easier for the case manager to do whatever needs to be done than to help the client do it. This temptation should always be resisted.

Patience and persistence are essential ingredients for providing effective support. It may take years for clients to accept needed resources, or it make take years for a needed resource to be available for a client. It is necessary for the case manager to be clear about the long-term treatment goals and to seize upon opportunities when they occur. To illustrate, one case manager worked with a client with schizophrenia who had a poor housing situation, which exacerbated the client's symptoms and interfered with functioning. Suggestions to refer the client to a cooperative housing program were repeatedly rejected for several years. However, when the client's landlady threw out some of her cherished papers, she became so upset that she wanted to leave, and then accepted a referral.

One of the long-standing goals of another client was to be a counselor in a mental health program. The case manager initially thought this goal was unrealistic and tried to divert the client toward other work opportunities. Again, these suggestions were steadfastly refused for years. It was only when a mental health consumer organization developed a peer counseling program in a local hospital that there was an opportunity for the case manager to help the client achieve her goal.

Mobilizing Resources

Some resources are necessary before clients can obtain other resources. For instance, mentally ill individuals cannot effectively access many forms of treatment without housing. Developing autonomous functioning requires both money and the ability to use it appropriately. Similarly, some clients can succeed in gainful employment only after mastering interpersonal skills. Therefore, when implementing a service plan it is necessary to link a client to resources that meet basic needs first, and then to resources that can provide access to further options.

The client's family and other support system members can also be enlisted in the linkage effort. These individuals can provide resources directly, assist clients in obtaining resources, or help bolster motivation. For instance, families often provide housing and economic support for their mentally ill family members; a client's girlfriend or boyfriend can help the client apply for entitlements; and friends can encourage a client to participate in a day treatment program. It is the role of the case manager to identify and mobilize the client's natural resources. This entails educating support system members about client needs, and supporting them so they can support the client. It is helpful for the case manager to make explicit what the case manager and others will do for the client, with the case manager standing ready to step in when others fail to follow through.

A case manager was able to assist a woman with bipolar affective disorder to live independently in the community by utilizing several support system members. First of all, the client's mother, who lived out of state, was willing to send some money to supplement her income as long as the case manager could assure her that the money would be well spent. A friend, when informed about the client's illness and its symptoms, agreed to see the client regularly and inform the case manager of sudden changes in her mental status. The manager of the client's hotel agreed to encourage the client to go to the clinic on appointment days to obtain medications.

Strategies for Working With Community Resources

As detailed above, there are many issues presented within community resources that can interfere with effective linkages. The strategies to overcome the obstacles presented by community resources require a level of knowledge and skill that parallels those involved in overcoming the obstacles to linkage presented by clients. The process of working with a particular resource in linking a client is as important as working directly with the clients. It may also take as much time and effort as working with the client, and may have to continue throughout the period that the client needs the resource.

Strategies for working with resources fall into three general categories: providing education, providing support, and utilizing a relationship.

Providing Education

There are several ways that education can help in gaining acceptance for clients. To begin with, there are many myths and misunderstandings about mental illness throughout most communities. This lack of understanding is quite pervasive and extends to service providers, family members, and the general public. It is not uncommon for even mental health providers to have misconceptions about the treatment needs and capabilities of people with serious mental illnesses. Inadequate knowledge can lead to both fear of those with mental illness and uncertainty regarding how to help these clients. Fear and uncertainty lead to the exclusion of clients from needed supports.

It is important that there be education about mental illness in general and about the situation and needs of specific clients. People in a client's support system need to have accurate and up to date information about mental illness and its treatment. This includes the names of the illnesses, the symptoms, the treatments, and the prognosis with treatment. This must be provided in simple, straightforward, nonpejorative language. One must be willing to respond to questions and, in order to provide more accurate information, must also pay careful attention to the misconceptions that people might have (McGill & Lee, 1986). The purpose of education about mental illness is not only to provide specific information, but also to deliver the message that mentally ill individuals are suffering from legitimate disorders deserving of attention and support, and that with adequate treatment and support they can make good family members, friends, employees, neighbors, and community residents.

In providing general information it is important to remember the cultural background of the listener. Most of the "facts" that are known about mental illness are based on Western, scientific, and medical model orientations. These viewpoints are frequently not shared by many clients and others in their culture, who may have other explanations for the behaviors. It is almost never helpful to either argue with or discount someone's beliefs. Rather, it might be a better strategy to suggest that another approach is being presented, one that has proven useful with other people like the client.

Although providing general information can play a role in reducing the stigma of mental illness, it is equally necessary to educate those in the client's support system about the specific problems and needs of that particular client. Of course, this can only be done with clients' consent, or within the confidentiality laws of the area in which the case manager practices. This is best done with the clients' participation, explaining how the illness affects them personally, how they feel about it, what is helpful to them, and what they want in life.

When discussing particular clients it is most important to emphasize how the illness affects the individual in terms of symptoms, overall functioning, and specific behaviors. In large part people want and need to know both what to expect and what to do when unexpected and difficult situations arise. It is equally important to explain the client's needs and what people can do to meet those needs.

When encouraging a program to accept a client, it is helpful to define the client's needs in terms of things that the program can do for the client. As an example, a woman with rapid cycling bipolar affective disorder, a history of polysubstance abuse, and dozens of hospital admissions was quite ambivalent about referral to a residential treatment program because of the many program requirements. The program staff sensed the ambivalence and questioned the woman's motivation. The case manager acknowledged the client's limited motivation, but also explained how it would be helpful to have the client in a structured setting, where her medications could be monitored, her substance use could be controlled, and she could work on interpersonal skills.

It can also be helpful to describe interventions and strategies that have been successful with a client in the past. When referring or re-referring a client to a program that has previously rejected the client, or in which the client has failed, it may be necessary to describe how the client has changed or grown since the last referral.

Providing Support

If they have support and backup and do not feel alone, programs and individuals are much more likely to take a risk and try helping a client they are not sure about. A case manager is, by virtue of the definition of the role, in an excellent position to provide supports that will help make linkage occur.

One support case managers can provide is sharing responsibility for the client. Because case managers provide continuous care, they can also provide continuous support for other services or resources to which they refer the client. This will help with the acceptance of clients, because the program will not be left with sole responsibility if things do not work. Support is also provided by the continuing availability of the case manager to furnish backup for the program. This backup can include problem solving, encouragement to continue, and, if necessary, removing the client and making other arrangements.

In the previous example, a woman with bipolar affective disorder was referred to a residential treatment program. With reservations, the program accepted the client, but only on the condition that the case manager would arrange hospitalization whenever the client became psychotic. The case manager met this expectation twice. This was the primary reason that the residential treatment program accepted the client back after both hospitalizations.

In utilizing community resources it is necessary for the case manager to have good knowledge of the available resources, including their capabilities and limitations. It is not helpful to push a resource to accept a client it cannot effectively help. Therefore, it is necessary to be realistic about what a service or individual can do, be responsive to the needs of the service or individual, and be flexible in providing support to achieve a common goal on behalf of the client. In this regard, if staff or individuals are resistant to helping the client, it can be most helpful to understand this resistance and work with it. Foisting an unwanted client on a resource will almost always result in the client's not receiving the benefit of the resource.

Utilizing a Relationship

The success of a case manager is primarily dependent on the quality of the relationships developed. This is true for the relationships with clients as well as the relationships with members of the client's support system and other community resources.

Relationships are best fostered by face-to-face contact. Although one may speak to a colleague in another agency dozens of times on the telephone, it makes a qualitative difference in the relationship to actually meet the person. Therefore, referrals and linkage stand a better chance of success if the case manager will go to the program and meet the staff. This is also true with family, friends, hotel managers, employers, and so forth.

To establish and maintain positive relationships it is particularly important for the case manager to be straightforward and honest—in terms of both information about the client and what the case manager will do. It is equally important to follow through consistently on agreed-on expectations.

It is also helpful to be available when needed or requested. This includes answering telephone calls quickly and meeting with people in their settings and on their terms. Maintaining high visibility with community resources will make it easier to identify problems and issues while they are small and more easily solvable.

When problems do arise a case manager must be ready to intervene quickly, with consultation or more active support. When a large number of individuals or services are involved in a client's care, it is often very useful to organize a case conference on behalf of the client. This helps those involved share not only pertinent information but also the burden of caring for the client. It also helps in both developing and implementing a consistent approach toward the client.

To summarize, linkage is the process of helping clients gain the benefit of available community resources. It requires that case managers be resourceful and skillful in overcoming the obstacles to linkage that are presented by both the clients and the community resources.

Monitoring

Monitoring simply means observing the client over time. It is one important aspect of continuity of care. This is the mechanism through which a case manager becomes aware of changes in a client's condition or needs and can then intervene and respond to those changes.

Of course, the purpose of case management is to bring about change. Clients do change over time; hopefully for the better, but not infrequently for the worse. Change can happen quickly or slowly, dramatically or incrementally, planned or unplanned. Nevertheless, change inevitably occurs, and case managers must respond by changing their treatment plans and interventions.

To detect change the case manager must stay in touch with the client. This is usually done directly by seeing the client on a regular basis. All aspects of the client's life require routine review, including mental status; medication response including compliance, symptom reduction, and side effects; relationships with family, friends, lovers, and service providers; housing and finances; functioning in areas such as daily activities, living skills, and/or employment; health, dental, legal, and recreational needs; and any other aspect of the care plan.

One component of case management that requires particularly close and continuous attention is the relationship between case manager and client. The case manager must determine whether engagement is occurring and trust is developing. If not, it could be because the client does not find the case manager helpful, possibly because of inactivity or insensitivity, or even because the case manager has been so active that the client is feeling overwhelmed by the attention. Similarly, a client may repeatedly require acute care services because insufficient supports have been arranged; or a client may become regressed and overly dependent because unnecessary support has been provided.

These examples make it clear that different interventions will have different effects on clients, and it is not easy to predict what interventions are needed. Therefore, it is necessary to monitor the effect of all interventions, and the effect of the relationship overall, in order to shift approaches as necessary.

One goal for many clients will be to learn to monitor themselves. This can be an aspect of helping clients manage their illnesses and take control of their lives. Clients can monitor their own symptoms, such as hallucinations or changes in mood, and can learn such methods for reducing them as adjusting medications, obtaining social support, meditation, or shopping. Clients can also monitor side effects of medications, social relationships, ability to function in various roles, and progress toward their goals.

Nearly anyone in the client's support system can assist with monitoring. Support system members can observe the client at times when the case manager is not available. They will also see the client from different viewpoints, which can provide important insights. Those who might assist in monitoring are mental health and human service providers, family members, friends, pastors, employers, landlords, and neighbors. For instance, one case manager taught the girlfriend of a client with schizophrenia to recognize his prodromal symptoms, so that she could let the client know that he needed to reduce his activity, and also let the case manager know that his medications needed to be reviewed.

Although many people may be helpful with monitoring, it is equally important that the client not be made to feel intruded on, spied on, self-conscious, or uncomfortable because of this attention. Therefore, clients should be active in decisions about who the case manager will discuss them with, giving their permission and participating in the process.

Some state laws allow case managers to discuss the client with other mental health services providers without the client's permission. In any case, the case manager should let the client know what discussions are occurring and with whom. Although confidentiality laws limit who a case manager can give information to without consent, they do not restrict the case manager from receiving information about the client. This means that case managers can listen to family member, friends, and others concerned about the client, and act on the information received even if the client does not approve. For instance, a client's parent can notify the case manager that the client has discontinued taking medications and is becoming paranoid and threatening.

Another aspect of monitoring involves overseeing the care the clients receive in other programs. This requires discussing with clients their experiences with these services, as well as watching for the expected benefits of these resources. It also involves staying in touch with the other providers serving the clients.

Like the other case management activities, monitoring is an ever-changing process. Early in the relationship a case manager may need to stay in frequent contact with the client, while only infrequent contact may be required later on. The degree of monitoring necessary is dependent on the client's psychiatric stability, the availability of social and practical supports, and how well the case manager knows the client. For instance, a newly referred client, who has been recently discharged from a hospital to a tenuous housing situation with few supports, may need daily contact to assure successful community placement. On the other hand, a client who is psychiatrically stable, has meaningful daily activities, and has a history of contacting the case manager when help is needed, may require contact only when the client requests it.

The degree of monitoring is also dependent on the clients' participation and wishes. Some clients will not want to be worked with too closely, and others will require that the case manager work with them only at their pace.

As case management services are generally provided on a voluntary basis, a case manager must respond to the clients' clear and consistent statements that they do not want the case manager to work with or stay in touch with the them. Some clients will move and not let the case manager know where they are. In these instances the case manager is expected to stand ready to work with the client again if the client resurfaces or requests help.

In summary, monitoring is an essential case management function by which the client's circumstances and needs are continuously observed by the case manager, by the client, or by members of the client's support system. This allows for timely responses to ever-changing needs.

References

Fariello, D. F. (1991). Presentation to Division of Mental Health and Substance Abuse Services, Department of Public Health, San Francisco, CA.

Kanter, J. S. (1985). Psychosocial assessments in community treatment. In J. S. Kanter (Ed.), *New directions in mental health services* (Vol. 27, pp. 63-75). San Francisco: Jossey-Bass.

Lovejoy, M. (1982). Expectations and the recovery process. *Schizophrenia Bulletin, 8*(4), 605-609.

McGill, C. W., & Lee, E. (1986). Family psychoeducation intervention in the treatment of schizophrenia. *Bulletin of the Menninger Clinic, 50*, 269-286.

Nickens, J. (1989). Presentation at Seminar on Community Mental Health Services, University of California, San Francisco, at San Francisco General Hospital.

Rapp, C. A. (1992). The strengths perspective of care management with persons suffering from severe mental illness. In D. Saleesby (Ed.), *The strengths model of social work practice* (pp. 45-58). New York: Longman.

Segal, S. P., & Baumohl, J. (1980). Engaging the disengaged: Proposals on madness and vagrancy. *Social Work, 25*(5), 358-365.

7

Advocacy and Case Management

CARLOS E. MORALES

The functions of a clinical case manager reflect a multifaceted combination of interconnected roles. One role of these roles is advocacy. The advocate role entails arguing, debating, negotiating, urging, challenging, and manipulating those in the environment on behalf of the client (Compton & Gallaway, 1984). Advocating on behalf of the severely mentally ill adult population poses some unique considerations and challenges for the clinician. Responding to these challenges requires a variety of skills.

The skills needed to effectively advocate for client and systemic changes are often omitted from discussions of case management. The clinical case management model addresses the clinical dimension of advocacy as an extension of clinical skills and a sanctioned area of practice. It also incorporates skills required to work within the client's environment, which includes the client, other individuals, programs, and policymakers. The flexibility of this model of care allows for creativity, which increases the likelihood of improved care for severely mentally ill clients.

This chapter will describe advocacy for individual clients, clients as a group, and systemic changes from the perspective of a case manager.

Advocacy for the purpose of this chapter is those activities done with a client or for a client or client system that are in response to both the lack of services and the obstructions or barriers to the client's obtaining services, supports, or opportunities from the environment. The environment for purposes of this chapter is everything affecting a client's life outside the clinician's relationship with the client. The environment encompasses both the physical and social environment of the client and includes but is not limited to family, extended family, significant others, community, programs, and services. The clinical case manager combines comprehensive care with a clear focus on the person in the environment. The clinical case management model of care views the clinical contacts with the client as not restricted by time or location. For instance, such contacts can take place while meeting with a landlord to advocate that a client retains housing, or attending the appeal hearing for Social Security benefits. This expanded perspective of clinical work with the client's environment not only affords the clinician additional material for ongoing assessments and interventions but also increases the opportunities and avenues for advocacy. Clinicians challenged by clients' environment must exercise their knowledge and authority, together with their skills, to advocate for positive outcomes for their clients.

The advocate role is closely interconnected to the linkage and mediating roles of the clinical case manager. The processes of linkage and mediating are often not easily distinguishable from advocating and may take place simultaneously. When linkage is not successful or problems arise, the clinician may adopt an advocacy role to secure the resource. For instance, while attending a clinical case conference with the client's residential treatment providers, the clinician is in the role of a mediator. If the providers suggest a premature discharge plan, the clinician adopts the role of an advocate to argue for the client's remaining in residential treatment. Advocacy is often not seen as a distinct role unless there is a clear adversary.

The advocacy role, a concept that social work borrowed from the legal profession, is one that requires the ability to manage conflict. Attorneys advocate specific legal issues for a client or group of clients and then close the case. Clinical case managers must advocate with the knowledge that they will be providing services to a client over a long period of time. They must also modify their advocacy efforts with the knowledge that there is a limited amount of resources and that they may have to advocate again with the same provider. Case managers are comfortable in the role of supporting and encouraging colleagues but may feel uncomfortable in the role of arguing, debating, and challenging colleagues to meet the special needs of the severely mentally ill population. Advocacy may also target making changes within one's own program, or making changes in the availability of services within the mental health service system, and thus may entail conflicts with supervisors and administrators.

Overview of the Severely Mentally Ill Population

The process of deinstitutionalization of severely mentally ill individuals requires that clients fend for themselves in the community. Hospitals may compound patients' problems by making them "institutionalized." Patients may be forced to awaken and eat at certain times; their meals are prepared for them and their clothes are washed for them; and they may be told when to bathe and when to take their medication. As a result, patients become increasingly dependent on others for survival. When they return to their homes and communities, they may not have the skills to live independently (Dinitto & Dye, 1987). Many of the services that were provided for the clients in the institution must be replicated in the community. Clients must obtain food, shelter, and clothing for themselves. They have to negotiate a fragmented array of services in the mental health and public health systems, which often are not receptive to their needs. They have to manage money, while some are required by Social Security to have payees. Simple tasks of daily living, such as using a laundromat, shopping for food and clothing, or getting a haircut, can become overwhelmingly negative experiences for some of these individuals.

The severely mentally ill population returns to the community with the same illnesses that led society to institutionalize them. Many of the clients are stigmatized for the symptoms of their illness, and are often denied access to or receive limited resources from both the public and private sectors. Some of the consequences of limited accessibility of resources for this population are that many experience periodic homelessness and often, through errors in judgment, are incarcerated. In addition to living with a mental illness, many clients suffer from the effects of poverty, racism, sexism, and homophobia. The incident rate of alcoholism and drug abuse is high among these clients; and clients who present with problematic behaviors are often denied services and are at high risk of being hospitalized or incarcerated. The clinical case manager is both sanctioned and obligated to establish relationships with public and private providers to ensure that clients and groups of clients obtain the necessary resources to not only stabilize their lives but also enhance the quality of their lives. In practice many of the goals of the clinical case manager require advocacy. Clinical case managers advocate by using their knowledge of both clients and resources, working toward the goal of providing or securing those resources for the clients.

Knowledge Is Power

Clinical case managers must draw on an eclectic knowledge base, which they apply in practice to address the multiple problems of the diverse clients they serve. The knowledge requirements of case advocacy are fourfold: knowledge of the clients or the systems in which they function; knowledge of one's own agency; knowledge of the workings of other agencies; and knowledge of community resources (Sunley, 1983). The individual/environmental interface requires knowledge of both traditional casework and community organizing. This knowledge, combined with the authority of both the case manager and the case management program, empowers the clinician to intervene on behalf of clients.

To effectively advocate, the clinician must have a thorough knowledge of mental illness and its treatment, and must be able to both communicate effectively with other mental health providers and provide informational influence. The clinician must also be able to mobilize mental health resources that are responsive to the real needs and abilities of the client and advocate, based on interventions that are clinically sound, with a focus on long-term work with the client.

The case manager becomes a repository of knowledge of the client's past and present psychiatric history. The clinician, through repeated contacts with the client in different settings, becomes aware of the client's needs, goals, strengths, and weaknesses. Through knowledge of the client's past psychiatric and personal history, and present level of functioning, the clinician determines what advocacy efforts, if any, are indicated to meet the client's needs and goals. If clients are capable of advocating for their own needs, the clinical case manager should not, for the sake of expediency, intervene on behalf of the clients. The case manager may only need to support the clients' problem-solving skills and engage them in developing their own strategies. The clinical case manager must refrain from rescuing clients, through advocacy efforts that can be clinically inappropriate and may set up a dynamic between clinician and clients, where the clients' expectations are that the clinician will always advocate for them in any situation. For example, a client with a history of violent episodes attacked and severely battered his girlfriend while under the influence of alcohol and was subsequently arrested for assault and battery. The client requested that the clinician attempt to influence the court for his release, based on his mental illness. The clinicians' assessment did not indicate any barriers or obstructions to the client's receiving services or benefiting from a structured environment that could contain his violent impulses.

The clinical case manager explained to the client that she would not advocate for the client's release, based on his mental illness, but would advocate that he receive psychiatric medications and participate in substance abuse treatment while incarcerated, and when the client returned to the community, she would continue to treat him.

Case managers must familiarize themselves with different modalities of treatment available in the mental health system. Mental health programs are designed to meet the needs of target populations that may or may not be responsive to the needs and goals of the client. For example, many day treatment programs require that clients arrive during the scheduled hours of operation and participate daily in a variety of activities. For some clients, traditional service delivery styles, such as daily activities and mandatory participation, may limit the utilization of and accessibility to the resource. The case manager must advocate that mental health services reflect the individualized needs and capabilities of the client. The case manager may advocate that the day treatment program allow for an engagement phase of several months, during which the client can drop in or participate selectively in scheduled activities, or the case manager may advocate that the client receive individualized services that are tailored to what is meaningful and meets the subjective needs of the client. This is often in conflict with traditional service delivery styles of community mental health services.

Knowledge of the dynamics of organizational behavior is critical to effective advocacy. Through interacting with the program the client is utilizing, the clinical case manager becomes aware of the organization's culture and norms and the values that make up the service delivery style of the agency. The case manager must get close enough to understand the organizational behavior but maintain enough distance to not be co-opted by the agency's norms and values. It is necessary to hold the interest of the clients as paramount and not be intimidated by the professional culture or the norms of the agency. The case manager must not be swayed by arguments that protect the norms or values of an agency and meet the needs of the program or the providers. Mental health and human services providers must sometimes be reminded that they are employed to serve clients and not to meet the needs of providers or their agencies.

Clinical case managers cannot rely solely on community mental health resources to meet the needs of their clients. The case manager is sanctioned with authority and with the permission of the client to interact with all the systems in the client's environment. The case manager must be familiar with the array of existing resources and the delivery model and dynamics of these resources (such as AIDS services; substance abuse counseling; medical, legal, educational, recreational, familial, cultural, and spiritual resources). Case managers should also be aware of community resources, such as free meal sites, homeless shelters, and available housing in the area in which they practice. Additionally, they should become aware of private vendors, such as local stores and restaurants and laundromats, who are accessible to clients and are willing to service mentally ill clients. Finally, case managers need to be familiar with the accessibility of religious and other nonprofit organizations to the severely mentally ill population. This knowledge is obtained through direct experience with clients, with resources, in discussions with colleagues, and during clinical supervision.

To effectively advocate for clients when attempting to obtain resources from their environment, the case manager must be familiar with the policies of the resources, so that demands on the resource can be appropriately presented. For example, a case manager spent several hours a day over the course of a week advocating with the local Medicaid office over a client's share of cost. After researching current policy, the case manager began arguing with the site supervisor over her client's rights under the Pickle Amendment. The case manager had conducted her research prior to advocating and was able to save the client money.

The case manager becomes knowledgeable through experience of systems that are not accessible to clients or will not accommodate their special needs. This information, along with other experiences by colleagues, can provide necessary data to involve the case management program in advocacy efforts on behalf of groups or clients. For example, a money management program was not flexible enough to meet the special needs of the case management clients. That particular program mandated that it would not have any client contact, and was either reluctant or unwilling to provide daily disbursements for clients who exhibited poor budgeting skills. The clinical case management staff formed a committee to address these complaints and make suggestions. The staff began to individually and collectively put organizational pressure on the program to change and better serve clients. The program did become more responsive to the needs of clients but was still unable or unwilling to modify the program to address all the suggestions of the clinical case management staff. The case management administration provided documentation of the money management program's inability to meet the social needs of its clients to the community mental health administration, who decided to award the money management contract to another program that would better meet the needs of this population. Through program pressure, the clinical case management program's advocacy efforts improved the delivery style of the money management program, which will benefit other clients who need this service.

The case manager becomes knowledgeable about both the multiple problems of the client and the gaps in available resources while providing direct services, because the case manager is in a good position to assess the gaps in services and make suggestions as to what comprehensive services are needed. For example, the collective experience of the case management team may indicate that substance abuse is high among their client population. The collective experience of the case management team may also indicate that traditional substance abuse programs are not receptive to the needs of the clients, and that programs which serve the dually diagnosed are not able to accommodate the number of referrals made to them. Collectively, the case managers must encourage, support, and demand that the case management leadership and administration advocate for resources to reduce or eliminate these gaps in services.

Case managers becomes knowledgeable about the limitations of their own program while practicing and must advocate for changes in the program. These changes may be for expanding services or developing additional interventions.

The case manager must also be knowledgeable about mental health advocacy groups and their various positions. This is important information because these advocacy groups can become allies in advocating for the clients. According to Stockdill (1992), there are four major groups that make up the mental health system. First and foremost are the clients or consumers of services, those having a mental illness. Second are the family members, friends, and significant others. Third are those known as the providers or caregivers, including the entire range of human service providers and not just mental health specialists. And finally, there are the mental health administrators and policymakers. This group includes the legislators, financing agencies, mental health administrators, and judges who develop and interpret the legislation, regulations, and policies that influence the interaction of the other major groups. Stockdill suggests that administrators should develop relationships not only with the leaders of these groups but also with grass-roots members. Clinical case managers should also be encouraged to develop relationships with mental health advocacy groups. Collectively, case managers should encourage, support, and demand that case management leadership and administrators establish relationships with these groups to further the advocacy efforts on behalf of their clients.

Skills

Clinical case managers must be skilled at developing relationships. They must develop relationships with clients that are meaningful and helpful to their lives, and relationships with colleagues and providers that are collaborative in providing comprehensive service to clients. They also must become skilled at developing relationships with providers, business people, advocates, and local citizens that can evolve into advocacy efforts on behalf of their clients.

It is necessary for the case manager to develop skills such as negotiating, arguing, debating, and challenging the environment to meet the client's needs. They must also develop skills in providing information, educating providers, clarifying conflicts, suggesting alternatives, and problem solving to achieve positive outcomes for clients. They must become skilled at mobilizing mental health resources through collaboration, or through using their program to place pressure on other programs to bring about changes.

The process of advocacy, which develops out of the clinician's relationship with the client, unfolds by utilizing the relationship with the client and articulating the client's needs, abilities, and impairments. Optimally, the advocacy efforts should both reflect the client's needs and abilities and be participatory. Some of the goals of advocacy are to obtain resources for clients and also promote self-determination and empowerment by engaging the clients in the advocacy process.

The severely mentally ill population can be difficult to engage in a trusting and working relationship. By advocating with the client for the provision of a concrete service, advocacy can be the formative process to engaging the client in a therapeutic relationship. The expectation is that clients will participate either to the best of their ability in the advocacy process, in order to effectively utilize their own skills, or minimally, which can demonstrate the value of having a case manager.

Advocating can enhance the relationship between the clinician and the client by sharing experiences that can build trust and understanding. The case manager begins by listening to the client's concerns and using the client's defined problem as a means to further the relationship. For example, a client complained to the case manager that her hotel manager was harassing her and threatening to evict her. The case manager seized the opportunity to be useful to the client and, with her approval, accompanied her to the hotel. The hotel manager complained that the client's behavior was bizarre and that she kept others awake all night. The case manager described both his relationship to the client and the mental health agency where he was employed. The case manager also impressed upon the hotel manager that his client is a tenant, and that it would be in their mutual interest to avoid a lawsuit. The case manager left the hotel manager with his business card and promised to check in on the client weekly at the hotel, to monitor her behavior in the hotel and the progress in her treatment. Negotiating with the hotel manager to keep the client in her housing legitimized the case manager in the eyes of the client. Through this experience, the client began to engage the case manager in a working relationship that later developed into a trusting relationship.

Through the modeling of appropriate behaviors and problem-solving techniques used in the process of advocating, the clinician can demonstrate to the client methods of obtaining resources for themselves.

Case managers establish relationships with a network of resource providers, in both the private and public sectors, through their contact with these providers on behalf of their clients. One purpose of this network is to identify allies who can assist in overcoming resource delivery obstacles and increase accessibility for the clients. This network can also be used for advocacy efforts. For example, a storekeeper who has established a relationship with a client may be willing to write a letter on behalf of the client to establish community ties during a probation revocation hearing. A substance abuse counselor who had provided service for several case managed clients in a detox setting was solicited in advocacy efforts to have his program formalize provision of services to the mentally ill clients.

The case manager becomes both a salesperson and spokesperson for the client. The case manager emphasizes the clients' strengths and the benefits they would receive if provided the service. The case manager attempts to balance the concerns of the providers with the needs of the client. Successful advocacy is facilitated when case managers articulate patient assets and deficits, empathize with the concerns of providers, and offer them ongoing support and consultation (Kanter, 1989). Successful advocacy also ensures that patients' rights are respected. The provider must also be made aware that the case manger is not acting alone and is receiving ongoing support and consultation from the case management program.

Strategies

Advocating for severely mentally ill adults demands patience and creativity. The diversity of this population requires individualized strategies. Each client's problem must be examined within the context of experience with the client and the environment. The client must be apprised of the advocacy efforts and counseled in regard to the possibility of failure. The client must also be made aware of the possibility that services may be secured, but the providers may still be unwilling to provide quality services, and that the case manager will continue to monitor the program's provision of service. The client needs to agree with the advocacy efforts and contribute to the process, if possible.

Once a problem has been defined, a strategy must be developed and an action plan implemented. The target system that the clinician's change efforts are directed toward must be well understood in respect to what the system has to gain or lose; or what advocacy efforts will be needed, in respect to time and resources, to obtain the desired outcome. The desired outcome must be definable. The pros and cons must be thoroughly explored prior to advocating. Brenda McGowan (1983) has identified some of the major questions confronting the advocate:

- What is the source of the problem?
- What is the appropriate target system?
- What is the objective?
- What is the sanction for the proposed intervention?
- What resources are available for the intervention?
- How receptive is the target system?
- With whom should the intervention be carried out?
- At what level should the intervention take place?
- What methods of intervention should be employed?
- What is the outcome?
- And finally, if the objective has not been achieved, is there another approach that can be employed? If the immediate objective has been achieved, has another problem been identified that requires additional advocacy?

The answers to these questions are intended to guide the advocate's decision-making process and shape the activities.

This section of the chapter will describe some strategies for changing the client's environment. Case managers use the resources and collective experiences of the case management team to change its own program's services for its clients. Case managers also work toward changing the response of other programs to the severely mentally ill population. In addition, they work toward changing the availability of services in the clients' environment.

The clinical case management program can not rely solely on advocacy efforts directed at changing other programs' accessibility or accommodations for severely mentally ill individuals. Despite both individual and collective advocacy efforts by case managers, agencies and programs tend to change incrementally. Advocacy is often done with the knowledge that the efforts must continue on a prolonged basis in order to obtain results. A strategy for changing services available to one's clients is to develop services in-house. For example, the leadership of a case management program became aware that many of their clients had some contacts with forensic services, and a few clients had repeated contacts. A forensic case manager position was developed. The forensic case manager was given jail clearance and was sanctioned to work with the forensic systems, judicial and correctional, that the clients interact with. The forensic case manager was acquainted with probation officers, public defenders, and judges who routinely work with severely mentally ill inmates. Presently, the demand for long-term case management exceeds the caseload of the forensic case manager, so the forensic case manager and the supervisor and program administration are advocating for several additional forensic case managers. They are also attempting to influence both forensic services and mental health services to work together to improve linkage and the provision of services to the severely mentally ill clients who have experienced incarceration.

The clinical case management program must be flexible and willing to change to meet the needs of its clients. The consumer movement has been advocating that community mental health programs be consumer-focused. Consumers have suggested various ways such a focus can be achieved, from integrating clients with self-help groups to hiring clients to provide services. For instance, staff on one case management program were interested in bringing a consumer focus to the team by hiring mental health consumers to work with case managers to deliver direct services. They recognized that there could be an empathy gap between providers and clients. With the approval of the case management administration, and the direction of a supervisor, an implementation project was established. An implementation team was created, comprised of one clinical case management supervisor and two clinical case managers, a representative of a local consumer group, and representatives from a local family organization. This collaborative effort resulted in the creation of four peer case manager positions. Through the peer case management project, other agencies and programs will be influenced to hire consumers, either by example or through advocacy efforts to develop a consumer focus. The efforts of consumer advocates, family member advocates, and providers can translate into organizational pressure placed on community mental health systems to develop a system-wide consumer focus.

Establishing formal liaison roles with programs and agencies can affect and change the way these programs provide services to severely mentally ill individuals. The case management leadership should establish liaison positions with all programs having high utilization rates by the clients of the program. These liaison positions are responsible for periodically attending other agencies' staff meetings to share information, provide input, and monitor the provision of services to these clients. The liaisons periodically report back to the team any new developments within the operations of agencies with which they are working. For example, the case management team may establish liaison roles with all of the area inpatient psychiatric hospitals, day treatment centers, and vocational services. The case management team may also consider establishing liaison positions with homeless shelters, residential programs, and entitlement and benefit programs. These liaison roles can facilitate reciprocal learning between programs of their service delivery styles. These relationships can further advocacy efforts through direct input by case managers to service providers on the accessibility and accommodation of their services to the clients.

Another useful forum for case managers is interagency case conferences, which can be used to address the needs of individual clients and groups of clients. They can also be used for network building among case managers and providers, as well as serving as avenues to promote advocacy efforts on behalf of individual clients and groups of clients. During a case conference, case managers can convey their perspective of what the client's needs are and whether they are being met. The case manager may advocate that, because of the clinician's knowledge of the client's past psychiatric history and level of functioning, a more flexible and tailored approach to treatment be considered to meet the client's needs. The case manager may also advocate on behalf of a group of clients. For example, a residential program developed a reputation among case managers for discharging African-American males at a higher rate than other males prior to completing the program. The case manager, while attending a case conference, shared his observations that African-Americans seldom completed the program and that there were no African-American staff members. The case manager suggested that the staff obtain consultation on working with African-Americans and also suggested several possible consultants.

A case manager, when participating in or developing task forces, can be a valuable source of information on the provision of services to the severely mentally ill population. It could be helpful if case management programs seek representation and an active role with local task forces and coalitions.

The following are suggestions for organizing advocacy efforts but are not intended to be an exhaustive list. These suggestions also define the role of the clinical case manager in the advocacy efforts, and the complexity and multiple variables and factors entailed in advocacy.

1. Information and Data Collection. Case managers gather information on service gaps and document needs and the costs of not meeting the need. The case managers use their experience with their caseload, and the collective experiences of their colleagues, as a starting point. They may need to solicit assistance from various graduate schools, from programs such as Social Welfare, Public Administration, and Public Health, to conduct research and evaluations. The case managers need to stay current in new developments in the field through the reviewing of relevant literature, so they can use this information to be credible with others when advocating for clients.

2. Charging One's Own Agency to Make Changes. Case managers must be sanctioned and expected to advocate for changes in their own program with their supervisors. They have to be willing and able to voice their opinions on how to enhance the services delivered by their agency. They may request additional service roles, such as those of peer case managers, vocational counselors, and substance abuse counselors.

3. Changing the Response of Other Programs to the Severely Mentally Ill Population. Case managers can use case conferences with other agencies to effect changes in their delivery styles, by using information about the accommodation and accessibility of their services for clients. The case conference can be an effective vehicle to involve administrators from all involved agencies. The use of liaison roles with different agencies can increase the understanding and the sharing of information. They can also be used to influence the agency and advocate for improved services.

4. Interagency Committees. Participation on these committees can enhance the services by having participants problem solve on issues concerning difficult clients. They can also serve to place pressure on agencies to provide services that they are capable of but may be unwilling to provide. These committees may also develop into allies with other agencies, who may be experiencing similar problems with a system or service delivery approach.

5. The Use of Task Forces and Coalitions. Case managers who participate in ad hoc, standing, or coordinating advocacy groups will have the advantage of working with various organizations with similar agendas for change. They may be able to develop allies who can use their collective pressure to bring about systemic changes that will benefit the clients.

6. Identifying and Working With Other Advocates to Obtain Resources. Each locality has its own advocacy groups. Groups such as homeless coalitions, consumer advocates, and the Alliance for the Mentally Ill are excellent sources of information and are often allies for advocacy efforts. These organizations may be willing to support a case manager's advocacy efforts and may already be working for the same outcomes.

7. Educational Activities. Case managers can participate in professional conferences, presentations, panels, brochure preparation, and media contacts. The purpose of these contacts is to influence different segments of the population. The use of the media may rally support for a program and gain resources for clients.

8. Political Advocacy. Case managers must be aware of the need to adapt to such changing conditions as funding cuts, new political realities, and shifting community needs. The case management program should use some staff meeting time to discuss political issues that affect the program and the severely mentally ill population. Case managers should be encouraged to participate in political activities on the local, state, and federal levels of government. Engaging in letter writing and telephone calls to legislators, on behalf of clients and programs that work with severely mentally ill clients, should be a norm. Providing informational influence through formal and informal meetings with legislators should be undertaken.

9. Demonstrations and Protests. Case managers need to participate in and, if possible, organize street demonstrations and protests. They must familiarize themselves with such methods of protest as marches, sit-ins, picketing, and street drama. These activities are especially important in the era of cutbacks and budget deficits. Clients may also be encouraged to participate in peaceful demonstrations. The purpose of the demonstrations should be to attract media attention and to influence legislators and policymakers.

10. Using Legal Decisions. Case managers must be informed about and willing to use legal decisions to benefit clients. For example, a legal decision resulted in a consent decree mandating fines for overcrowding in the local jails. This motivated the local sheriff's department to support diversion projects to reduce overcrowding. One of the diversion projects created was a jail aftercare program, which linked mentally ill clients to mental health services in the community. Legal decisions on the county, state, and federal levels may be used to benefit clients. Presently, the Americans With Disabilities Act may evolve, with persistence from helping professionals, into benefits for mentally ill individuals.

Conclusion

The importance of the clinical case manager's advocate role cannot be minimized. In order to provide the highest quality of care to severely mentally ill clients, the clinical case manager must be an effective advocate. The case manager must be able and willing to advocate for resources and services for clients, on both the direct service level and the indirect service level. Advocacy activities must be sanctioned and encouraged by administrators of case management programs, or the programs will not be effective and will fail the clients. Advocacy efforts by case managers should be undertaken with the knowledge that changes in systems are usually incremental, and will not take place unless advocacy efforts are persistent and prolonged.

References

Compton, B., & Gallaway, B. (1984). *Social work process*. Homewood, IL: Dorsey.

Dinitto, D., & Dye, T. (1987). *Social welfare politics and public policy*. Englewood Cliffs, NJ: Prentice-Hall.

Kanter, J. (1989). Clinical case management: Definition, principles, components. *Hospital and Community Psychiatry, 40*, 361-364.

McGowan, B. (1983). The case advocacy function in child welfare practice. In H. Weissman, I. Epstein, & A. Savage (Eds.), *Agency-based social work* (pp. 141-149). Philadelphia: Temple University Press.

Stockdill, J. W. (1992). A government manager's view of mental health advocacy groups. *Administration and Policy in Mental Health, 20*, 45-55.

Sunley, R. (1983). Family advocacy: From case to cause. In H. Weissman, I. Epstein, & A. Savage (Eds.), *Agency-based social work* (pp. 155-168). Philadelphia: Temple University Press.

PART III

Clinical Case Management Issues

8

Treatment of Substance Abuse and Mental Illness

DAVID F. FARIELLO

Substance abuse among severely mentally ill clients is so widespread that anyone treating this population must be prepared to routinely address the co-occurrence of these two problems as part of the treatment plan. It is estimated that half of the severely mentally ill adults have problems associated with the misuse of alcohol and/or drugs (Ridgley, Osher, Goldman, & Talbott, 1987). Studies of specific mentally ill populations have shown rates of substance abuse problems ranging from 25% to 75%, with rates being higher in hospitalized populations (Bergman & Harris, 1985; McCourt, Williams, & Schneider, 1971; Test, Wallisch, Allness, & Ripp, 1989; Wolfe & Sorenson, 1989). One case management program with an acute recidivist population found, in an unpublished review of cases, that 60% of severely mentally ill adult clients also had a substance abuse problem.

Diagnostically, this population, which is often referred to as dually diagnosed clients, encompasses a broad spectrum of psychiatric disorders, including schizophrenic disorders, affective disorders, and personality disorders (Drake & Wallach, 1989; Kay, Kalathara, & Meinzert, 1989; Lyons & McGovern, 1989). Similarly, these dually diagnosed individuals utilize all classes of substances and frequently use polysubstances (Drake & Wallach, 1989; Szuster, Schanbacher, & McCann, 1990; Test et al., 1989).

The consequences of adding substance abuse to a severe mental disorder are disastrous for the client and the client's support system. The client's ability to comply with treatment, even assuming a modicum of motivation, is limited. This is due to the client's being less cognitively available to remember appointment dates or medication regimens, to participate in socialization or vocational rehabilitation, and so on. Symptoms such as affective lability, poor impulse control, disorganized thinking, paranoid delusions, depression, suicidal ideation, and social isolation will all be exacerbated rather than controlled. The client will be at high risk for self-inflicted injury, violent acting out, repeated arrests, psychiatric rehospitalizations, and accidents. Medical complications of substance abuse, such as liver damage, pancreatitis, abscesses, compromised immune system, cardiac disorders, and communicable diseases, impede the functioning of psychotropic medications, add stress to the client's life, and reduce the life quality and longevity of the client. Consequent to all of the above, clients often develop organic brain impairments, such as memory loss, inability to change cognitive sets during problem solving, or psychomotor disturbances. Clients' behaviors often result in the loss of the precious few resources that they may posses, such as stable housing, disability entitlements, the support of friends and/or family, part-time or sheltered work, and so forth. In short, substance abuse is a debacle for severely mentally ill clients (Drake & Wallach, 1989; Kay et al., 1989; Minkoff, 1989; Pristach & Smith, 1990; Surber, Winkler, Monteleone, Havassy, Goldfinger, & Hopkin, 1987; Szuster et al., 1990).

This population does not receive adequate treatment. Barriers to effective treatment include the difficulties of the clients, organization and funding of the mental health and substance abuse treatment systems, as well as the respective treatment paradigms of each system. These individuals are difficult to assess because the complex interaction of both disorders can not only cause similar symptoms but also mask symptoms. Additionally, both disorders are frequently denied by those who suffer from them. The acuity of these clients' symptoms, the unpredictability of their behavior, and the resulting chaos of their social support system all serve to discourage even the most optimistic treaters of this population.

Funding and licensing of mental health and substance abuse programs may specifically preclude concomitant treatment of both disorders by the same agency. Stringent patient confidentiality policies make communication between mental health and substance abuse agencies exceedingly difficult. The expectation that such severely impaired clients could and should link with two treatment programs, much less the other components of a complex and fragmented human service systems, grossly overestimates the social functioning capacity of such an impaired population.

Mental health providers often ignore or minimize substance abuse in their clients. They are not trained to perform assessments for substance abuse disorders. Asking "Do you use alcohol?" for example, will not elicit specific and useful information, but will instead signal the client which topics should be avoided. When unmistakable signs of substance abuse arise, mental health providers are often quick to ascribe them to "self-medication," or an expression of unresolved dependencies as an indication for chemotherapy and/or psychotherapy; not understanding that substance abuse, no matter what its origin, quickly takes on a life of its own and must be addressed in its own right. Similarly, clinicians are apt to minimize the significance of recovery and relapses, or ignore "recreational" or occasional drug use. Because many clients suffer from a biologically caused mental illness and are not personally responsible for their symptoms (including substance abuse), mental health professionals may seek to ameliorate the negative consequences of that abuse, inadvertently making it easier for clients to continue the abuse. As the abuse persists and clients' behaviors become more erratic, mental health providers may become overwhelmed, rejecting the client as "treatment resistant" and insisting that mental health treatment cannot continue until the client has achieved sobriety.

Substance abuse treaters often miss significant signs of mental illness, ascribing them to the secondary signs of prolonged substance abuse. Additionally, they often insist that mentally ill clients abandon all medication, even nonaddictive psychotropics, without which many severely mentally ill clients cannot function. Substance abuse treatment relies heavily on confrontational group treatment, which can easily overwhelm the fragile ego functioning of severely mentally ill clients, resulting in psychiatric decompensation or addiction relapse. Furthermore, the treatment is premised on a notion of personal accountability that discourages treaters from providing a safety net when the client relapses. This is because it is thought that clients often must "bottom out" before they choose to seek treatment. For those who have significant problems negotiating reality even when stable, the process of "hitting bottom" can be a life-threatening experience.

The irony of this great division between mental health providers and substance abuse treaters is that both pathologies have much in common, and so should their treatments. Minkoff (1989) has pointed out that both illnesses can be understood as incurable illnesses, with a hereditary predisposition and an expectation of periodic relapses. Both illnesses require lifelong attention to treatment, with denial a prominent feature of the illnesses as their victims often attempt to curb their effects through willpower alone. Both psychiatric restabilization and substance abuse recovery can be premised on a recognition that accepting one's individual powerlessness over these diseases is a first step toward accepting help from others and learning to manage the illnesses and minimize their negative consequences.

Increasingly, treaters of dually diagnosed clients try to facilitate referrals between the mental health and substance abuse systems (both residential and outpatient). This is usually unsuccessful with severely mentally ill substance abusers. They are often unable to tolerate the multiplicity of relationship formation required by such a strategy. They have to undergo intake evaluations, medication evaluations, and group participation at two facilities instead of one. In the substance abuse outpatient or residential facility, dually diagnosed clients have to mix with nonpsychotic clients, making both parties uncomfortable and group work unproductive. It is suggested here that severely impaired clients should, instead, be treated by a single, long-term program that can provide comprehensive psychiatric and recovery services.

Clinical case management provides a conceptual framework in which the treater can integrate clinical expertise with direct involvement in the client's support system sufficient to construct a flexible, responsive, and therapeutic plan that will maximize the potential for both the client's psychiatric stability and reduction of or abstinence from substance use.

Such treatment must begin with a clinical assessment of clients' ego functioning at baseline and during periods of decompensation. Clients' capacity to use any form of treatment will be limited by their ability to organize new information, tolerate group settings, initiate social interactions, identify their emotional state, recall recent or remote incidents, and so on. This is not to say that one should never challenge the dually diagnosed clients to expand their abilities, but that it is not possible to create a treatment plan premised on capacities that the clients have not yet demonstrated.

An Approach to Treating Dually Diagnosed Clients

Fariello and Scheidt (1989) have developed an outline for treating dually diagnosed clients that breaks the recompensation and recovery process into discrete stages, allowing the client to get support for specific ego functions while gradually confronting the consequences of substance abuse and/or psychiatric decompensation. The stages are as follows: (a) the crisis, (b) detoxification and recompensation, (c) breaking the cycle, (d) re-creating a new lifestyle, and (e) psychodynamics of addiction and chronic mental illness.

The Crisis

In most cases the dually diagnosed client comes to the attention of case managers through a crisis, such as a psychiatric hospitalization, an arrest, or an eviction. This is an opportunity for the case manager to engage the client by offering to be of use with concrete assistance. The assistance must be of immediate value to the client, while not encouraging the client to ignore the cause of the crisis, that is, an unmanaged illness. Behavioral reinforcements must support further treatment involvement. For example, if the case manager negotiated with a landlord for the client's return without eliciting the latter's commitment to a medication trial, or regular participation in AA, then the case manager has not helped the client understand the connection between the crisis and the untreated illness.

A crisis presents a good opportunity to assess the client's support network by noting who calls, offers resources, or otherwise demonstrates concern during the crisis. The case manager must begin to forge an alliance with members of the client's network, identifying a common goal of recovery and restabilization.

These clients are often chronically vulnerable because of low ego functioning, poor impulse control, persistent thought disorders, or debilitating depression. If a case manager is responding to a crisis in an outpatient setting, the client must be repeatedly assessed for suicidality; the potential of danger to others; or the inability to provide food, clothing, or shelter; and will have to be hospitalized, if necessary.

Detoxification and Recompensation

Detoxification and psychiatric recompensation may need an arena with medical resources adequate to manage the severity of the client's intoxication, and appropriate psychopharmacological interventions, as psychiatric or withdrawal symptoms emerge. This means that acute psychiatric inpatient programs must additionally be prepared to manage detoxifications of dually diagnosed patients.

It is useful for dually diagnosed patients to be assessed for the appropriateness of receiving long-acting injectable phenothiazines. Medication compliance is a major problem for this population, as they become easily confused about when and how to take an oral regimen on their own, or may have little understanding of the importance of medication in the first place. Often, clients in denial offer less resistance to monthly shots than to daily oral medications, perhaps because it is a less constant reminder of obstacles in their lives.

Education about substance abuse and mental illness should begin with the client and support system members before discharge from a facility. If the restabilization is being attempted on an outpatient basis, regular, brief check-ins between case manager and client are essential. The client must be encouraged to give the case manager permission to communicate and coordinate with all parts of a support system, including family, psychiatric emergency services, a landlord, entitlement agencies, and the like. This is a time when there is a high risk for splitting to occur in the client's support system, as ambivalences about treatment are played out by various support system members.

Breaking the Cycle

After restabilization, the case manager must move to address the cycle of substance abuse, noncompliance with medications, decompensation, and crisis. Using the assessment of the client's support system and capacities to negotiate it, the case manager can begin active intervention to restructure the system so that sobriety and treatment compliance are rewarded. For instance, money management might initially reduce the client's access to money for drugs or alcohol, while ensuring stable housing, or family and social service agencies may agree to respond only when the client is sober and exhibiting civil behavior. Continued education in clear, uncomplicated, and nonjudgmental terms with written materials must be a regular intervention. Such materials must explain mental illness and its management as well the nature of addiction and its effects on mental illness.

This is usually not the time to explore the client's early history, repressed feelings, or other dynamics, as this may cause the client to become more anxious and avoid treatment and sobriety. Psychodynamic interpretations may also serve, at this point, as a distraction from the most important issues of this stage: denial about addiction or mental illness, and acceptance of oneself as a recovering, mentally ill addict. Denial will come in many forms, including equating addiction to street drugs with a lifelong dependence on psychotropic medications, expressing hopelessness about the possibilities of recovery, or denying the importance of abstinence.

The case manager must help the client construct a written plan for responding to the impulse to either abuse drugs or discontinue needed medications or treatment. This should include identifying precursors, such as a depressed or elated mood, boredom, isolation, and the like. Consideration should also be given to those in the support system who could be available to give a consistently helpful response; what environment might reinforce sobriety and compliance; and where to go if exterior controls are needed (a psychiatric emergency room or a drop-in detoxification facility, for example). With the client's support, everyone in the support system needs a copy of the plan so that universal support can be sustained.

Generous praise is in order for each step the client takes. This is a very difficult stage, and relapse is to be expected. Termination of treatment by the case manager is not an appropriate response to such an expected course of illness; rather, a return to the tasks of an earlier stage of recovery is in order.

Re-creating a New Lifestyle

The case manager must, at the next stage, help the client relearn social skills basic to re-creating a new lifestyle. Learning to start conversations with new people, using public transportation, being assertive about one's needs are a few of the basic building blocks needed to help the client break away from the locations and acquaintances of prior binges and decompensations. The negative symptoms of severe mental illness, such as inertia, anhedonia, and social isolation, all contribute to continued patterns of socializing with "bottle buddies" or abusing substances alone in one's room. Abstinence and treatment compliance can leave a large vacuum in the client's life, and with only a limited capacity to fill that void, these clients are at high risk to withdraw and commit suicide. Paradoxically, because the client is medically stable and abstinent, the case manager can be lulled into thinking that this is a low-risk period for the client and may inappropriately reduce the intensity of contact and exacerbate the problem.

Consistent use of *The Big Book* (Alcoholics Anonymous, 1976) and other 12-Step materials can serve at this stage as a prelude to the client's participation in Alcoholics Anonymous or Narcotics Anonymous groups. Care, however, must be taken in locating such groups for dually diagnosed clients. Standard AA and NA groups may be too large and stimulating, and may include people who have little understanding or sympathy for the issues of severely mentally ill clients. Similarly, clients may feel out of place in their dress and manner in such meetings. Case managers should encourage and support the formation of smaller AA or NA groups, led or co-led by recovering consumers of mental health services. By initially attending several meetings with the client, the case manager can underscore the meetings' importance, while facilitating a firm alliance to the AA or NA group.

The client must also begin to address the consequences of prior binges or psychiatric decompensations. This may include an inventory of ruptured relationships, unresolved legal consequences, or untreated medical problems. A dispassionate assessment of the damage and needed restitution is in order, rather than recriminations or despair.

A new lifestyle also raises the issues of spirituality, a topic with which many mental health professionals are exquisitely uncomfortable. This is a time to help the client explore connectedness (or lack thereof) to others and to notions of something larger than the self. Simple-minded efforts to impose values on clients must be avoided. Instead, helping clients to find a meaning for their lives, how they connect to others and/or some larger force in the world, can serve as an inspiration in struggling toward a substance-free sanity.

Psychodynamics of Addiction and Chronic Mental Illness

After prolonged sobriety and psychiatric stability, the case manager should begin raising issues of the underlying dynamics of recurrent substance abuse and/or noncompliance with psychiatric treatment. It will also be important to address the developmental tasks that were interrupted by the client's addiction and psychosis. Like others, severely mentally ill people are able to examine and address the patterns of their lives and resolve conflicts that prevent future growth. Case managers must, however, listen carefully to the client's communications about the pace and limits of this work.

It is to be expected that some clients will choose to engage in only the most rudimentary stages of treatment and recovery, if any at all. The clinical case manager's assessment of the reasons for the client's lack of engagement, as well as the possible consequences for the client and the community, will guide the case manager's choice of treatment response. A comprehensive treatment plan must consciously delineate when and what kinds of active involvement are called for by treaters, which interventions should be tried next, as well as when it is appropriate to withhold active interventions and what indications would call for a reappraisal of that decision. For example, it may be decided that despite a lack of client motivation, the case manager should continue managing the client's money, supporting family members, and monitoring the client for grave disability or danger to self and others, because the immediate risk to the client or the community is otherwise too high. Or it may be decided that the client's survival skills are adequate, that the withholding of active intervention is unlikely to precipitate an imminent threat to self or others by the client, and that "hitting bottom" may serve as an incentive for the client to become more involved in treatment. Treatment planning must always be done in concert with other support system members, specifying when and which other interventions will be employed by whom. The withholding of active intervention by a case manager cannot be done unilaterally or out of frustration with a client's behavior.

Case Example

Pete was a 45-year-old, single, white male with long hair and a beard. He was pleasant and cooperative; oriented to time, place and person; with flat affect and concrete, tangential thinking. He described auditory hallucinations that recede when he takes phenothiazines. During past psychotic episodes he had been repeatedly jailed on misdemeanor charges, such as public drunkenness or pulling fire alarms. Pete had little memory of his behavior during these episodes and even less insight into their causes, as he attributed his frequent psychiatric hospitalizations and arrests to police harassment. He described an almost daily use of beer and wine, as well as marijuana when he had sufficient funds. He carried a diagnosis of chronic, paranoid schizophrenia and polysubstance abuse. He was prescribed Stellazine and Artane, but had poor compliance.

Pete was the youngest child in a large family, and reported that both of his parents abused substances and physically abused the children. There was an extensive history of substance abuse in Pete's extended family and among his siblings. Pete began sniffing glue at age 9, drinking alcohol by age 11, and left home by age 14. He joined street gangs, began using barbiturates intravenously at age 17, and later abused LSD, amphetamines, peyote, and other street drugs.

Pete had his first psychotic break at age 19 while he was in the military. Within 10 years, he was drinking continuously, hearing auditory hallucinations almost all of the time, and sought treatment for neither.

I. The Crisis

Pete had numerous crises in the first 2½ years of treatment. His case manager was unable to use the crises to reinforce Pete's participation in substance abuse or mental health treatment. He was subsequently sentenced to 60 days in jail for his repeated misdemeanor offenses. His case manager suggested that Pete use the jail sentence as an opportunity for prolonged sobriety and medication compliance, rather than fleeing the state, as Pete had planned.

A. *Identity Support Network.* Pete's family contact was by telephone to his aged mother living in a distant state. She repeatedly refused Pete's requests to live with her, but encouraged him by phone to engage in treatment. His only other source of support was his case manager, whom he saw three or more times a week.

B. *Lethality.* Pete was neither homicidal nor suicidal. His repeated patterns of being seriously injured while living on the streets, as well as his inability to manage food, housing, and medical care, put him at high risk for accidental death.

C. *Behavioral Reinforcements.* The case manager contacted the treatment programs that would likely encounter Pete. They agreed that Pete would not be seen when he was intoxicated, and that help in acquiring housing, entitlements, and other interventions would depend on Pete's agreeing to address substance abuse issues with his case manager.

D. *Appropriate Arena for Detoxification.* Pete had been previously admitted to voluntary detoxification programs, but could not tolerate the stimulus of the milieu nor the confrontation of group therapy. Pete chose to go to jail because he could not leave as soon as his check arrived.

II. Detoxification

Since Pete was using jail as a detoxification and restabilization facility, the case manager communicated with jail personnel regarding Pete's recent alcohol abuse and consequent medical risks during withdrawal, as well as his psychotropic medication regimen. The case manager met with Pete in jail to discuss what his discharge plans would be when his time was served.

III. Breaking the Cycle

A. *Social System Assessment.* Pete lived alone in a tiny room, located in the basement of a residence hotel, and received $640 a month in disability entitlements. The physician for the case management team signed a form assessing Pete as needing a subpayee for his entitlements, so that his monthly rent would always be paid. He knew few people outside of the mental health programs and his "bottle buddies" with whom he drank. Pete's social skills in one-to-one, familiar situations were adequate. In groups or in new circumstances, Pete would become confused, isolated, and withdrawn. Despite repeated attempts, Pete would not return to AA groups, because he felt out of place and could not follow the content of the discussion.

B. Educate the Client. Pete had never received an explanation of either schizophrenia or alcoholism, nor how the two interact. The education was concrete, nonjudgmental, and repetitive. Pete agreed to take Prolixin Decanoate after learning more about his illness, because he now had the understanding that it might help him control the disorganization and hallucinations that had previously overwhelmed him.

C. Instill Hope. Pete repeatedly asked, "Will I ever be normal?" The case manager suggested that even though Pete would always have both alcoholism and schizophrenia, he certainly could decrease the impact on his life. He also pointed out Pete's genuine strengths, such as personal warmth and his interest in art and world events, as resources in rebuilding a social life and making connections to others.

D. Predict Consequences. The case manager helped Pete to expect the unpleasant side effects of psychotropic medications and how to minimize them, as well as the positive consequences of being less confused and not hearing voices. He also told Pete to anticipate increased social isolation from his "bottle buddies," as they had little in common while he was sober. Finally he predicted a decrease in the amount of "harassment" he might experience from the police, and fewer trips to the hospital or jail.

E. Avoid Interpretations. Initially, Pete wanted to spend sessions with his case manager exploring the childhood causes of his depression and substance abuse. Such discussions only increased Pete's anxiety, depression, and impulses to drink, so they were avoided.

F. Predict Impulses. The case manager encouraged Pete to drop in for brief visits when he felt an urge to drink. Pete would describe where and when such impulses had occurred, and together they planned how to avoid similar situations. These interventions, often made daily, also served to mitigate some of Pete's loneliness.

G. Encourage Acceptance of a New Identity. Pete's identity was firmly anchored in the late 1960s counterculture and its reverence for drugs and alcohol. He and his case manager spent time mourning the passing of the 1960s and the loss of Pete's youth. They then focused on the advantages of the "new Pete." One indication of this transition was that Pete shaved his beard and cut his hair.

H. Identify Denial. Much of the case manager's work was identifying and gently confronting Pete's denial. Pete often stated: "I don't want to have to depend on medications my whole life." The case manager would point out that Pete had been using dangerous street drugs since age 9, and that it would be better for him to use less dangerous phenothiazines to manage such a debilitating illness as schizophrenia.

I. Educate the Family. Pete's family was not available to involve in treatment. However, his case manager helped him write letters to his mother about his illness and his improvement, so that she would be less worried about him. This increased Pete's positive connection to her as well as his feelings of competence.

IV. Re-creating a New Lifestyle

This was a very difficult stage for Pete, because it required him to draw on very limited ego functioning.

A. Social Skills. The case management program's weekly social skills group helped Pete learn to make new friends who are not abusing substances. The group has focused on such skills as how to initiate a conversation, how to use public transportation, how to refuse a request from others, how to find something to do, and so on.

B. Building a Support System. Pete's support system grew from his case manager to include peers in the social skills group. Progress was slow as Pete rarely initiated discussion in the group, but responded to specific, concrete questions.

C. The Social Vacuum. Pete's relapses were usually associated with events: (a) his birthday, which invariably brought up loneliness and hopelessness and precipitated decompensations for 4 years; and (b) old drinking buddies, who recontacted him and urged him to drink again. Pete and his case manager made special efforts to fill his time when either of the above events loomed.

D. Relapse Prevention. Pete had only a rudimentary program for relapse prevention: identifying his urge to drink, getting away from the stimulus and easy access to alcohol, seeing his case manager as soon as possible to review events, and staying on injectable antipsychotic medications so as to quell the voices as one cause of drinking.

E. Address Problems Generated by Addiction and Decompensation. Pete's legal difficulties were resolved after serving his jail term. His physical problems from years of self-abuse and neglect will be slower to remedy, especially since Pete dislikes medical appointments. His relationship with his mother is improving because he seldom calls her while intoxicated and angry.

V. Psychodynamics of Addition and Severe Mental Illness

These issues remain largely unaddressed, as Pete has not yet attained a prolonged period of stability and sobriety. Such issues might concern his unexpressed anger at such neglectful and hurtful parents, his difficulties with intimacy, the mourning of his lost vocational potential, and his considering new opportunities.

Pete continues to struggle with both his mental illness and his substance abuse. Denial of both conditions and repeated treatment failure continue to be a recurrent theme in his life. However, he has remained in stable housing for longer periods, his binge abuse is less persistent with longer periods of sobriety between episodes, and for the first time in years Pete celebrated a birthday without a psychiatric decompensation and hospitalization.

Summary

Treaters of severely mentally ill adults must be prepared to assess and respond to the presence of both substance abuse and psychiatric disorders. By recognizing how much the two pathologies have in common, and by using the flexible conceptual framework of clinical case management, a five-stage treatment model has been devised, which allows for a variety of interventions that pay close attention to the specific level of functioning the client is currently demonstrating.

References

Alcoholics Anonymous. (1976). *The big book.* New York: Alcoholics Anonymous World Services, Inc.

Bergman, H. C., & Harris, M. (1985). Substance abuse among young adult chronic patients. *Psychological Rehabilitation Journal, 9,* 49-54.

Drake, R. E., & Wallach, M. A. (1989). Substance abuse among the chronically mentally ill. *Hospital and Community Psychiatry, 40*(10), 1041-1046.

Fariello, D., & Scheidt, S. (1989). Clinical case management and the dually diagnosed patient. *Hospital and Community Psychiatry, 40*(10), 1065-1067.

Kay, S. R., Kalathara, M., & Meinzert, A. E. (1989). Diagnostic and behavioral characteristics of psychiatric patients who abuse substances. *Hospital and Community Psychiatry, 40*(10), 1062-1064.

Lyons, J. S., & McGovern, M. P. (1989). Use of mental health services by dually diagnosed patients. *Hospital and Community Psychiatry, 40*(10), 1067-1069.

McCourt, W. F., Williams, A. F., & Schneider, L. (1971). Incidence of alcoholism in a state mental hospital population. *Quarterly Journal of Studies on Alcohol, 32,* 1085-1088.

Minkoff, K. (1989). An integrated treatment model for dual diagnosis of psychosis and addiction. *Hospital and Community Psychiatry, 40*(10), 1031-1036.

Pristach, C. A., & Smith, C. M. (1990). Medication compliance and substance abuse among schizophrenic patients. *Hospital and Community Psychiatry, 41*(12), 1345-1348.

Ridgley, M. S., Osher, F. C., Goldman, H. H., & Talbott, J. A. (1987). *Chronic mentally ill young adults with substance abuse problems: A review of research, treatment and training issues.* Unpublished manuscript, University of Maryland.

Surber, R. W., Winkler, E. L., Monteleone, M., Havassy, B. E., Goldfinger, S. M., Hopkin, J. T. (1987). Characteristics of high users of acute psychiatric inpatient services. *Hospital and Community Psychiatry, 38*(10), 1112-1114.

Szuster, R. R., Schanbacher, B. L., & McCann, S. C. (1990). Characteristics of psychiatric emergency room patients with alcohol or drug-induced disorders. *Hospital and Community Psychiatry, 41*(12), 1342-1344.

Test, M. A., Wallisch, L. S., Allness, D. J., & Ripp, K. (1989). Substance use in young adults with schizophrenic disorders. *Schizophrenia Bulletin, 15*(3), 465-475.

Wolfe, H. L., & Sorenson, J. L. (1989). Dual diagnosis patients in the urban psychiatric emergency room. *Journal of Psychoactive Drugs, 21*(2), 169-175.

9

Clinical Case Management of Personality Disordered Clients

DAVID F. FARIELLO
SHIRLEY POWERS

Kim is a 37-year-old, single, white male who has identified as "a woman trapped in a man's body" since early adulthood. Kim never underwent surgery for a sex change, despite several opportunities in his early adulthood, blaming others or circumstances beyond his control. However, Kim cross-dresses, identifies as a she, and takes female hormones to promote breast development. Despite being of average intelligence, strongly motivated, and having completed his high school education, Kim has never worked for any length of time. He quickly finds himself at odds with co-workers who "never understand me." Kim has been hospitalized psychiatrically 22 times, with countless psychiatric emergency visits beginning in late adolescence. He typically is admitted after drinking or using street drugs and making a suicide attempt, often of a bizarre and/or serious nature: for example, ingesting cleaning fluid, drug overdoses, or cutting his left wrist. The hospitalizations follow periods of depression and hopelessness after Kim has been rejected, victimized, or abused by the "love of my life," who is usually a recent casual acquaintance. Kim comes to see his case manager in the midst of a crisis as often as several times a week, but will often feel unsupported or misunderstood and leave in a rage. Other times he will avoid treatment for weeks, despite committing to regular appointments, since he feels he has nothing to say and gets very anxious during these sessions. He has requested admission to numerous residential settings, day treatment, and vocational training programs, only to be unable to follow program rules, splitting staff and clients, and being involuntarily discharged.

Mental health staff in the public outpatient sector are faced with the task of treating clients such as Kim. These extremely dysfunctional clients share most, if not all of the following characteristics:

1. Confusing diagnostic pictures on Axis I and II. Client inpatient and out-patient records typically display a confusing array of clinical assessments, such as adjustment disorder, dysthymia, schizoaffective disorder, atypical psychosis, antisocial or borderline personality disorder, and/or malingering. A high incidence of complicating substance abuse increases the likelihood of diagnostic confusion.

2. Intense and rapidly shifting affective states. Clients may experience intense rage or self-destructive impulses, depression, gnawing emptiness and anxiety, euphoria and optimism, often in rapid succession.

3. Bizarre and/or unstable identity. Clients experience serious difficulties in maintaining a coherent understanding of who they and who those around them are. Identity at the most basic level—clients' sex and sexual orientation, values and aspirations, affiliations and commitments—are unintegrated, fractionalized, contradictory, and rapidly shifting.

4. Clients exhibit overall severe psychosocial dysfunction, despite periods of apparent lack of symptoms or even demonstrated ability to problem solve. Clients repeatedly fail to maintain interpersonal relationships, to manage funds, to keep jobs, or to maintain housing, medical care, financial entitlements, and other critical social services.

5. Clients maintain a stormy and ambivalent relationship to mental health services and providers. They are often voracious consumers of services, attempting to satisfy their feelings of deprivation and neediness by searching for yet another program that will solve their problems. They are invariably disappointed by the search, because no program or provider is able to perfectly mirror their internal states, leaving them feeling abandoned and enraged. In a parallel process these clients often fail to meet the programs' goals or observe their rules, and are discharged for treatment noncompliance.

6. Clients depend on primitive defenses, such as splitting, primitive idealization, projective identification, denial, and omnipotent control and devaluation.

7. Clients suffer from periods of impaired reality testing. Here it is important to differentiate the bizarre delusions and prominent hallucinations of clients suffering from thought disorders, in which the ability to organize thoughts is dramatically impaired by loosening of associations, concrete interpretations, ideas of reference, and the like, from the reality distortions of primitive defenses employed by clients suffering severe personality disorders, during which, nonetheless, they maintain the ability to organize and communicate their thoughts.

These difficult clients appear in the literature as part of the "young, adult chronic patients" (Bachrach, 1992; Lamb, 1982; Schwartz & Goldfinger, 1981; Surber, Winkler, Monteleone, Havassy, Goldfinger, & Hopkin, 1987) or within the notion of the "nonpsychotic chronic patients" (Adler, Drake, Berlant, Eilison, & Carson, 1987) or as "severe personality disorders" (Kernberg, 1984). These severe personality disordered clients all exhibit a very low level of ego functioning, characterized by borderline, narcissistic, and/or schizotypal features. All authors agree that these clients are difficult to engage; consume a disproportionate share of time, energy, and resources; evoke strong negative countertransference; and often result in little clinical progress.

Many outpatient therapists have concluded that the most severe of this population is not amenable to treatment and should be excluded from services. Selzer, Koenigsberg, and Kernberg (1987) contend that clear behavioral limits must be delineated with severe personality disordered clients, and that when a client violates the conditions of treatment, the therapist must consider an entire gamut of responses, including termination of treatment. Additionally, therapists may have differing tolerances for the onslaught of primitive affect, behavior, and verbal abuse typical of such clients and must decide if working with such regressed clients is possible for them. But the price of having no one in the public mental health system treating such dysfunctional clients is too high for the clients, for their families, and for society. Without a successful strategy for linkage and intervention, severe personality disordered clients will soon exhibit behaviors that result in emergency room visits, inpatient stays, incarceration in jail, and/or serious medical injury. This is a population that has repeatedly demonstrated high-risk and high-cost behaviors.

Clinical case management provides a framework out of which a successful strategy for intervening with this population can be developed. Close attention to an ongoing clinical assessment of the client (especially transference and countertransference issues), a wide continuum of intervention strategies that includes supportive psychotherapy, direct support system manipulation, continuity of care throughout the treatment system and over time, coordination of client accessibility to public resources including the mental health system, and a flexible use of role will allow the clinical case manager to develop a treatment plan tailored to the individual needs of these clients that can change with the dramatic vicissitudes of their illnesses. However, the same flexibility and the same comprehensive approach can also lead the clinical case manager into serious errors with this population.

The goal of work with severe personality disordered clients is to provide a continuous, safe, dependable, and positive arena, in which the client can work through issues about being in a relationship with the clinical case manager, regardless of the intervention strategies chosen by the treater. This arena can act as a base for the client out of which accumulated psychic resources and ego functioning can be applied to other relationships in the outside world, with a consequent improvement in problem solving and social skills.

Interventions with severe personality disordered clients are fundamentally different from those used with higher functioning clients. Severe personality disordered clients often feel wounded, shamed, and increased self-hatred in response to interpretations of their behavior or labeling of their defenses. At times almost any intervention may be rejected by clients because it is experienced as foreign, threatening, or intrusive. Exploration of early life material, or other ways of promoting client regression, should be avoided because that raises the risk of telescoping current events into past traumas and undermining the client's reality testing. By experiencing a therapeutic environment of containment and holding, the client can authentically feel valued and believed, allowing for the possibility of self-acceptance. A holding environment is one in which the case manager primarily provides listening, understanding, and acknowledgement of the client's pain, rather than interpreting the behavior prematurely. Such an environment will provide the client with the trust necessary to maintain an alliance in the face of clinical confrontations or limit setting.

The clinical case manager must pay close attention to the client's use of primitive defenses, especially projection, which are used to ward off those aspects of the client's self that are found to be intolerable. Respect and understanding of the need for these defenses is critical to therapeutic progress. The clinical case manager should avoid the impulse to either deny the projections or try to convince the client of their inaccuracies, because this will inevitably be met with increased defensiveness. Instead, the goal is to join with the clients in their viewpoint and explore the experience of such projections. The more the clinical case manager highlights and seeks to understand the client's experience, the more heard and seen the client will feel, and the more trust will be fostered.

The clinical case manager need not feel compelled, however, to validate the accuracy of the client's projections. For example, a client may tell the case manager of a residential counselor who is cruelly trying to effect the loss of the client's housing. The case manager could remark, "It must be terribly frightening to believe your counselor is trying to harm you," without agreeing that in fact that the counselor's motives are malevolent. The fear could be explored, recognizing where else in the client's life it comes up, and discussing how the client could feel safer in the face of the fear. Interventions in such instances aim at increasing the client's sense of cohesion, and decreasing fragmentation, until such time as the client has the ego capacity to own the projected parts of the self.

Encountering clients' projective identification is a challenging but central ingredient of work with severe personality disordered clients. This severe and intense variation of projection occurs when the client splits off the intolerable primitively aggressive self-part and projects it onto the case manager. The client now responds to the feared rage of the case manager by attempting to control and attack the perceived source of sadistic aggression (see Ogden, 1982, for a more thorough discussion of projective identification). The boundaries between the case manager and the client blur dramatically in such instances, challenging the equanimity of even the most grounded, self-aware clinician. The task of the case manager is to hold the client's infantile rage until the self is strong enough to own this unwanted part. This requires tolerance by the case manager, as well as firm limit setting in the face of any threats or abuse from the client. Limit setting assures the client that the case manager will act to preserve the relationship, contains the client's affect, and support boundary development, as well as provide a role model for protecting oneself from abuse or injury. This dynamic will need to be repeated over and over within the context of a trusting client/case manager relationship.

Sally is a 31-year-old woman with psychotic defenses within a borderline personality structure. She had several psychiatric hospitalizations before admission to the case management program. She has never held a job, yet is very intelligent and articulate. She never misses her twice weekly supportive psychotherapy sessions, but often uses them to express wildly rageful accusations toward the case manager. The case manager's responses, especially if they demonstrate empathic failure, are met by Sally's skillfully targeted devaluations of the former.

The case manager primarily listened to Sally in the beginning of their relationship in order to promote a trusting environment, as even attempts to communicate understanding were experienced as threatening by Sally. Early limit setting of Sally's abusiveness only increased her rate. The case manager often felt held hostage and tormented by Sally. For example, Sally would accuse the case manager of sadistically and coldly participating in the relationship for the sole purpose of earning his paycheck, or tricking her into more opportunities to abuse her. The case manager began questioning his capacity to convey concern for Sally, in spite of his knowledge to the contrary. He struggled with fantasies of retaliating or discharging Sally from treatment, and felt hopeless about getting beyond this impasse. Sally was putting into the case manager her internalized, sadistic parent. It was some time before Sally could recognize how angry she was, and before her outbursts became less intense and less frequent. Very gradually, Sally came to tolerate the fact that the case manager was separate and different from her. She learned that she had suffered from severe childhood abuse and neglect.

Four years later, Sally is able to acknowledge her anger and its impact on others. There remain times when she is quick to feel abused and when the boundaries between herself and others blur in the face of her rage. She is now able to regain observing ego functioning more quickly, as well as use therapy to talk about her experience and to express her fears and her profound grief. She has not used the hospital or the psychiatric emergency services during these 4 years. Additionally, she is attending school and is hopeful about forming friendships.

The case manager may at times employ reality testing with the client to preserve the relationship or maintain client safety, but not as the primary mode of intervention. For example, the client may believe the case manager to actually be an abusive father. The case manager could respond by saying, "You seem to believe I am abusing you. That must be very frightening, but you should know that is not my intention." Later the case manager may be able to help the client understand that these confusions are also taking place with others, thus helping improve the client's social functioning.

The clinical case manager should expect to have strong personal responses to such primitive defenses as projection, splitting, devaluation, and so on. Being the container for such unwanted split-off parts of the client requires the case manager to be able to identify rage, feelings of being overwhelmed and helpless, euphoria, and other feelings elicited by the client. Processing these feelings with supervisors and colleagues will decrease the chances of the case manager acting them out with the client. Errors will be made, however, by the case manager in treating such difficult clients. In such instances, the case manager can identify the error to the client, apologize for any injury, and clarify the intentions, if necessary. This will allow the client to experience the case manager as a three-dimensional person, with imperfections as well as knowledge and abilities.

A safe relationship for such dysfunctional clients will also be premised on the existence of adequate food, clothing, shelter, physical safety, and other life-sustaining requisites. Since the client is often unable to develop support system resources and has limited skills to manage them, the case manager may need to provide a thorough inventory, often in vivo, as part of the psychosocial assessment of the case. It is important for the clinical case manager to pay close attention to the meaning for the client of such an assessment. Interventions outside the traditional boundaries of a 50-minute hour carry powerful intentional and unintentional messages to the client. Repeated exploration of the client's feelings and fantasies about such interventions is critical, as are repeated clarification and elaboration of the case manager's intentions and goals.

Severe personality disordered clients often present the clinical case manager with demands for practical intervention coupled with extreme helplessness. Such clients have often had early experiences of being loved or valued by caregivers only when they were weak or dependent, and abandoned or rejected when they acted independently. The case manager is at risk to replicate this scenario by rushing in to resolve a problem on behalf of the client. The case manager can, instead, avoid reacting to the drama of the client's demands or needs, offering to explore the issues when the client is calmer. It is important to ask such questions as: What is the client afraid of? What aspect of the problem is most troubling? What resources are available to the client? This will both help the client sort through the flood of intense feelings and support ego functioning. It will also help the case managers evaluate at what level they should intervene, and how they can best avoid disempowering the client.

Some clients, not having their requests or demands gratified, may respond with rage or self-destructive acting out, as the following example demonstrates.

Dan, a 29-year-old, gay-identified male, comes to see his case manager for weekly supportive psychotherapy. Prior to referral to case management services, he had a history of repeated psychiatric hospitalizations and psychiatric emergency visits, typically precipitated by real or perceived rejection and followed by alcohol abuse, explosive behavior, and the loss of his housing.

Since linking to case management Dan now presents at his case manager's office, rather than at the psychiatric emergency room, when he has lost his hotel room. He insists that the manager has treated him unfairly, and claims that if the case manager cannot help him he will perish from being homeless in the streets. The case manager has learned, however, that Dan's knowledge of community resources surpasses her own. When the case manager encourages Dan to use his knowledge to meet his needs, as well as confronting him on his need to abstain from alcohol, he becomes enraged, refusing to leave the facility; he has broken the facility front door on one occasion. Over time, however, Dan has kept his hotel room for longer periods of time, as well as paying for repair of the facility front door. Because the relationship with the case manager has been built on trust and firm limits, Dan has begun to consider the relationship between his behavior and his loss of housing. Additionally, he has for the first time expressed a desire to quit drinking, attend AA meetings, and decrease his rageful attacks.

A safe relationship must include clear and firm limits, allowing the client to know from the beginning that the case manager will intervene, as able and if necessary, to insure the safety of the client, the facility, and the community.

This subpopulation is at high risk to repeatedly commit dramatic and/or life-threatening self-destructive acts. For example, one client repeatedly swallowed sharp objects, requiring numerous surgeries for retrieval. Other clients either neglect treatment of or actively complicate physical illnesses, such as diabetes, grand mal epilepsy, and hemophilia, during self-destructive episodes. Clients may repeatedly provoke others to assault or otherwise abuse them, or may repeatedly abuse others. Despite the fact that the acts sometime occur in situations where help is readily available, it is misleading to minimize them by describing them as gestures, since the risk of lethality is so high and the client is often acting impulsively, with impaired reality testing.

If the case manager assesses the need for involuntary hospitalization, it is important that both the causes of the case manager's concern for safety and the purpose of hospitalization be explained to the client. It is likely that such an action will create a crisis in the client/case manager relationship, because the clients may feel threatened and devalued by the disparity between their own assessments of the situation and those of the case manager. The case manager needs to help the client contain rage, despair, or other tumultuous feelings, while demonstrating that the client and the case manager can have dramatically different observations and judgments, yet agree on a common goal: the client's safety and well-being.

During the hospitalization it is important that the case manager maintain contact with the client, perhaps as often as would occur on an outpatient basis. By actively participating in the inpatient treatment planning, the case manager can bring valuable information, a clear understanding of how the inpatient stay fits into overall treatment strategy, and the help to minimize splitting between the various staff that is wont to occur in treating such a difficult client. Additionally, the case manager should continue the relationship work with the client during the inpatient admission. This will help the client master fears of being abandoned by the case manager, during a time when the client has little control and may feel at great risk. It will also help the client understand that the case manager is capable of maintaining the same kind of relationship, although circumstances and environment may have changed significantly.

Hospitalization may, however, reinforce a client's feelings of helplessness and inadequacy, as well as reward acting out behavior. Prolonged hospitalization may also promote further regression on the client's part.

A systemwide treatment plan may help contain the client's acting out and forestall the need for hospitalization, as the following instance illustrates.

Mary repeatedly presents at the psychiatric emergency room with threats of suicide and complaints of being victimized by her case manager or others in her support system. When hospitalized, she repeats the scenario soon after her discharge to the community and upon confronting another stressful event. The case manager developed a plan with psychiatric emergency staff to hold Mary during these episodes, but not to admit her to the hospital. Her impulses to suicide usually pass within 24 hours, and an expensive inpatient episode is avoided. More important, Mary has the experience of surviving these episodes without hospitalization and has come to rely more on managing feelings of helplessness and rage, without acting out through her relationship with her case manager.

Other forms of boundaries and limits will be necessary to protect and preserve the client/case manager relationship. It is important, however, for the case manager to be aware of countertransference issues when setting boundaries. Too often, limit setting by staff can reflect sadistic impulses called forth by the client. A case manager may feel overwhelmed and defeated by the client's needs, for example, and tell the client that such needs are inappropriate and should stop being expressed. In effect, this blames the client for presenting symptoms that are predictably part of the pathology. The error is only compounded when the case manager insists the client agree to a contract, which will be predictably violated. In such cases the case manager will need to examine feelings of neediness that have been denied, with the help of supervision or psychotherapy.

In limit or boundary setting, then, it is important that the case manager clearly understand why the boundary is being set and take responsibility for it. In the above example, the case manager might state: "I know you would like to see me daily when you are feeling anxious, but I don't have the ability to do that. I am sorry; I understand how important our sessions are. I can, however, see you 'x' times a week and talk on the phone Friday afternoon. What other resources are available to you for times when I am not available?" Thus, a boundary was set for the case manager's well-being and for the maintenance of the client/case manager relationship, while at the same time acknowledging the client's needs and looking for resources to respond to them.

It is also important that setting boundaries not become an exercise in determining who is in control of the relationship. For a relationship to be safe, it must be clear that the case manager is ultimately responsible for it. Thus, once a limit has been set, it must be maintained until there is reason to change it. If the client is allowed to dispute limits, changing them through stubborn argument, the boundary between the client's and the case manager's roles will become confusing, complicating the already chaotic identity of the former.

For a limit to have impact, there must be a consequence for its violation. The consequence must be nonjudgmental and consistent with the maintenance of the client/case manager relationship, since there can be no clinical improvement without a relationship. The case manager must be able to help the client differentiate between the behaviors and value as a human being. Consequences that are clearly connected to the problem created, which do not require the clients to feel bad about themselves, but are consistently enforced, will help maintain the client/case manager relationship and act as a reality test about what happens in the world. For example, if a client breaks facility property while acting out, the case manager could cause the client's subpayee to reimburse the facility, and/or the client could be seen in another setting until impulse control is restored.

The amount of practical intervention by the case manager often varies dramatically over the course of the relationship. While helping to forge an alliance, practical activity can complicate boundary issues with clients who might have little experience with therapists who are involved so intimately in their lives. Questions as to what the therapist's ultimate intentions are; the parameters of what the client and therapist can do together; or even if the therapist is fundamentally a separate person from the client, or just an extension of the client's desires or needs, can begin to occur for the client. The case manager, then, needs to clarify such concerns from the very beginning, without overwhelming the client with a wealth of issues that have only begun to emerge. Thus, the therapist is helping define the purposes and parameters of the relationship as it unfolds. This requires case managers to think clinically at the same time that they are concentrating with clients on a specific task at hand. The thinking should consider such questions as: What ego deficit causes this client to have difficulty performing this alone? What abilities or resources does the client imagine that the case manager possesses, enabling the latter to perform this? What does this client believe is the case manager's motivation in helping accomplish this task? How will the solution of this task make the client's life easier and/or more complicated? At what point will the case manager urge the client to attempt more of the task? Are there circumstances in which the case manager should refuse to help the client with a task? If so, how would it be explained to the client? The point is that one must not only attend to the specifics of the issue at hand but also consider the past, present, and future meanings of the task to the client.

The use of medications is another important issue in the treatment of clients suffering severe character pathology. Clients have often been given trials of various mood stabilizers, anxiolytics, and/or antipsychotic medications; usually with limited success. This may reflect the complicated diagnostic issues presented by such clients, as well as the dramatically shifting array of intense symptoms they suffer from. It may also mirror the client's feelings of being helpless and overwhelmed, and the hope that some powerful, idealized person like a psychiatrist will intervene to contain the turmoil. Again, it is important that treaters track their countertransference so they do not join the client in this fantasy of omnipotence.

Medication assessments should target specific symptoms experienced by the clients, and require clear communication by all members of the treatment team, because symptoms may not always be evident to the psychiatrist during the evaluation. Medications may be another issue around which the client struggles to assert control, as they become symbolic for the client of the need to be gratified by taking things in. Again, limit setting in such instances requires the treater (the psychiatrist, in this case) to clearly delineate options and boundaries, not to argue with the client over them, and to change only when the treater is clear about the need for such change. Dispensing medications must always take into consideration the potential for abuse or use in self-destructive acting out. The case manager can be helpful in responding to this latter concern, by working with the client and the client's support system to help manage the medications safely.

As was noted above, substance abuse has a high comorbidity rate among clients suffering from severe personality disorders. There is an ever-present impulse to drink and/or use drugs among clients who get little symptom relief from prescribed medications and are also at high risk for self-destructive acting out. As with all dually diagnosed clients, persistent substance abuse takes on a life of its own and cannot be understood exclusively as attempts at self-medication. Otherwise, the case manager is at risk to address only psychiatric symptoms, expecting the substance abuse to dissipate of its own accord, rather than to respond to both the chronic mental illness and the substance addiction concomitantly (see Chapter 8: Treatment of Substance Abuse and Mental Illness).

Unlike with dually diagnosed clients suffering from psychotic disorders, the case manager must use practical intervention into a client's support system much more carefully, as described above. Additionally, clients suffering from severe personality disorder may be able to tolerate and benefit from limit setting more readily than clients suffering from psychosis. Similarly, as the latter clients may have great cognitive difficulties processing and organizing the stimuli of groups such as AA, the former clients may feel contained by the unity of purpose and consistency of meeting structure, while not being overwhelmed by intimacy.

Severe personality disordered clients challenge treaters with their extreme behavior, with the intense countertransference they evoke, and with their seeming inability to manage any areas of their lives. Despite such deficits, these clients can be treated successfully through a slowly constructed, trusting relationship. Progress requires a judicious combination of the treater's patience, limit setting, optimism, flexible and imaginative use of interventions, close attention to transference and countertransference, as well as support system interventions when warranted. Clinical case management, then, can be understood as a broadening of the parameters of the traditional clinical relationship to give the treater more options and flexibility in treating a seriously dysfunctional population, such as those suffering severe personality disorders.

References

Adler, D. A., Drake, R. E., Berlant, J., Eilison, J. M., & Carson, D. (1987). Treatment of the nonpsychotic patient: A problem of interactive fit. *American Journal of Orthopsychiatry, 57*, 579-586.

Bachrach, L. L. (1982). Young adult chronic patients: An analytical review of the literature. *Hospital and Community Psychiatry, 33*, 189-197.

Kernberg, O. (1984). *Severe personality disorders*. New Haven, CT: Yale University Press.

Lamb, H. R. (1982). Young adult chronic patients: The new drifters. *Hospital and Community Psychiatry, 33*, 465-468.

Ogden, T. H. (1982). *Projective identification and therapeutic technique*. Northvale, NJ: Jason Aronson.

Schwartz, S. R., & Goldfinger, S. M. (1981). The new chronic patient: Clinical characteristics of an emerging subgroup. *Hospital and Community Psychiatry, 32*, 470-474.

Selzer, A. M., Koenigsberg, W. H., & Kernberg, O. F. (1987). The initial contract in the treatment of borderline patients. *American Journal of Psychiatry, 144*, 927-930.

Surber, R. W., Winkler, E. L., Monteleone, M., Havassy, B. E., Goldfinger, S. M., & Hopkin, J. T. (1987). Characteristics of high users of acute inpatient services. *Hospital and Community Psychiatry, 38*, 1112-1114.

10

Managing Problematic Behaviors

DEBORAH BEGLEY

Most clinicians in community mental health can provide detailed examples of clients with problematic behaviors. Such behaviors include suicidality, aggressiveness, substance abuse, behaviors resulting from severe character disorders, and noncompliance with medications. These behaviors impair a client's functional ability and may alienate service providers. Clinicians' and other service providers' countertransference responses to clients' problematic behaviors can enhance or impede treatment.

This chapter will describe problematic behaviors, describe characteristics of clients with such behaviors, provide management guidelines, and discuss transference and countertransference issues.

Describing Problematic Behaviors

Frequent Suicidal Ideation, Gestures, or Attempts. This can mean serious suicide attempts, frequent threats of self-harm, reports of an overdose by a client who then presents to the therapist's office or medical emergency room, or more unusual and self-destructive tendencies, such as eating lightbulbs or reopening physical wounds. While the possibility of suicide by a client is part of the chosen profession, the frequency and intensity of threats can result in countertransference reactions that lead to a referral of the client to another program for unmanageability or an exclusion from services altogether. That severely mentally ill clients may make fatal or near-fatal attempts can only increase a clinician's anxiety.

165

History of Violence, Threatening Behavior, or Assaultiveness. The threat of violence is a common reason that clients are refused services at traditional outpatient clinics. Many clients have a history of and continued potential for physically assaulting others, destruction of property, threatening others, and other aggressive, intimidating, and frightening behaviors. They are often refused services at outpatient clinics for such behavior as yelling or shouting threats in waiting areas or at the therapist, threatening to blow up the clinic, throwing objects through clinic windows, or brandishing a weapon. Police may be called to intervene and have often played a significant role in many clients' lives. All of these events serve to alienate service providers, particularly when there are much less provocative and anxiety-evoking clients seeking treatment.

Severe Substance Abuse and Intoxication. Many clients abuse or depend on alcohol and/or drugs. This interferes with the ability of clients to comply with treatment, and they may even end up in jail for drug possession or public intoxication. These clients may often miss therapy or medication appointments or come intoxicated and create a scene, being loud, demanding, and perhaps verbally abusive while refusing to leave the clinic. They may spend much of their time and money procuring, using, and withdrawing from the intoxicants, and they are often broke the day after receiving their entitlement check. Preexisting symptoms are frequently exacerbated when a client is intoxicated. Clients may become more depressed, more suicidal, and more impulsive when under the influence of drugs or alcohol, and often end up in psychiatric emergency rooms. Denial of the problem abounds. Such clients will have little use for the mental health system while under the influence, but should they seek treatment, outpatient clinics often refuse services until the clients can demonstrate they are in alcohol or drug treatment. Clinicians are naturally frustrated by clients who consistently fail to keep appointments due to intoxication, or when they find themselves "talking to the drug" instead of the client. They may wish to refer these dual diagnosis clients elsewhere.

Behaviors Resulting From Severe Personality Disorder. Some clients, usually those diagnosed with borderline or antisocial personality disorders, do not endear themselves to mental health clinics and are often seen as manipulative or "just acting out." The unspoken belief with such clients is that they could get better if they only wanted to, and somehow they are less deserving of treatment than clients with only Axis I disorders. It has been found, however, that of chronically mentally ill individuals, 44%

who had an Axis I disorder also had an Axis II diagnosis (Harris, 1990). Such clients may present as very demanding or entitled, insist on help and then reject any offer made as not good enough. They may try to split one staff member or system from another. They may be hostile, verbally abusive, blaming and sarcastic, or they may be chronic liars. When combined with substance abuse, the problems quickly alienate clients from the very services they need. While their provocative behavior may seem intentional, and they often reject the very services they demand, it seems that with frequent emergency room visits they use the mental health system in a different way than providers want or expect them to.

Noncompliance With Psychotropic Medication and Treatment. All public sector clinicians can describe the revolving door syndrome—the frustration of watching a client stabilize on medication while in the hospital, only to refuse medication when released, leading to quick rehospitalization for decompensation. For example, a 41-year-old male with schizophrenia consistently wins his release from the hospital because his mental status improves due to the medication he has obtained there. Once discharged, however, he refuses to take his medication, becomes psychotic and confused, and is unable to provide for his basic needs. He often puts himself and others in potentially dangerous situations by such behaviors as throwing rocks at landing airplanes, walking into traffic, and not eating. His refusal to take medication results in repeated hospitalizations, with repeated releases. Clinicians may feel they are tilting at windmills.

A related problem is noncompliance with treatment. While clinicians in the private sector are accustomed to clients faithfully keeping appointments, today's community mental health clients are less likely to do so for a variety of reasons. Some clients are called treatment resisters or, more accurately, system resisters (Goldfinger, Hopkin, & Surber, 1984). Two different systems are in force here: one based on clinic need, the other based on client need. Clinicians and administrators often believe that if clients are in need, they will keep their appointments, and this line of thinking is difficult to resist. There are only so many appointments, particularly given shrinking resources, and failed appointments and open times mean less productivity and fewer clients seen. Service providers become frustrated (out of countertransference responses of anger, helplessness, and the like) with clients who continually miss scheduled appointments, because these valuable slots could go to clients who are viewed as more responsible and in need and motivated to keep appointments.

The ability to keep appointments, however, is simply not a good indicator of need. Clients may be on a different kind of time, that is, "street time." They may not even know what day it is, or it may not be important for them to know. There are many reasons a client will not keep an appointment, such as oversleeping due to medication, no transportation, confusion or disorientation, or the need to choose between waiting in line for a meal and attending a therapy appointment.

It should be noted that these problematic behaviors are not discrete entities, but tend to overlap. For example, a 25-year-old male demonstrated severe borderline personality disorder symptoms, made repeated suicidal gestures, missed appointments, refused to take needed medications for physical disorders, often lied, was frequently drunk and sometimes verbally hostile when intoxicated. It is the combination of these behaviors in clients that can make them particularly difficult to treat.

Characteristics of Clients With Problematic Behaviors

Demographic Characteristics

The majority, although certainly not all, of case management clients with problematic behaviors fit some elements of what has been described as the Young Adult Chronic Patient population or a subgroup of it (Pepper & Ryglewicz, 1984; Sheets, Prevost, & Reihman, 1982; Surles, Blanch, Shern, & Donahue, 1992). Characteristics of these groups have been reported to include suicide attempts, history of violence, rejection of treatment, drug and alcohol abuse, and multiple hospitalizations. McClelland and Kerr (1991) also note a group of patients whose "aggression or socially embarrassing" behavior can be problematic, and whose treatment is complicated by lack of cooperation and stable residences and a fragmentation of care.

There is a range of diagnostic categories: Schizophrenia, schizoaffective disorder, other psychoses, and bipolar affective disorder are the most common, often with secondary personality disorders. Major depression or dysthymia, adjustment disorders, and organic syndromes are underrepresented.

Most clients are supported by public entitlements or awaiting decisions on appeals. While some may have a previous work history, most have not been able to maintain any period of employment. They may often express a desire to work but are unable to follow through due to substance abuse, psychotic symptoms, disorganization, and so on. Many have had some forensic involvement and most live in single-room-occupancy (SRO) hotels, residential care homes, shelters, or on the streets. Almost all are single or divorced. They represent the chronically disenfranchised.

Living on little money is a very difficult task for all of us, but it can be particularly devastating for those with a mental illness. Many clients spend much of their money on a hotel room because supported housing is either scarce or unreceptive to them. Some clients will choose to live in shelters and save their money for food and cigarettes. Robbery is also a frequent occurrence for clients and can precipitate a crisis. Poverty is, at the very least, dehumanizing.

Many clients are often without family or social support. Despite heroic efforts, families may no longer feel able to deal with the client's behavior, so they decrease or cut off contact. They may blame the client and project all problems on the individual, without seeking support, such as the National Alliance for the Mentally Ill (NAMI) or Alanon, for themselves. Some clients may be so disruptive to family life, threatening members with weapons or stealing family resources, that restraining orders are necessary.

Often it is the client who withdraws from the family out of fear, hurt, or anger. The family may be dead, dispersed, or in a different state. Many clients also live in rather squalid rooms in transient hotels, which only serves to further their isolation. Communication with some landlords may pose problems due to different ethnic backgrounds, and interpersonal difficulties may be exacerbated by language barriers.

Clinical Characteristics

Inability to Form Stable Relationships. Most case management clients, and problematic behavior clients in particular, have a great deal of difficulty establishing relationships, and may treat others as objects. Many have had horrendous histories of abuse and abandonment while growing up, and have not only had no one consistently emotionally available to them, but have also never learned the skills or possessed the ego strength to interact with others. A strong sense of isolation prevails. Frequently, the client's assaultive behavior has through the years alienated caregivers and reinforced the inability to establish and maintain relationships. These clients often live alone in SRO hotels.

Inability to Problem Solve. Clients will frequently demonstrate the same reaction to handling stress, repeatedly engaging in behavior that in the short run removes them from a troublesome situation, but does not lead to a lasting stress reduction, or which creates a different problem altogether. One male client's solution to perceived rejection was to drink and cut himself. He then felt bad about his behavior and would drink some more, further alienating him from potential friends who could be of support. Another male client with schizoaffective disorder borrowed money from a hotel resident for alcohol, with no intention of repayment, and then was forced to vacate his hotel out of fear of reprisal, thus rendering him homeless. A third male client, also diagnosed with schizoaffective disorder, sold items for less than he had just paid for them in order to buy cocaine, and then had no money for food. What often happens with such clients is that they repeatedly end up on the doorstep of the psychiatric emergency service.

Poor Impulse Control. Many clients respond to perceived rejection, anxiety, and frustration at not getting their needs met with violence against self, others, or property. Responses can range from verbal abuse or threats to actual physical violence. This impaired impulse control is often exacerbated by the influence of such substances as alcohol, cocaine, or PCP. For example, a 40-year-old Caucasian male with schizoaffective disorder spent all his money on alcohol and drugs, and then presented to the clinic for food and shelter. When this was not forthcoming, he threatened to kill the people in the parking lot and his therapist, who was standing in front of him.

Many clients have a history of violence and have spent time in jail. The question arises: To what is the violence in the current clinical presentation due? In a review of the literature, it was found that the most common diagnosis related to violence was schizophrenia, followed by personality disorders and organic brain syndrome (Krakowski, Volavka, & Briser, 1986). It was noted that violence can reflect emotional upheaval or an inability to adhere to social restraints. Clients with personality disorders can manifest violence as a relatively stable trait, irrespective of emotional upheaval. The meaning of violence will be different for each client, and this must be taken into account when dealing with such clients; for example, is it intentional, out of fear, manipulation, frustration, or intimidation? (Smith, 1983). Reid and Balis (1987) also reviewed the literature and found similar diagnoses in violence in emergency rooms. Tardiff and Koenigsberg (1985) found, however, that in outpatient assaults the diagnoses were more likely to be personality disorders.

How one has learned to deal with situations in the past, that is, individual patterns of behavior, must be taken into account in addition to the actual environmental influences. Many clients with problematic behaviors are intimately involved in street life, where violence is a common way of dealing with problems. One female client threatened to have her friends beat up her landlord, with whom she was experiencing difficulty. This was an expression of borderline rage that did pass. The client, however, continues to live in a violent and disruptive neighborhood, and chooses for companions men who are quite streetwise. She has impulsively called the police when another resident called her "a bitch," and pulled a knife on another resident to show she meant business in a dispute. She has had a chaotic life filled with abandonment and abuse, which continues to manifest now because that is what she has learned.

Labile Mood. Clients may quickly switch from pleasant mood to explosive rage, cheerfulness to paranoid-based hostility. Combined with poor impulse control, this can make for potentially dangerous situations.

Lack of Daily Living Skills, or Institutionalization. Many case management clients have invariably spent years in and out of state hospitals, long-term locked facilities, structured programs including residential care homes, hospitals, and possibly jail. The clients have a great deal of difficulty with independent living and may seek the safety of the hospital when anxiety becomes too high. Independent living skills and problem-solving skills will be impaired, because all of their basic needs, such as food, clothing, shelter, companions, and handling money, have previously been managed for them. Decisions have been made for them. Clients may understandably rely on institutions to provide both ego and superego functions. These issues will invariably arise during treatment and recur over time.

The Role of Victim and Victimizer. Finally, clients with problematic behaviors can often be characterized as both victim and victimizer. This is a self-perpetuating dynamic among clients, institutions, and others. Many outpatient clinic staff become increasingly frustrated by clients who return again and again for crisis visits, but never follow up on referrals; or they present intoxicated with no place to stay, having just spent all of their money on drugs and alcohol. This frustration is heightened by an increasing lack of resources within the mental health system, as well as the system's inability to legally detain clients, who then quickly decompensate and recycle back. As a way of dealing with such frustration, staff may blame clients for their refusal to stick with treatment referrals. Clients may blame staff for turning what feels to be a deaf ear to their needs, or for restraining or medicating them against their will. There can be an "Oh, no, not you again" mentality on the part of all parties concerned. Family members or shopkeepers may also feel victimized by clients who are threatening and abusive, or who eat in restaurants without paying ("dine and dash"). There usually arises the question of who has jurisdiction: mental health, jail services, or substance abuse services? The question itself is a way of expressing frustration. No one wants the client, yet each system blames the other for its failure to solve the problem. Coid (1991) also describes how "difficult to manage" clients are referred from one agency to another, rather than helped to develop ways to meet their needs. As indicated in this book, the blending of these arenas is one of the reasons clinical case management is needed.

Management of Problematic Behaviors

General Guidelines

Safety. Safety for all concerned is of paramount importance. Where one sees clients is a key factor in managing problematic behaviors. Depending on the level of potential assaultiveness, a client may be seen in a locked emergency room setting, where other staff are familiar with physically restraining a client should the need arise. The locked setting itself can have a containing effect on the client.

Most if not all mental health clinics have a policy that clients turn over all weapons before being seen. Once in the interview, the position of the chairs is important. Some therapists believe they should never get between a client and the door, but it is the rule of this clinician to sit closer to the door, so as not to be barred from the exit by a hostile and threatening client. Clinic staff should also receive regular training, including verbal and physical interventions, in the management of assaultive behavior.

The therapist should never see a client alone in a hotel room if there are reservations about the client's unpredictability or one's own safety. Previous threatening behavior, sexualizing behavior, impulsivity, and showing no remorse over past aggressive behavior are good indicators *not* to see a client alone during a home visit, particularly when a therapeutic relationship has not been established. Other team members, or even the police, may be needed to accompany a clinician on an outreach. For example, the primary therapist of a 43-year-old male, who was being asked to check out of his hotel room due to threatening others with a knife, asked another clinician to accompany her on the outreach. While the client was loud and demanding, he was not assaultive, due to this added precaution.

Use of the Relationship. The use of one's self is the single most important tool in psychotherapy. It is what a therapist has to offer beyond theory and technique. With difficult clients it may take multiple efforts to connect, and realistically, some clients just will not link, despite the persistence of the therapist.

Each clinician must come to a decision about how far to go and how much to do to engage a client. Engagement often requires vigorous outreach, in sharp contrast to traditional outpatient therapy. The engagement process must be individualized for each person. Where one might check on a disorganized or severely depressed person for failure to keep an appointment, this would not be indicated with a client whose marked hostility and sexual preoccupation might lead either to a misinterpretation of the outreach or to hostile behavior. It is a clinical decision to take another team member on an outreach, or to wait for the client to resurface. Problematic behavior clients may also be especially difficult to engage because their defensive mechanisms serve to keep others at a distance. They may project angry impulses, blame others, deny they have any problems, all to protect themselves from overwhelming anxiety or to guard against intimacy.

The therapist must be a real person. This does not mean unbridled disclosure, but rather a sense of genuineness, honesty and directness, a sense of humor, and a true sense of caring about the client. One client, in describing why he liked one psychiatrist, stated: "She shakes my hand, she asks me how I'm doing, she treats me like a real person, not like I'm just some piece of paper." Clients also rely on a therapist for reality testing and will feel they cannot trust a therapist who pretends that all their behavior is appropriate, due to the therapist's own anxiety about confronting it.

Providing Resources. Clinicians often take for granted the satisfaction of their basic needs and their abilities to do so. But for many case management clients, it is a daily matter of survival. Recognition of the powerful effects of poverty on clients and their ability to cope with stress is essential. Therapists must ask themselves how they would respond if in a similar situation, and to do so without negative judgments. The use of concrete resources, such as bus tokens, bag lunches, or housing, can facilitate the beginning of a therapeutic connection and offer acknowledgement of the client. In fact, the provision or coordination of concrete resources is often the only way to initially connect with a client. The first several years of work may be geared toward stabilization of food, clothing, and consistent shelter.

Help with housing is a frequent request. Many clients have been homeless, and the odds of psychotic decompensation increase without shelter. Referral for a week of emergency housing can stabilize a client until the next check comes. An overnight stay in the psychiatric emergency room can be used, depending on the presentation of the client, or referrals to shelters may be made. There are, of course, both the potential and the reality of abuse of emergency resources. Some clients have relied on it for years while they spent their money on drugs. In this case, such housing would not be indicated, particularly if the client was not on money management; but referrals to shelters would be offered, as well as a suggestion for assistance with money management and/or referral to drug treatment programs.

Many clients are required to have a payee for their entitlement funds. Some choose family members or "partners," others have their funds administered by a formal social service program. One female client in her forties had gone through a series of male payees, who would invariably give her a fraction of the check and keep the rest. She is now on a formal representative payee program and receiving checks four times a month, and is able to consistently have food, clothing, and a decent residence. Case managers may serve as a link between clients and their money. While this may be helpful to clients to ensure they have money throughout the month and that their rent is paid, it inevitably brings up issues of power and external control, which will be addressed later.

Linkage and advocacy with other agencies are also important means of management. These issues are addressed in depth in Chapters 6 and 7.

While clients may seek food or housing, they may not be as enthusiastic about another resource, medication. Many clients, as noted earlier, refuse all medication, or accept prescriptions and never fill them, or sell the drugs on the street. Some seek inappropriate medication. For instance, a client insisted that only Valium would help with his paranoid delusions and auditory hallucinations and became quite upset when it was not forthcoming. He was unwilling to take other medication and drank daily when not hospitalized.

Other clients recognize that medication can be helpful, even if they do not like taking it. Medication can prevent hospitalization and can help clients avoid the disabling results of psychotic symptoms. Clients may see an offer of medication as an acknowledgement of themselves, a validation that the clinician takes their concerns seriously. For example, a 30-year-old client with schizophrenia had expressed his ambivalence toward medication by insisting that someone had come into his room and stolen his medication. He had been given pillboxes to ensure compliance. Through coordination with his therapist and psychiatrist, who themselves were in close consultation, he was able to maintain a reduction in medication and obtain prescriptions rather than having pillboxes filled (thus increasing independence). He was able to report that *he* now had control of his medication, not someone else. This was directly related to his sense of being listened to about the issue of medication and side effects and feeling a sense of control.

Use of Involuntary Hospitalization. Clients should be legally detained if a danger to themselves or others or gravely disabled (unable to provide for food, clothing, or shelter) as a result of a mental disorder, depending, of course, on the laws of the particular state. There may be times when a clinician does not feel a client will harm self or others, yet is in need of some containment. This may be caused by increased anxiety or depression, feelings of exhaustion, need for a time-out from a stressful situation, or to prevent a client from being overwhelmed. The client may be asked to voluntarily sign in to a psychiatric emergency clinic or hospital. Clients may also be legally detained to convey to them that their threats/ideation are being taken seriously, or to avoid a power struggle if clients will escalate to dangerous behaviors if not legally held.

Clients often ask to be legally detained, either verbally or through self-destructive behavior, and are relieved when it is forthcoming. This represents for them control and safety. They may initially become angry when told they will stay in a psychiatric emergency service, but their intentions often become clear. One male client with borderline personality disorder presented to the psychiatric emergency clinic just before dinner and complained of suicidal ideation. When reminded of his appointment with his case manager in the morning, he insisted he must be detained, that he would hurt himself if released. He then appeared jovial and ate two helpings of dinner. When he discovered he would have to sleep on a mat on the floor that night due to crowded conditions, he quickly recovered, declaring his suicidal crisis resolved and affirming his intention to keep his appointment the next day. He was released and kept his appointment. Another time he was legally held by his case manager for suicidal ideation. Held overnight, he told the case manager he felt better and not suicidal, and was released. However, clearly ambivalent, he became angry over his release, took a mild overdose, and presented to the medical emergency room, where he was again detained. In the next session this incident was processed, regarding his feelings about being released and how he dealt with them.

Some clients strenuously object to legal detention, and the clinician may need police back-up if in the community. If there is any question of safety for anyone concerned, the police should be called to provide such back-up. However, if safe, the clinician should be prepared to wait with the client until the police arrive. Any time the client is legally detained by the therapist, this needs to be processed in the next session if possible. Issues to be considered include the reasons for the detainment, the client's reactions, possibilities for different behaviors, transference, and trust issues.

There is, of course, the question of power and coercion in the use of involuntary hospitalization, and the therapist must be aware of and accept the feelings that arise concerning this issue. There is the clear obligation to provide for the safety of the client and others. A less clear-cut area may be the question of grave disability. When is one unable to care for oneself due to a mental disorder? The therapist may be reluctant to legally detain a client on these grounds, given the purpose of helping clients maintain themselves in the community. Factors to consider include weight loss from not spending money on food, or inability to keep a hotel room due to paranoid ideation, or failure to shower or change clothing for weeks due to disorganization. It is at these times that clients may protest the most, believing that they are capable of independent living, and there may never be agreement. This can also be acknowledged and discussed with clients, as tolerated by them. For example, a 37-year-old man with schizoaffective disorder spent money impulsively on movies and cab rides and had no money left to pay for food. He had lost weight to the point where it jeopardized his health and refused to shower or change clothing on his own. He had no insight and could not understand his hospitalizations, insisting he was fine. The case manager could only acknowledge the difference of opinion around his many hospitalizations, while continuing to take the necessary protective measures for him.

Managing Specific Behaviors

Suicidality. In the course of work with clients, suicidal or self-destructive feelings will at times need to be tolerated by the client and the therapist without any action. There should be an effort to identify alternative means of support, such as a friend, Suicide Prevention, medication, or a psychiatric emergency clinic when the clinician is not available. A no-self-harm contract can be entered into with a client whom one feels can honor this arrangement.

Many times the suicidal ideation can be managed by talking about it in session, and the client obtains relief. Hopefully, by now, the myth that talking about suicidal feelings increases the likelihood of acting on them has been laid to rest. If the clinician has any doubts about the client's intentions, one should simply ask. If the feelings/intentions do not decrease, and the clinician feels the client is in danger of acting on the impulses (e.g., has a plan and the means to carry it out), then a legal hold should be instituted. If a therapist is in an outlying clinic, and the client agrees to go voluntarily to the psychiatric emergency clinic, this can be arranged; otherwise, an involuntary hospitalization will need to be coordinated. Clients who spend the night in the psychiatric emergency clinic will often report a decrease in suicidal feelings.

A therapist may be concerned about a suicidal client who does not keep an appointment, and an outreach to the hotel room may be indicated. One client casually reported to the therapist on the outreach that he had ingested 31 Cogentin tablets the night before. Although he seemed fine (and his story seemed suspect), he was escorted to the medical emergency room, where he was treated with charcoal, an indication that while he might not have taken it seriously, his therapist did.

Frequently, clients say they are suicidal, and it is clearly a manipulation to obtain housing and food, avoid anticipated negative consequences, and so on. The clinician will perceive a lack of genuineness from clients, or the clients may seem markedly more distressed when they know someone is observing them. This can lead to a discussion of what clients mean or hope to gain when they say they are suicidal. Is it a way to hook the therapist; is the client depressed; is there secondary gain besides attention; or is there genuine suicidality? Sometimes a client will express suicidal feelings out of a familiar pattern and without any intent, and both the therapist and client know the client won't act on the feelings. The clinician can then respond that certainly that behavior is the client's choice, and not get stuck in the struggle. This frees the client from an entrenched way of being with the therapist and opens up access to other areas of need. There may be anxious times when the therapist lets a client go, and indeed self-destructive behavior may result. There may also be a need to hold a client, not necessarily for suicidality but to avoid a power struggle. One young man would write consistently more urgent and creative notes to the staff and his therapist in the psychiatric emergency clinic, describing his demise, to ensure that he would be hospitalized. As with many clients diagnosed with personality disorders, a day or two of containment gives them time to regain some equilibrium.

Actual suicides are very hard on everyone involved with the client, and all sorts of emotions can arise. Psychological autopsies, in which the cause of death, contributing factors, recent events, and progress in therapy are examined, are a useful way to review what has happened and to lend support to the therapist involved. Chronically mentally ill clients with severe problem behaviors and lack of social and environmental support are, unfortunately, probably at greater risk for suicide than the general client population.

Violence, Assaultiveness, and Verbal Abuse. Violence in whatever form is upsetting to the clients and everyone around them. Clients need to know that someone is in control when they are not and that there are consequences to their behaviors. Often it simply takes a recognition of their feelings to defuse the situation. The clients should be encouraged to talk about their feelings if possible. The therapist should remain calm and in a nondefensive stance.

It is important for therapists to set clear limits with threatening clients. If someone is a danger to self or others, then that person should be legally detained. If specific threats have been made against someone, then the intended victim and the police must be informed (this is California law; other states will vary in their reporting laws). Should clients be verbally abusive in session, they can be asked to leave until they feel more in control, with the assurance that the clinician will see them when they are less threatening. If clients are verbally abusive over the telephone and unresponsive to interventions, the therapist can inform them that the conversation can resume when they can speak in a less threatening manner, but that the discussion is being discontinued for now. This conveys the idea of limits and control to the client, and also that the therapist is also a human being who is not there to be abused. There should also be degrees of escalation of response to the situation. It is not necessary to ask someone to leave who is just venting anger.

The expectation should be conveyed to the client that, even when upset, the client can and will remain in control, or leave the clinic. Clients familiar with any psychiatric emergency setting know that control (in the form of seclusion and restraint) may be provided if they cannot maintain it. Many of them have been in seclusion and restraints before, however unjust they felt it to be, and this can serve as a deterrent and an avenue to further discuss their feelings.

The therapist needs to model appropriate behavior. There must be an acceptance of angry feelings, but not of acting on them. The client may indeed opt to leave or storm out of the office. If a therapist has difficulty with anger, this will inevitably be conveyed to the client, who will not feel safe to deal with it appropriately and will only become more anxious or feel out of control.

A distinction needs to be made between the client and the behavior. It is not the client who is unacceptable, but some behaviors are. This should be clearly stated to the client, who, while perhaps needing external controls, does not need rejection.

The meaning of the violence or abuse must be considered. Why now; what is the client feeling; how do the people around the client respond; what is being communicated to the therapist? People, including clinicians, have different thresholds of response to violence. The use of the therapeutic relationship is very important here, as well as one's sense of what is occurring with the client. For example, one client became quite agitated in session and threatened to kill his therapist. The therapist felt that he was frustrated and upset about not having his needs met and was also quite paranoid. But, based on the relationship they had, the clinician felt there was no danger of his acting on these feelings. Limits were set with him around the expression of threats, and he was allowed to leave. Two days later he returned in a much more pleasant state, but totally denied having had those feelings and, in fact, denied he was ever in the room. The therapist did not press the client as to the nature of these impulses, because it became clear they were too threatening to discuss at the time. They were able to return to it much later.

It is also important to consider what the gain is in the expression of violence or threatening behavior. For many people it is the only way they have learned to deal with frustration. One female client revealed that the only way she felt she could get what she wanted was to yell. And while clinicians may be frightened by threatening or violent behavior, it is often the fact that such hostile behavior is based on fear and the clients are much more afraid than the clinicians ever are.

Substance Abuse and Intoxication. The dual diagnosis client is seen more and more frequently, and presents quite a challenge. There have been differences of opinion between mental health and chemical dependency professionals on how to treat someone with both a psychiatric and a substance abuse disorder. It is quite difficult to watch clients continue to drink or use substances in spite of the negative consequences, including loss of housing, money, social supports, and self-esteem, but it is not through the therapist's eyes that the client sees. Clients have often dropped out of treatment in the past, or it has been refused them until they got into drug and alcohol treatment. They are often unable to negotiate the maze of acceptance procedures for a program (the logistics and waiting list would try anyone's soul) and thus end up with no help at all.

Clinicians will need to decide on an individual basis how to respond when a client comes in intoxicated. Clients may be told to come back when sober and be given a return appointment, with the therapist explaining that the client's intoxicated state makes it impossible to meet at that time. The therapist may also decide to meet briefly with the client and point out the connection between the client's current problem (if the client is in crisis) and the drug use. Referrals to AA or other drug treatment programs should be made, and efforts in sobriety encouraged, while the therapist and client continue to work on these issues in ongoing psychotherapy. The provision of concrete services can also be linked to not drinking, that is, for the client who is consistently broke because of spending money on drugs and alcohol, the therapist can refuse to assist with a specific form of housing, or whatever it is the individual wants, until the client does get into drug or alcohol treatment. This does not mean the therapist abandons the client. In the above example the therapist would provide the client with free shelter information, rather than another free week in an emergency hotel. It does, however, give recognition to both the problem and that the therapist is not willing to collude with the client in denial of the problem (see Chapter 8 for further discussion).

Behaviors Resulting From Severe Personality Disorder. Clients with severe personality disorders do not have a lofty reputation in the mental health system. They may be demanding, entitled, verbally abusive, blaming, or rejecting of the very help they insist on. They know exactly how to "push the buttons" of providers. They are often in need of the structure an outpatient clinic provides, but seek it through a psychiatric emergency room setting. They are, however, the ones least likely to get services, particularly in the present-day budget limitations. They are often seen as malingering or "just borderline," with the sole purpose of manipulation. They may be told they are not crazy enough to come into a psychiatric emergency setting, and this response indeed may activate their variable coping skills. On the other hand, clients may continue to feel overwhelmed and become more regressed. Some clients may need the structure of a psychiatric emergency setting, for a few hours or overnight, for the containment of anxiety. They may indeed even require a brief period of hospitalization. One must take into account the client's current mental status, previous coping patterns, precipitating stress, availability of other resources, and the significance of the client's presentation for emergency treatment.

Clients with severe personality disorders require both support and limit setting. There will be much testing of the therapist by the client, and the therapist must remain steady in the face of verbal onslaughts as well as overidealization. There should be consequences for assaultive behavior or property damage, such as pressing charges if necessary and appropriate. The therapist should not get swept up in the content of the presentation, but should look for the broader message the client is trying to convey.

The importance of the "interactive fit" between client and clinician has been noted (Committee on Psychopathology, 1987). It has been pointed out that clinicians' expectations for clients, for example, to assume "normal" roles, can create problems in the therapeutic relationship, and that therapists may need to lower their expectations, while still maintaining hope. Identification of the impact of countertransference reactions on the client and clinician during the main stages of engagement, contract negotiation, contract maintenance, and disengagement has also been emphasized in regard to managing difficult behaviors.

It is often easy to underestimate the level of a client's pain—at the moment the client may be incapable of acting otherwise—and much of the management of the difficult behaviors of the client with a severe personality disorder is in the management of the clinician's own countertransference, which will be discussed later. Also, see Chapter 9 for further discussion on the treatment of clients with personality disorders.

Noncompliance With Treatment or Medication. Compliance with medication is a goal that must often be worked toward slowly. Much education can be done around the nature of the psychiatric disorder (depending on the functioning and insight of the client) and medication. For example, a 40-year-old male diagnosed with schizoaffective disorder and substance abuse was able, through clear and consistent discussion, to identify his "red flags"—his warning signs, such as the onset of auditory hallucinations—and how his medications helped.

One can also find something the client wants and work toward that goal, including the role of medication in attaining it. For example, a therapist may suggest that taking medication may, by helping the client become less fearful and anxious, assist with the goal of staying out of the hospital or maintaining stable housing. Peer counseling can also be quite helpful, as other consumers share their experiences of what it is like to be on and off medication.

Many clients have been involuntarily medicated in the past and naturally are quite resistant. In cases where medications are clinically indicated, the clinician should continue to encourage compliance, not just by examining with the client the meaning of taking medication, but also by providing psychoeducation, including the responsibilities of the client in taking the medication. Such responsibilities include knowledge of the particular medication the client is taking, the purpose and side effects of the medication, safeguarding the medication, and the importance of discussing any questions the client might have about the medication with the prescribing psychiatrist. The clinician will need to work closely with the psychiatrist to coordinate the treatment plan, and in this regard, flexible schedules are a must. Issues around side effects must be discussed. When a client who has been noncompliant expresses interest in taking medication, understand that this is a significant movement by the client.

Many clients, of course, do not come to the clinic at the appointed time, so the clinician needs to be flexible without unduly compromising treatment. Drop-in visits may be used, and some clients will not have regularly scheduled appointments—they come when they need to. If a clinician cannot see a client who does drop in, the clinician should simply and honestly say so and give the client a better time to return. Outreaches may also be done for clients who miss appointments and medications. It may be the first time clients feel someone is interested in them, although it may also be met with initial hostility.

Cultural differences as to time should also be considered. The assumption that European-Americans represent the appropriate cultural yardstick requires questioning. The European-American culture places a high priority on time and punctuality, whereas those of African-American and Latino cultures may be less concerned with a linear or future-oriented time perspective (Akbar, 1991; Hall, 1977; Jones, 1991). It is the difference between being *on* time and being *in* time (Lefley, 1990). The clinician should attempt to assess whether missed or late appointment times are due to cultural factors, resistance, disorganization, or some other factors, and intervene accordingly.

Transference Issues

The recognition of and response to transference and countertransference issues are necessary in the management of problematic behaviors. Without such recognition the clinician may blame the client, fail to understand the needs of the client, and feel angry and overwhelmed, with the risk of doing damage to both client and clinician. Transference has been variously defined, but for general purposes refers to the unconscious experience the client has of the therapist, based not on the reality of who the therapist is (although there is some basis in reality for all transference reactions) but on remnants of relationships earlier in life, particularly with parental figures (Greenson, 1967; Langs, 1983). Each client will, of course, bring different transference issues to the therapeutic relationship, and potentially these can be explored over time, depending on the functioning or readiness of the client. They may be addressed or commented on throughout treatment, but the client may not be ready to acknowledge them. Some common transference issues that transcend the difficult behaviors discussed in this chapter follow.

Issues of Trust and Control. How does one establish trust with a client who has felt controlled and coerced by the mental health system? For many clients who need the safety and containment of a structured setting, there may be fears, both initially and sporadically throughout treatment, that if they do come to see a therapist, they may not be released. The clinic may be seen as an aversive place, one that deprives them of their rights. These fears should be openly acknowledged. In meeting initially with clients, it is important to stress that the relationship is an outpatient therapeutic one. The clinician's role is to help that person stay out of the hospital or jail, and the client will be involuntarily detained only if there is a danger to self or others, or grave disability. The feelings of being in a structured setting, indeed of being in treatment, can and should be explored over time.

The use of self in the relationship is important here. If the client senses that the therapist means what is said, the client will be more inclined to trust the therapist. Some clients will be met in the community first to build that trust. One client, a male in his thirties with schizoaffective disorder, was quite confused, disorganized, and grandiose on the streets, and he refused to come and get his money at the clinic. The therapist met him on a bench outside the clinic, which was the beginning step in establishing a relationship with him. The therapist continued to meet with him in the community after his release from the state hospital. Unfortunately, he had to be rehospitalized after 7 months because of his refusal to take medication and his subsequent psychotic decompensation. There is often tension around issues of control, coercion, and dependence, and a therapist must be able to listen to a client while providing reality testing, and intervening when necessary.

Clients need acknowledgement of their feelings, not necessarily an acquiescence to them. They do need to feel they are in control in a place that represents control and that they can leave when they want. This is an issue of trust in establishing the relationship and it will be tested many times over, particularly for those who feel no one has ever had their interests at heart. Clients may also feel safe with the therapist, but not with the clinic, and can thus be seen in more neutral places (assuming, of course, the safety of all concerned) until such time as a move to the clinic is indicated. The reasons for refusal to come to the clinic, which should be explored, may include fear, dependency, entitlement, or other issues.

The Therapist in Parental Role. Clients will often see the therapist as a parental figure, and there can be a multitude of both positive and negative feelings toward the clinician related to the client's experiences of parental figures. If the therapist does indeed take on the role of parent, which the client often wishes for, these feelings can be reinforced and complicated.

By virtue of providing concrete services, such as help with housing, food, or even bus tokens, the therapist will be seen as a nurturing figure. The client will come to look to the therapist for help with the basics as well as "shelter from the internal storm." If, however, the clinician does not grant a request for specific services, the therapist may be viewed as punishing. For example, a 40-year-old African-American male with schizoaffective disorder, substance abuse, and very poor money management skills requested his weekly check early to pay off two men he owed for cocaine. He became quite angry when his case manager refused, accusing the case manager of wanting him to be killed. Three days later he could, with encouragement, acknowledge his responsibility for the trouble he had been in. Clients see case managers as both nurturing and authority figures —one who gives and sets limits, one who provides and denies. Limit setting can be anxiety-provoking, particularly if the client has had too much or too little during childhood and is always looking to be either abandoned or engulfed.

Dependency and Autonomous Functioning. In conjunction with issues regarding therapists as parental figures, clients often feel disenfranchised and powerless and in serious conflict about dependency, particularly if reliant for many years on institutions for their basic needs. The client may need continued assistance with meeting these needs, yet experience intense anger at feeling dependent. This can result in the attention-seeking but help-rejecting behavior often seen, where a client continually requests assistance yet rejects as unsuitable every effort made (Kanter, 1988).

Along with dependency issues comes the wish for (or fear of) autonomous functioning. The conflict between independence and dependence is a very common one. Clients may feel frequently infantilized, particularly if on a money management or subpayee program. Clients often want to believe that they can immediately maintain their own apartment, work, and manage their money, and they are often impatient to build the skills to accomplish these goals. But as independent living occurs, clients may become anxious and sabotage any further steps toward independent living (Kanter, 1988). Kanter (1989) also suggests the need to make clear assessments about when and how to titrate support. Withdrawing support too quickly can lead a client to feeling abandoned and overwhelmed; yet, continuing to offer support when it is unnecessary may convey the message that the client is incapable of higher functioning, which in itself may be devastating.

One client, the 40-year-old African-American male, mentioned previously, who owed money to drug dealers, was very ambivalent about living independently. He sought hospitalization in a long-term, locked facility when he was stressed by the demands of daily life. His functioning was jeopardized by his remarkably impulsive spending, which resulted in his being broke the day after he got his check, regardless of the amount. His case manager generally informed him that he was just not ill enough to be locked up and focused instead on helping the client tolerate some anxious feelings, problem solve in a real and immediate way, and examine the conflict he felt about being independent. There have been times that residential programs have been utilized instead of hospitalization. The client wanted increased independence when in this kind of program, yet became anxious when a move to a more independent level of care was initiated. He responded once by pouring white paint on his head, necessitating a delay in transition (as well as revealing internalized racism). He and his case manager have experimented with various forms of payment schedules through the money management program. In the past, the case manager assisted him in finding hotels, but because of his tendency to move frequently, that task has now been left up to him. The case manager has remained available to assist him, but will not do things he can do for himself, such as making phone calls. He sometimes accuses the case manager of being racist when his wishes are not met. At the same time, he acknowledges the helpfulness of their work together. It is simply a question of *true* compassion—a therapist should support a client's strengths, not limitations (Hayes, 1992).

Accepting the Role of Mental Health Client. Many clients are in denial about having a mental disorder and will need to come up with some explanation for why they see a therapist. (Some clients, of course, are in such denial they do not come at all and do not link to care.) Clients may also view therapists as a tangible reminder that they have a mental disorder, and may become furious with them.

Clients may use euphemisms to explain being in treatment. One female client with schizophrenia angrily stated, "I am *not* crazy," but she did describe herself as nervous from time to time. It is important to find out what clients mean when describing themselves: What is their self-concept, what is their concept of mental illness? For most, if not all, mental illness is a very difficult thing to accept, and the therapist must abide by the cardinal rule in psychotherapy: Start where the client is. Do not push, but join in discovering what reality is like for the client. As Shainberg (1983) points out, beginning therapists in particular often feel that therapy should go a certain way, but that "there is 'no way' " and that "it is in the mutual participation of discovering the essential quality of the patient that the healing takes place" (p. 164).

Countertransference Issues

Countertransference has been defined similarly to transference—reactions to clients, which, while having some source in present life, are also based on past relationships (Langs, 1983). Giovacchini (1989) described *homogeneous countertransference reactions*, in which most therapists would react to a particular situation with similar responses, and *idiosyncratic countertransference reactions*, wherein a therapist has a uniquely individual response to a client, based on his or her own early relationships. It should be noted that with clinical case management, however, behavior that might traditionally be considered to stem from a countertransference reaction, such as helping a client find an apartment or working with the client on financial matters (Chessick, 1983) is an *integral* part of treatment.

As Geddes and Pajic (1990) note, countertransference issues or feelings either can be used to inform the clinician as to what the client is experiencing, or can be viewed as something that must be managed for the therapy to progress. It is the premise of this chapter that one must take into account one's feelings about the client and the nature of the relationship, and also be vigilant about unconscious or conscious invitations by the client for the therapist to behave nontherapeutically. Clients showing the range of difficult behaviors may elicit a range of feelings from the therapist, who must be fully aware of the feelings and the potential for acting on them. The clinician must also observe feelings that arise in relation to how the client is feeling, and remember that the management of those countertransference feelings can assist clients in managing their feelings.

It has been said that the clinician working with difficult clients must possess "tolerance, flexibility and resilience . . . a sense of timing . . . persistence . . . in the face of abuse and rejection . . . and realistic expectations" (McClelland & Kerr, 1991, p. 614). Stein (1992) has suggested that the individual case manager model is inadequate to provide integrated and available services and that what is needed is a multidisciplinary continuous care team.

Whether individual or not, the following are issues that may induce countertransference reactions, and suggestions for handling them.

Appearance and Hygiene. Case management clients are not the well-dressed, well-groomed individuals usually seen in private practice, and the therapist may experience countertransference reactions in response to their appearance. With chronically mentally ill clients, hygiene is often quite poor, particularly in decompensation, and can be viewed as a diagnostic sign. There will be many times that a therapist is confronted with clients unaware of their appearance and will need to recognize one's own feelings in these situations. In the clinical case management model, there can be an incredibly intimate relationship between therapist and client, and clinicians must examine their own level of comfort and how they respond to clients. For instance, does the clinician avoid or keep sessions short with a client who has not bathed for a week or two? In a direct and respectful way, the clinician can point out the need to improve hygiene and help the client to find ways to do that.

Violence. As Lion and Pasternak (1973) point out, some anxiety in dealing with potentially violent clients is warranted. But fear and anger can result in both a distortion of the actual threat and inappropriate action. They note that denial of anxiety can result in the therapist's failure to ask relevant questions regarding indicators of violence. The clinician can also overestimate or exaggerate the client's potential for violence, leading to unnecessary legal detainment or to rejection. The fear may not be based on objective reality.

Clinical case managers may minimize the potential for violence when doing outreaches, or become so used to seeing violence every day that they take unnecessary risks. Clinicians are not invulnerable and they should also be aware if they are pushing limits or being provocative. It is important to seek consultation in all such cases. Limit setting and ending sessions early due to threatening behavior should also be incorporated.

Suicidality. The idea of suicide certainly makes therapists question themselves, and inevitably, feelings of loss, grief, and anger arise. Even the threat of suicide or an attempt will make a therapist anxious. Maltsberger and Buie (1974) have noted the countertransference hate that suicidal clients evoke in the therapist, and the danger when defenses against such feelings as aversion and malice go unrecognized. This increases the likelihood of inappropriate behavior on the part of the therapist, and may increase the likelihood of self-destructive behavior by the client. As with the violent client, the therapist may be too anxious and overprotective with a client who threatens suicide and may too readily detain a client or suggest hospitalization. This can convey to a client that the therapist is unable to tolerate such affect and is frightened by the client. On the other hand, the therapist may be angry with a client who constantly threatens suicide and may minimize or dismiss serious clues to suicidality. It is important that the therapist be constantly alert to such feelings, refrain from acting on them, and again, seek consultation.

Substance Abuse and Intoxication. Many clinicians have had little experience dealing with substance abuse and have strong personal feelings about continued abuse by their clients. One client, who resisted all efforts of engagement, was found by police, unconscious in a doorway, and died 3 days later from a cocaine overdose. It can be frustrating to hear clients continually deny there is a problem, even when they have no money for food or shelter, having drunk or shot it away. It is equally frustrating to hear clients admit they have a problem and that they plan to stop, only to see them continually engage in substance abuse. Many clients use detoxification programs merely for shelter. Therapists (and other people) often feel that if clients just had willpower they would quit. They become quite angry and feel the client is wasting resources, particularly if the crisis is repeatedly alcohol- or drug-related. Clinicians may also become frustrated with AA meetings that are not sensitive to medication issues, whereby clients who are taking psychotropic medications are told that all medications are no good. Drug and alcohol treatment programs may also not accept clients with a psychiatric disorder, or amazingly, may demand the client have a month of sobriety before entering the program.

As mentioned previously, therapists might refuse, out of anger, to work with clients until they get into drug treatment. Or they might overlook important emotional cues, out of anger and frustration at the substance-abusing client. Both approaches ignore the reality of the client and what is needed. Continued education and consultation regarding dual diagnosis and treatment of chemical dependency are imperative. Therapists should also be familiar with 12-Step meetings in the area, attend some open meetings to gain first-hand experience, and even attend support groups themselves, such as Alanon or specific codependency groups for therapists.

Dependency. A client may have such strong dependency needs, and such limited internal resources, that there are daily visits or phone calls to the clinician. A therapist's own issues around dependency can be triggered by this and may result in a countertherapeutic reaction of withdrawal or anger. A therapist can react to the client's neediness by becoming frustrated and pushing the client to be more independent when that is not appropriate (Kanter, 1988) or by limiting services. Conversely, a clinician may promote dependency and not reinforce steps toward independent living due to the clinician's own need to be cared about or to be in control. By being aware of one's own issues around dependency, the therapist will not unconsciously reject the client and will have an expanded understanding of what the client is experiencing. Consultation should also be considered. (See Chapter 13 for further discussion of dependence issues.)

Clients With Personality Disorders. Other common countertransference reactions have been reported by Harris (1990), particularly in the treatment of personality-disordered clients. Denial of serious pathology in the client may result in feelings of false hope. This may result in the client's not being given appropriate referrals to such programs as drug treatment, and the clinician may ultimately feel demoralized or betrayed when the degree of pathology is finally realized.

Harris also notes that grandiosity and the failure to accept personal limitations can be problems. Clinicians may feel they are the ones who can ultimately heal the client and may engage in inappropriate heroics. Being unaware of one's limits may also interfere with the ability to provide the needed limits for clients. Harris further points out the issue of sadism and inappropriate helping as ways of expressing anger toward clients. Making clients more dependent on the clinician through inappropriate helping may reflect the clinician's hostility rather than compassion.

Noncompliance With Treatment and/or if the Client Gets Worse. Therapists may get angry when the client does not do something the therapist wants done, such as keeping appointments or going to day treatment; or does something the therapist does not want done, such as abusing drugs. Anger comes in many forms for many reasons. Therapists, despite their best intentions, may get caught up in the moment and retaliate, whether by an inappropriate comment, a hostile tone of voice, lack of engagement, thinly veiled disgust, or being abrupt when a client finally drops in for an appointment or presents repeatedly with superficial wounds. Winnicott (1949) also discussed objective hate in the countertransference when working with psychotic clients, and how critical it is that the therapist be aware of it.

Protectiveness is a common reaction among therapists that can be directed toward both the client and the clinic, in addition to one's self. Clinics will often, in not so subtle ways, let the clinician know the client may not be welcome, particularly if the client has been acting out in the waiting area. A clinician may want to protect the client from a hostile environment, and at the same time want to shield the clinic from the client's behavior. A clinician needs to preserve the relationship with both, and be swayed by neither.

Searles (1982) points out that therapists as managers must be objective about their own experiences of helplessness and effectiveness, and that the latter may, in part, be due to "strength unconsciously borrowed . . . from the idealizing patient" (p. 479). In addition, therapists may have sadistic impulses toward clients as a reaction to the therapists' own sense of helplessness.

There is a need to redefine "being with" the client, which brings to mind Winnicott (1965, 1971). Kanter (1990) describes Winnicott's contributions as the environmental holding and dealing with countertransference reactions in the management of psychotic clients. Clients have so often been rejected by service providers, and this "being with" the client is best exemplified by being with them in their element, in the community with an expanded view of the holding environment.

Systems Issues. On a systems level, there will be inevitable feelings of frustration at the lack of available resources for severely mentally ill clients. There are lengthy waiting lists, particularly for drug and alcohol treatment programs, and as such counselors know, the optimum time for treatment is when the client says "yes," not later. What happens to this frustration on the part of the clinician? The danger is that it may then be transmitted into blaming clients for the lack of resources and taking it out on them.

There are institutional reactions to the severely mentally ill client and to the clinician. It is possible that clients may be viewed more favorably if they are linked with a case manager who is known within the mental health community. On the other hand, the therapist may be viewed as "the problem," as the one who is bringing difficult clients to the treatment agency's doors. One is reminded of the apt saying, "Don't shoot the messenger." Institutional reactions also highlight the issue of who is responsible for the client's behavior, a question that arises in conjunction with countertransference reactions.

There is a clear need to educate the mental health system, and other service providers, about what is and is not clinical case management. This does not mean, however, that there will necessarily be agreement on the treatment plan, and that the varying expectations of treatment can be explored through case conferences and clear communication. It should be remembered that there are no instant cures.

Finally, how therapists take care of themselves cannot be overlooked. It is important to note that clinical case management with severely disordered clients is intense work, and the potential for burnout and disillusionment is high. Several guidelines to help a clinician manage this include:

1. Be patient and have compassion for oneself, one's clients and one's colleagues. This is long-term work that is done *together.*
2. Do not take the job home. The severity of clients' pain and impairment can be gripping, and it is important to have other interests and ways to use and rejuvenate oneself.
3. Ask for help. Avoid the trap of believing that one person can do it all, or is so powerful. Consultation and peer supervision help the clinician not to feel alone.
4. Be aware of oneself. The awareness of and management/use of countertransference responses are crucial to continuing to effectively perform

the clinician's duties. The use of consultation and peer supervision is invaluable to examine such issues, problem solve, develop creative strategies, and help clinicians know they have support. It is helpful to remember that these are very difficult clients, and that one is human. It also helps to remember to be grateful for all that the clients give back to the clinician.

5. Finally, and most important, have a sense of humor. Humor is protective and also very healing; it is a way to open one's heart. There is great joy in being alive and helping one another. If we forget to laugh, we forget to live.

References

Akbar, N. (1991). The evolution of human psychology for African-Americans. In R. L. Jones (Ed.), *Black psychology* (pp. 99-123). Berkeley, CA: Cobb & Henry.

Chessick, R. D. (1983). *How psychotherapy heals: The process of intensive psychotherapy.* Northvale, NJ: Jason Aronson.

Coid, J. W. (1991, March 16). "Difficult to place" psychiatric patients. *British Medical Journal, 302*, 603-604.

Committee on Psychopathology: Group for the Advancement of Psychiatry. (1987). *Interactive fit: A guide to nonpsychotic chronic patients.* New York: Brunner/Mazel.

Geddes, M. J., & Pajic, A. K. (1990). A multidimensional typology of countertransference responses. *Clinical Social Work Journal, 18*(3), 257-272.

Giovacchini, P. L. (1989). *Countertransference triumphs and catastrophes.* Northvale, NJ: Jason Aronson.

Goldfinger, S. M., Hopkin, J. T., & Surber, R. W. (1984). Treatment resisters or system resisters?: Toward a better service system for acute care recidivists. In B. Pepper & H. Ryglewicz (Eds.), *New directions for mental health services: Advances in treating the young adult chronic patient* (pp. 17-27). San Francisco: Jossey-Bass.

Greenson, R. (1967). *The technique and practice of psychoanalysis* (Vol. 1, p. 154). Madison, CT: International Universities Press.

Hall, E. T. (1977). *Beyond culture.* New York: Anchor Press/Doubleday.

Harris, M. (1990). Redesigning case-management services for work with character-disordered young adult patients. In N. L. Cohen (Ed.), *Psychiatry takes to the streets* (pp. 156-176). New York: Guilford.

Hayes, P. (1992, September). Concept of "true compassion" discussed in workshop on "Dharma," South Fallsburg, NY.

Jones, J. (1991). A cultural analysis of the problem. In R. L. Jones (Ed.), *Black psychology* (pp. 609-635). Berkeley, CA: Cobb & Henry.

Kanter, J. S. (1988). Clinical issues in the case management relationship. In M. Harris & L. L. Bachrach (Eds.), *New directions for mental health services: Clinical case management.* San Francisco: Jossey-Bass.

Kanter, J. S. (1989). Clinical case management: Definition, principles, components. *Hospital and Community Psychiatry, 40*(4), 361-368.

Kanter, J. S. (1990). Community-based management of psychotic clients: The contributions of D. W. and Claire Winnicott. *Clinical Social Work Journal, 18*(1), 23-41.

Krakowski, M., Volavka, J., & Briser, D. (1986). Psychopathology and violence: A review of literature. *Comprehensive Psychiatry, 27*(2), 131-148.

Langs, R. (1983). *The technique of psychoanalytic psychotherapy* (Vol. 2, p. 148). Northvale, NJ: Jason Aronson.

Lefley, H. (1990). Culture and chronic mental illness. *Hospital and Community Psychiatry, 41*(3), 277-286.

Lion, J. R., & Pasternak, S. A. (1973). Countertransference reactions to violent patients. *American Journal of Psychiatry, 130*(2), 207-209.

Maltsberger, J. T., & Buie, D. H. (1974). Countertransference hate in the treatment of suicidal patients. *Archives of General Psychiatry, 30,* 625-633.

McClelland, H. A., & Kerr, T. A. (1991). Long-term difficult-to-manage patients—their need for continuity of care: Discussion paper. *The Royal Society of Medicine, 84*(10), 613-614.

Pepper, B., & Ryglewicz, H. (1984). Treating the young adult chronic patient: An update. In B. Pepper & H. Ryglewicz (Eds.), *New directions for mental health services: Advances in treating the young adult chronic patient* (pp. 5-15). San Francisco: Jossey-Bass.

Reid, W. H., & Balis, G. U. (1987). Evaluation of the violent patient. *APA Annual Review, 6,* 491-509. Washington, DC: American Psychiatric Press.

Searles, H. F. (1982). The analyst as manager of the patient's daily life: Transference and countertransference dimensions of this relationship, In R. Langs (Ed.), *International journal of psychoanalytic psychotherapy, 1982-83* (Vol. 9, pp. 475-486). New York: Jason Aronson.

Shainberg, D. (1983). Teaching therapists how to be with their clients. In J. Welwood (Ed.), *Awakening the heart: East/West approaches to psychotherapy and the healing relationship* (pp. 163-175). Boston: New Science Library.

Sheets, J. L., Prevost, J. A., & Reihman, J. (1982). Young adult chronic patients: Three hypothesized subgroups. *Hospital and Community Psychiatry, 33*(3), 197-203.

Smith, P. (1983). *Professional assault response training.* Unpublished working papers, State of California.

Stein, L. I. (1992). On the abolishment of the case manager. *Health Affairs, 11*(3), 172-177.

Surles, R. C., Blanch, A. K., Shern, D. L., & Donahue, S. A. (1992, Spring). Case management as a strategy for systems change. *Health Affairs,* 151-163.

Tardiff, K., & Koenigsberg, H. W. (1985). Assaultive behavior among psychiatric outpatients. *American Journal of Psychiatry, 142*(8), 960-963.

Winnicott, D. W. (1949). Hate in the countertransference. *International Journal of Psychoanalysis, 30*(2), 69-74.

Winnicott, D. W. (1965). *The maturational processes and the facilitating environment: Studies in the theory of emotional development.* Madison, CT: International Universities Press.

Winnicott, D. W. (1971). *Playing and reality.* London: Tavistock.

11

The Psychiatrist's Perspective

JERALYN JONES

"A process that is defined by a conceptualization of mental illness and treatment . . . clinical case management is as much a way of thinking about care as it is providing specific interventions" (Chapter 1). The clinical case management paradigm assumes that serious mental illness may affect many areas of individuals' lives. Traditional mental health services may be unable to provide the comprehensive approach to care that severely mentally ill clients need. Clinical case management expands psychiatric services so that clients' needs are more fully explored, managed, and treated.

The clinical case management model places case managers at the fulcrum of the mental health system. Case managers become the primary mental health providers for their clients. They provide access to psychiatric services clients would otherwise be unable to utilize. In this model, psychiatrists are an integral part of the system, working collaboratively with case managers to augment mental health care.

In this chapter a variety of psychiatric issues will be addressed, including diagnostic dilemmas, medication issues, cultural factors, and transference/countertransference phenomena. These particular topics are chosen because of their practical relevance in treating severely mentally ill clients. A discussion of psychiatric assessment will highlight the need for communication between psychiatrists and case managers. Diagnostic complexity and its effect on decision making are stressed. Treatment response may be diminished by poor medication compliance; and potential reasons for noncompliance will be outlined. Also considered are aspects of dynamic relationships among psychiatrists, case managers, and their clients. This chapter's intent is to provoke thought about psychiatric treatment within a clinical case management framework. An appreciation of ambiguity will be noted throughout this chapter. The case management model provides a practical way to deal with ambiguities of treatment. Collaboration may clarify ambiguity; but if it persists, team members may still work together to find practical treatment solutions. Representative case examples will be used to highlight specific treatment situations, suggesting a treatment approach that combines psychiatric and clinical case management solutions.

Diagnosis

Psychiatric specialization emphasizes assessment for *Diagnostic Statistical Manual Third Edition, Revised* (DSM-IIIR) diagnoses, biopsychosocial formulation, and treatment. Assessment begins with observation and management of the client's behavior. A disruptive client may need to be restrained or emergently medicated. Determinations of danger to self or others must be made. While acute observations can provide immediate information about the client's mental status, history is almost always needed to clarify the clinical picture. Severely mentally ill clients are frequently unable or unwilling to discuss their current mental state or psychiatric history, because of internal preoccupation, intoxication, language barriers, or even fear of incarceration. Additionally, they may not have conscious memories of previous psychoses or periods of intoxication, and so cannot relate such history. The psychiatrist relies on the case manager to provide needed history on the severity of illness and prior response to interventions, such as medications and hospitalization. The client's baseline mental status may also be related by the case manager. Someone who is constantly suicidal, for instance, will be handled differently from someone who has never complained of suicidal thoughts. The basic assessment question "Why now?" is answered when the clients' presentation is contrasted with their history.

An example of how case managers and psychiatrists can work collaboratively is the case of Maurice, a 27-year-old client who scheduled to see the team psychiatrist. Upon entering the office, he immediately yelled, "Do you hate your job? You psychiatrists are all alike. You all ask questions and then never do a thing for me." The psychiatrist knew that the case manager had worked for several months to convince the client to have an evaluation for medication. The case manager had informed the psychiatrist about the client's history of adversarial relationships with authority figures, including psychiatrists. Equally important, the case manager had also provided past psychiatric history. The client had managed to be thrown out of many mental health clinics, sabotaging treatment. His unspoken behavior, making the appointment, was thus historically a progressive and important step. Maurice's motivation for treatment encouraged the psychiatrist to continue with the evaluation. Alliance formation was based on a realistic understanding of Maurice's limitations and strengths.

Diagnostic assessment of case management clients is complex. People may present with complicated histories and multiple DSM-IIIR diagnoses. Someone may have diagnoses of a major mental disorder, a substance dependence disorder, and a personality disorder. When this person becomes ill, the reason may be unclear. Clients may be involved with multiple systems—family, social services, health, mental health, and criminal justice. These external factors also complicate assessment. Suppose a case management client with schizophrenia, unmedicated, walks into the psychiatrist's office smelling of vodka and experiencing auditory hallucinations. She hostilely demands a place to stay for the night. Should she be medicated, housed, hospitalized, or detoxed from alcohol? Answers depend on a comprehensive assessment. Here again the psychiatrist will contact the case manager, who can provide background history, including severity of the client's psychosis and alcohol use and history of response to interventions like hospitalization. The case manager can provide suggestions on how to best to evaluate the client's situation. Is she someone who is constantly in a crisis, or chronically internally preoccupied but usually behaviorally stable? The psychiatrist can then consider management strategies while formulating diagnoses.

Case management clients may carry dual diagnoses, consisting of both a major mental disorder and substance dependence disorder. Or substance abuse disorders may mimic major psychoses or affective illness. The paranoid ideation and delusions seen in crack cocaine abuse may appear to be symptoms of chronic paranoid schizophrenia, or may exacerbate existing psychotic symptoms. Alcohol abuse may mimic or disguise affective disorders—often morning hangovers mimic the diurnal variation in mood seen in endogenous depression, while the euphoria and agitation of intoxication may suggest mania.

Working with dually diagnosed clients requires special attention to alliance formation. Clients who can be truthful about their substance use, without being expelled from treatment or scolded for being bad, are more likely to be honest about their substance use, and may eventually request help with recovery. Generally, clients will admit to using when they know there will not be punishing consequences for telling the truth. Yet, despite the treatment providers' best efforts, clients may continue to hide their substance use. Gathering data from previous presentations to emergency rooms in crisis may help fill in vague histories. When clients continue to deny use, urine toxicology screens may be utilized.

A common cycle in the dually diagnosed client is discontinuance of medication, worsening of psychiatric symptoms, and an increase in substance use. Eventually client behavior becomes socially disruptive, requiring hospitalization. Clients often decompensate when they have stopped their psychotropic medication while using drugs or alcohol. Substance abuse and major psychiatric illness increase symptomatology and morbidity synergistically. A clinical vignette illustrates some of these complexities.

Susan was a young woman who had been diagnosed with bipolar affective disorder for 10 years. She refused mood stabilizers like lithium and Tegretol because trials had made her feel "weak and disorganized." Thus trials had never been adequate. She accepted small doses of neuroleptics to "help with sleep," she said, and took them very sporadically. At baseline she expressed magical thinking, like believing she could control other people's thoughts and had extrasensory perception experiences, but otherwise claimed she was symptom free. On one presentation with hypomanic symptoms, amphetamine use was discovered. She denied use and refused detoxification and rehabilitation referrals. She eventually proceeded to a full manic episode. Historically, her poor judgment had led to repeated victimization by men and an inability to maintain employment or volunteer work. Her daughter had been removed from her custody. In substance abuse language, she had "hit bottom" long ago. Despite her symptoms, she remained competent to refuse medication. Her only mental health contact was the case management team.

During the previous 2 years the case manager had established an alliance with Susan. She would rarely keep her scheduled appointment and would call in crisis, with no money or no place to stay. The case manager had consistently been willing to help Susan find housing and had occasionally loaned Susan money from the team's emergency fund. Their alliance was based largely on the case manager's willingness to respond to Susan's needs, without placing unrealistic expectations on her behavior. Susan's positive transference had extended to the team psychiatrist. Susan was allowed freedom to drop in for appointments and was seen, despite her unwillingness to accept conventional medications for her bipolar illness. When Susan's substance use was discovered, these preexisting alliances were the foundation on which therapeutic interventions were laid. Susan was confronted about her substance use. Rather than give up on her psychiatric treatment, the team looked at ways to encourage her sobriety, or at least persuade her not to mix cocaine with thioridazine. Here the case management philosophy of treating the clients "as they are" prevailed. Susan's tendency to present in crisis was considered. She was informed that crisis visits would now include urine toxicology screens, and that she would not receive medication if she tested positive for amphetamines.

This strategy was important for several reasons. In their willingness to continue seeing Susan, the team conveyed an acceptance of her struggle with bipolar illness and amphetamine use. They also set a therapeutic limit that was not overly punitive, but did show the seriousness with which the team viewed Susan's behavior. Susan was made familiar with the lethality of mixing psychiatric medications with cocaine. Finally, the setting of limits prevented the team from feeling used by an out-of-control client. The team felt comfortable about her treatment plan and were able to continue to work effectively.

A case management program may never observe some clients "substance free." Suppose an outpatient client refuses drug screens when symptoms appear to be substance induced. Inpatient histories may reveal a client's behavior when substance free. Case managers can obtain collateral information from the client's family and friends. Treatment can proceed, based on all the information known about the client. In this case, if substance abuse were discovered, treatment would include attention to this use, despite the client's denial of use.

A more conventional approach would be to refuse to treat someone psychiatrically who is actively using, until the client admitted use and requested help with sobriety. This approach allows the client's resistance to substance abuse treatment to overrule the real need for psychiatric treatment. The case management approach focuses on both the psychiatric and the substance abuse disorders.

Another factor obscuring diagnosis may be organic impairment. Mentally ill individuals are at high risk for contracting HIV (Kelly et al., 1992). A recent study revealed undiagnosed medical disorders in many psychiatric inpatients (Sox et al., 1989). Chronic substance abuse may also cause organic deficits. Due to both a lack of resources and many clients' hesitance to seek treatment, they may not have had adequate medical evaluations. The treatment provider must always consider organic impairment during assessment of chronic mentally ill clients. Assessment includes a thorough mental status exam, attention to records of previous medical diagnoses, and collaboration with team members, especially when the etiology of psychiatric symptoms is unclear. A useful screening device in assessing the organically impaired is the mental status exam. Questions about orientation to time, place, name, and reason for office visit can help screen for delirium. Memory deficits are often present in organicity and may also be uncovered. Attention to clients' state of alertness will also provide clues to their mental state. The person who is falling asleep during an interview may be overmedicated, intoxicated, withdrawing from drugs, or otherwise organically impaired. The last explanation considered should be the client's resistance to being interviewed. An appropriate reaction to such a client would include contacting the team psychiatrist or another physician. The intervention might even include accompanying the client to an emergency room. All clients who receive psychotropic medications require laboratory evaluation. Screening labs have to be performed periodically, and treatment with medications like lithium requires serum monitoring at least every 3 to 6 months. These screenings may uncover organic impairment. Again, the case manager and psychiatrist work as a team. The psychiatrist might suspect an organic problem, and the case manager helps the client receive an adequate work-up. Case managers may build alliances with medical clinics or individual physicians, creating access to these services for their clients. The case manager may assume responsibility for transporting clients to the outpatient laboratory or arranging clients' medical appointments. When appropriate concern is given to organic impairment, the client can receive appropriate treatment.

Medication Issues

Treatment strategies are considered throughout the assessment process. While the psychiatrist assumes primary responsibility for medication choice, the case manager suggests important symptoms or behaviors to be medicated. The client's compliance with medications, willingness to accept treatment, and previous response to medications will be considered. It is important that the psychiatrist remain cognizant of what may be the most difficult issue in medicating severely mentally ill clients—medication compliance. It is, therefore, a major aspect of case management treatment. Factors influencing compliance may include denial of illness, impaired judgment and poor impulse control secondary to substance use, intolerance to medication side effects, concomitant personality disorders, complicated medication regimens, medication inefficacy, transference phenomena, and cultural bias. Medication may also become incorporated into psychotic delusions and denial. These concerns will be described and elaborated on below.

Many clients experience physical discomfort from neuroleptics, mood stabilizers, and antidepressants. Clients who take neuroleptics may suffer serious side effects. Extrapyramidal side effects can be especially disabling for clients on depot medication who will not take side effect medication.

People with psychotic thought content, guarded behavior, or minimal speech may not articulate discomfort with medications, or may express complaints in ways that are difficult to decipher. Treatment providers must collectively gather information to obtain accurate clinical pictures.

Charles, a Cantonese-speaking man with a diagnosis of schizophrenia, had remained out of the hospital for 2 years, maintained on fluphenazine deconoate and benztropine. He remained withdrawn from both his case manager and his psychiatrist, although he always kept his appointments. During each medication visit he offered a dinner napkin, with the following complaints written in English: "hard to walk, constipated, shaky hands, headache, sick stomach, and poor vision." He expressed symptoms that could be medication induced, such as extrapyramidal and anticholinergic side effects. Attempts to explore his complaints in English and Cantonese proved futile. Fluphenazine was lowered, and anticholinergic medications were adjusted. He expressed no change in the type or severity of his complaints. A medical evaluation was negative. Family members who dispensed his medication insisted he took it as prescribed. The client's case manager educated the medication team on the psychosocial component of physical complaints in Chinese culture. The team collaborated on the presence of delusional thinking in other settings. Transference phenomena were questioned. Was he expressing his dissatisfaction with being placed on medication? Was he determined to express complaints in an effort to continue to receive help? His complexity forced exploration of all of these factors—medication response and side effects, medical evaluation, cultural influence, psychotic thinking, and transference phenomena. No simple or complete explanation for his behavior and symptoms was found. Case management team members did feel assured that most possibilities had been considered, yet they were never totally certain. Living with ambiguity is a part of working with complex clients.

Multiagent therapy is widely practiced in psychiatric settings, especially in patient settings. Clients like the woman with bipolar disorder, discussed above, may be started on combinations of mood stabilizers and neuroleptics, during acute hospitalization, with some benefit. Yet the continued decrease in number of hospital days per inpatient stay means that clients may be discharged while medication titration is incomplete and symptoms persist. For instance, introducing lithium carbonate will mean a twice daily dosing schedule, a series of phlebotomies, and a lag period, during which the medication is not yet clinically effective but must still be taken regularly. Outpatients may be too disorganized or unmotivated to obtain necessary laboratory evaluation. Providing external structure can improve compliance. Using weekly pillboxes or having medications dispensed at day treatment facilities, outpatient clinics, or by residential care homes may allow for fair medication trials. In many cases, compliance is better enhanced by simplifying medication regimens. For example, the symptoms of many clients with bipolar or schizoaffective disease would be best treated with lithium carbonate or another mood stabilizer; yet there are so many hindrances to compliance for someone with a severe mental illness. As mentioned above, factors like twice daily dosing, frequent serum assessment requiring laboratory visits, and a high risk of lethality on overdose may make lithium carbonate an impractical medication choice. Someone who is psychotic, with mood swings, might be much more likely to comply with monthly depot haloperidol or fluphenazine. The case manager may facilitate compliance by helping clients remember appointments or by accompanying them to medication appointments, where the case manager may relate client symptoms to the psychiatrist. The alternative medication regimen may stabilize a client so that lithium can eventually be a viable treatment option.

The efficacy of a medication—its ability to treat that for which it is being prescribed—is highly important when psychiatric remission and relapse rates are compared. Research indicates that approximately 70% of patients treated with neuroleptics have a significant decrease in symptomatology, while 30% have less than optimal response (Kaplan & Sadock, 1991). Many clients have persistent auditory hallucinations, intrusive thoughts, delusions, and other psychotic phenomena. Medications may control their behavior, rather than relieve their psychic suffering. People may become ill while on medication or may get better, even though they are medication free. Psychotic exacerbations may be based more on the waxing and waning course of illness than on treatment compliance.

Psychiatric diagnoses as defined in DSM-IIIR are based on psychological and social values of twentieth-century Western thought. They are the basis for medication prescription, which is also largely European-American value-laden. All subcultures of Americans—Native, Latin, Asian, and African—are treated based on this paradigm. Yet these cultures have their own assumptions about psychic health and disease, as illustrated below.

A Latin-American woman, Susana, took lithium carbonate and herbal medications for her bipolar affective disorder. She consistently asked her psychiatrist, "How do you find me? Am I healed?" In response, the psychiatrist might have explored or interpreted her question. The psychiatrist might also have responded with explanations about bipolar affective disorder and how it doesn't heal but rather remits, and that the probability of relapse is high, given her history. These responses are accurate, but are based on European-American training and values. They may have isolated Susana from her experience of life and her illness. She lived in a world saturated with religious significance. For instance, her hypersexuality during manic episodes was followed by remorse for her sins, during which she made many confessions and felt spiritually healed. When she asked if she was healed, the psychiatrist asked her how she was wounded. Allowing her to discuss both wounding and healing experiences strengthened both the psychiatrist's and Susana's understanding of her illness. The psychiatrist was then seen as an ally and not a threat to her beliefs. Perceptions of illness are intricately related to personal and social values in all cultures. The reader is referred to Chapter 3 for further discussion.

Any cognitive disturbance may impair a client's ability to remain medication compliant. Iatrogenic causes, including anticholinergic delirium, lithium toxicity, dehydration, oversedation, and milder cognitive impairments secondary to medication, can all impair cognition. This impairment can interfere with a client's ability to remain medication compliant.

Tom was a 68-year-old man diagnosed with bipolar affective disorder, alcohol abuse, and Alzheimer's dementia. At baseline he was forgetful and needed assistance organizing his daily medications. His day treatment facility filled his pillbox weekly, and a home health nursed visited his hotel twice weekly. His psychiatric medications included lithium carbonate, haloperidol, and benztropine. Over a period of several weeks, he became noticeably more confused, forgetting where he was and missing appointments he could usually remember. An observant psychiatric technician brought this subtle change in behavior to the psychiatrist's attention. Head trauma was ruled out; lithium levels were checked and were normal. The possibility of worsening Alzheimer's disease was considered. Another potential culprit, anticholinergic delirium secondary to benztropine and haloperidol, was also considered. If Alzheimer's disease were the culprit, no medication intervention could be made. So benztropine was discontinued (it was something that the psychiatrist could actively try), and the confusion cleared. Seemingly benign medications like benztropine may cause deleterious side effects in clients whose cognitive function is already impaired, and discontinuing such medication or substituting side effect medication may be necessary.

Clients with concomitant major mental illnesses and personality disorders also present a special challenge to medication compliance. For example, clients may be unable to articulate specific symptoms, stating their concerns globally or vaguely. They may have intense transferential reactions to caregivers, and caregivers may have intense counterreactions, influencing all aspects of treatment. The limit setting used in other areas of treatment may be applied to medication issues; yet the conventional strategies for medicating symptoms may also be applied to these clients. Many times reassurance and readjusting expectations may be all that are indicated when clients complain vaguely of "depression and anxiety." However, most people deserve several trials of medication at therapeutic doses to attempt alleviation of discomfort and to treat major psychiatric diagnoses, like major depression or generalized anxiety disorder.

Transference and Countertransference Issues

A psychodynamic understanding of clients facilitates clinical assessment and treatment. Relationships between treatment providers affect clients and may provide insight into client dynamics. The remainder of this chapter is devoted to a discussion of relationship patterns occurring between clients and staff of case management teams. It begins with a discussion of the psychiatrist/client dyad, then explores psychiatrist/case manager dynamics, and finally addresses the complicated nature of relationships in the case management system as a whole.

The client and psychiatrist hold inherent assumptions about each other, based on previous experiences in similar relationships. Generally, the psychiatrist in mental health represents authority and "the system," to which clients may respond with ambivalence. Clients may have been referred to the case management program from inpatient units and may have not consciously chosen their psychiatrist. A devaluing transference may emerge during this initial period of treatment. It may manifest as failure to keep appointments, medication noncompliance, or refusal to cooperate with assessment. A client's rage at victimization may be expressed by general distrust of treatment. Entitlement may represent a defense against feelings of powerlessness. Allowing the client expression of these perceptions without interpretation helps the client feel understood. Acknowledging the client's distress may defuse hostilities that can obstruct initial treatment.

More rarely, clients may idealize the authority figure. Although this transference is less unpleasant, it may be easier to miss and may be manifested in client's underreporting of psychiatric symptoms or medication side effects. Group and individual supervision are crucial for the clarification of transference phenomena. A group may be able to express support for the treatment provider by identifying transference issues that the provider has missed. Supervision concerning countertransference feelings will help uncover personal issues and also lead to a better understanding of the client's transference. Once understood, transference may be interpreted to the client. In some situations working within the transference may be more constructive.

Sam was a client who had been followed by case management for 5 years. He was known as an entitled man who never thanked or attempted to please his caregivers. Interpretations would send him out the door, swearing never to return to the clinic. This behavior was understood as Sam's method of distancing from his case manager, and as his reaction to feeling narcissistically injured by remarks he perceived as criticism. The case manager responded to Sam's entitlement with several interventions. He attempted to give Sam what he demanded, basically time and consistency, gradually eroding Sam's anticipation of disappointment. He also developed pet names for Sam's more angry behavior. Sam became known as "Raging Bull" around the clinic, and even in the neighborhood. The pet name gave Sam a separate identity, helping him distance when necessary. It also ultimately allowed Sam room to express more positive feelings toward himself (he referred to himself as "the bull") and others.

The experience of swallowing a medication that will alter mental life is deeply symbolic and culturally influenced. Historically, shamans transformed undesirable aspects of another through prayer, ritual, sacrifice, and "medication." Modern prescribing continues this tradition, which is where trust and control themes emerge. For example, clients who experience psychoses are asked to mistrust their internal perceptions while trusting mental health providers. While clients are encouraged to trust the psychiatrist, they are also expected to take medications that will interfere with their internal experiences, such as auditory hallucinations or delusions. Such clients may feel they have no choice about compliance. This situation may exacerbate paranoid fantasies/delusions.

Psychiatrists will also have varied reactions to clients, based on their own and client's dynamics. Devaluation may elicit feelings of impotence or inferiority. The psychiatrist may respond with defensive tactics if this dynamic is unconscious. Idealization may elicit the opposite response. Rescue fantasies can easily be ignited when clients who need so much have so little. Guarding against boundary violation is crucial when these dynamics are operating and providers are attempting to access comprehensive services.

More primitive feelings, such as extreme anger or disgust, may also be evoked by clients. Socially less acceptable, they might be defended against in a way that will disrupt the treatment and therapeutic alliance. The psychiatrist might avoid the client, attempt to abandon the relationship, become less tolerant of client complaints, or put forth a variety of other responses. While all of these reactions and counterreactions are understandable, in fact unavoidable, the responsibility for them rests with treatment providers. They must identify client dynamics and clarify personal dynamics, helping to remove barriers to effective relationships.

The psychotic client is often intensely ambivalent about treatment, wavering between fears of engulfment and abandonment. Uninterpretable on a verbal level, this ambivalence may be addressed in the treatment. Allowing the client to make either/or decisions about medication type or dosage rather than "medication or not" can be an effective bargaining strategy. Choosing between two antipsychotics, haloperidol and trifluop-erazine, may replace more dramatic decision making, that is, deciding whether to take medication. The following case example illustrates trans-ference and countertransference reactions between client and psychiatrist, and their effects on the treatment.

JoAnn was a 35-year-old African-American woman with a diagnosis of bipolar affective disorder, in partial remission, who was being treated by a 32-year-old Caucasian female psychiatrist. The client was maintained on lithium carbonate and chlorpromazine with psychotic symptoms largely in remission. She had fired many previous psychiatrists; the most recent firing had occurred after she had become toxic on large doses of multiple medications. She was separated from her physically abusive husband by whom she had a 2-year-old son. She was financially responsible for herself and her child. She had been unemployed for 10 years, due to mental illness, and monthly entitlements were her only income.

JoAnn's main complaints were insomnia and depressed mood. For her symptoms the psychiatrist attempted trials of several antidepressants. Each medication was given at therapeutic doses for several months before discontinuance, following JoAnn's complaint that the medication did not work. The psychiatrist identified the client's hopelessness and expressed empathy with the client. JoAnn denied affects other than what she identified as "physical depression," a term which was never clearly understood by the psychiatrist. During the treatment JoAnn's son was diagnosed with a life-threatening illness and began having lengthy medical appointments. Her husband returned to her home to help care for their son. He was actively using cocaine and was physically abusive. She began to feel more depressed, and focused more intently on the inability of the psychiatrist to relieve her suffering with medication.

While she insisted she felt like a guinea pig and resented multiple medication trials, she argued that she should be able to feel good and that the problem was the psychiatrist's inability to find the proper medication. She felt victimized by the system and entitled to more. The psychiatrist felt frustrated and impotent and began to see her less often, explaining that no medication would make JoAnn feel better. The team psychiatric technician began to see the client for medication refill appointments. JoAnn continued to have persistent complaints of depression and insomnia. She requested referral to another psychiatrist, but before the transfer occurred, JoAnn became pregnant. The psychiatrist began to see her weekly again because of her pregnancy. Her depression lifted, her sense of entitlement grew, and she became increasingly hostile, attacking the entire mental health system and eventually threatening the psychiatrist's life. Lithium carbonate had been discontinued during the first trimester and was now reintroduced. After a week, her attacks softened. She continued to complain of insomnia, but agreed that medication trials would be unwise, given her condition. She admitted that she tended to worry at night and that she often lay awake, fearful of what the next day would bring. She verbalized feeling abandoned by the psychiatrist when she was transferred to another mental health provider. She felt a restored sense of hope awaiting her baby's birth. Her life situation had changed and she felt better about herself.

In retrospect the psychiatrist saw how her unwillingness to continue seeing JoAnn contributed to her increasing despair. A power struggle had existed of which the psychiatrist was unaware. The psychiatrist held a perceived access to something that the client so desperately wanted—to feel better. The treatment dynamic changed when the client became pregnant and was feeling more powerful. She was then able to verbalize feelings that she had previously felt would make her more vulnerable. This change in the dynamic showed the psychiatrist, after the fact, that her behavior (transferring the case), had been fueled by a rationalization that was based more on unconscious countertransferential feelings than good clinical care.

Expectations and disappointments about treatment, medications, the system, and mental illness itself may all be displaced onto providers. Because the case management model offers a nontraditional relationship between the system and the client, special attention must be paid to the dynamics between all involved providers. Opinions case managers and psychiatrists hold about each other will affect clients.

Often clients will force providers to analyze assumptions about each other. For example, the client who complains to the case manager that the psychiatrist is too busy or doesn't listen may evoke the case manager's own feelings about psychiatrists. The case manager must remain aware of these feelings and respond objectively to the client's complaint. If the psychiatrist is idealized by the case manager, he may invalidate the client's experience. If the psychiatrist is devalued, the case manager may collude and rescue the client from the psychiatrist by assuming an advocacy position out of proportion to client need. When expectations of other team members remain realistic, the case management team functions effectively.

A devaluing psychiatrist may see the "bleeding heart case manager" as overly involved when performing outreaches or practical services for the client. Failing to recognize the case manager's expertise, the psychiatrist may suggest therapeutic neutrality. Psychiatrists may alternatively expect case managers to miraculously rescue clients from themselves or serve as family member surrogates. Personal and systemic dynamics of all parties operate on a full-time basis and deserve attention to education and self-awareness. All providers must consciously work at maintaining respect for one another. Case management provides an invaluable service to severely mentally ill individuals, and the varying perspectives of case managers and psychiatrists are vital opportunities for treatment to be creative and effective. Differences of view are necessary for collaboration. They must be acknowledged and respected for constructive work to ensue.

This chapter has highlighted some important areas of psychiatric assessment, medication administration, and compliance in severely mentally ill clients. Acknowledging potential hindrances to compliance may help providers develop realistic expectations for clients and themselves. As well, recognizing interpersonal dynamics between treatment providers and clients will facilitate treatment; understanding relationship patterns between providers will allow them to work effectively and collaboratively. Combining strengths, psychiatrists and case managers can expect better lives for their clients.

References

Kaplan, H. I., & Sadock, B. J. (1991). *Synopsis of psychiatry* (6th ed.). Baltimore, MD: Williams & Wilkins.

Kelly, J. A., Murphy, D. A., Bahr, R., Brasfield, T. L., Davis, D. R., Hauth, A. C., Morgan, M. G., Stevenson, L. Y., & Eilers, M. K. (1992). AIDS/HIV risk behavior among the chronic mentally ill. *The American Journal of Psychiatry, 149*(7), 886-889.

Sox, H. C., Koran, L. M., Sox, C. H., Marton, K. I., Dugger, F., & Smith, T. (1989). A medical algorithm for detecting physical disease in psychiatric patients. *Hospital and Community Psychiatry, 40*(12), 1270-1276.

12

The Power of Dreams

Supporting Client Goals and Meaningful Activities

ROBERT W. SURBER

"Respect the power of a client's dream," are the words of the stockbroker Dean Witter in the television advertisement, who continues, "and help them achieve it." This advice would also seem to apply to clinical case managers working with mentally ill clients. As noted in Chapter 1, the purpose of clinical case management is to support clients in their struggle to achieve their goals and pursue their dreams.

The goals and dreams of individuals with mental illness are not appreciably different from those of anyone else. When asked, many clients mention work, intimate relationships or marriage, and parenthood among their primary aspirations. They also include the wish to be a respected member of a family and a community, the need to support oneself economically and contribute to the lives of others, the desire to love and be loved in interdependent relationships, the striving to express oneself through creative activities and spirituality, and the search for meaning. The specifics of how these goals might be realized are as varied as the dreams of the general public. Also, it was Freud who defined functioning in terms of love and work (Erickson, 1950). These domains, then, define the work of clinical case managers.

This chapter will provide a brief overview of the considerable impediments case managers face in helping clients achieve their goals. This will be followed by a summary of the contributions of psychosocial rehabilitation and mental health consumers to these endeavors. The chapter will conclude with a description of how the clinical case management approach can be utilized to support clients in pursuing their dreams.

Impediments to Supporting Meaningful Activities

Goals and dreams may be more often spoken of by clients and case managers than they are achieved. A large number of seriously mentally ill clients are not employed, are often lonely, and complain of being frustrated and bored by not having the relationships and activities they would like to have in their lives.

It is suggested that the technology exists to help most individuals with serious mental illness live stable lives in the community most of the time. Essentially, this involves providing a single point of responsibility, through an individual provider or a team of providers, to deliver comprehensive and continuous treatment and supportive care (Goldman, Morissey, & Ridgely, 1990). This also requires sufficient resources in the client's community to meet such basic human needs as safe and decent affordable housing and adequate financial entitlements.

Sadly, the public mental health services, upon which most seriously mentally ill individuals rely for care, seldom have the resources to implement the available technology or provide for the basic needs of large numbers of the clients who need them. This often results in the overutilization of acute psychiatric and medical hospitals, and the overrepresentation of this population in jails and among the homeless. It also results in preventable death. These outcomes require public expenditures for high-cost services that do little or nothing to improve clients' lives, or their ability to live successfully in the community. This, when combined with the effects of the stigma of mental illness, leads to large numbers of mentally ill people living tragic lives that are suffused with despair for themselves, their families, and others who care for them.

Some of those with mental illness are fortunate enough to find support, from families, treaters, and others in their communities, to live stably with only intermittent and infrequent relapses. In recent years, assertive continuous treatment teams and case management programs have been implemented to provide the single point of responsibility for comprehensive and continuous care (Kanter, 1989; Thompson, Griffith, & Leaf, 1990). There is considerable evidence to demonstrate that these programs are effective in helping clients live more stably in the community, improve the quality of their lives, and reduce reliance on expensive institutional care (Jerrell & Hu, 1989; Robinson & Bergman, 1989; Stein, Test, & Max, 1975).

Yet even the best of programs have only limited success in helping clients achieve their goals in the areas of work or other meaningful activities, as well as with developing and maintaining significant interpersonal relationships. A large number of clients who receive comprehensive and continuous services, and who are able to live successfully on their own, still report that they have little that is constructive to do with their time, and few people with whom to spend it.

There are many obstacles that face clients and their caregivers in the struggle to achieve client dreams. These include not only the disabilities of the illnesses but also impediments that can result from treatment. Obstacles also include discrimination that results from the stigma of mental illness, and poverty that limits opportunities. These obstacles can result in psychological difficulties within the clients that further inhibit their progress.

Serious obstacles for individuals with major mental illnesses stem from the disorders from which they suffer. Their symptoms distort perceptions, interfere with cognitive abilities, disturb affect, and cause behavioral problems. Over the long term, they can interfere with normal developmental processes, which can further interfere with clients' abilities to maintain viable relationships and participate in constructive activities.

The treatments available to assist clients in managing their symptoms can also play a role in reducing their ability to fully function. Medications, which can be critical in controlling symptoms, also frequently have side effects that induce lethargy and other discomforts that limit clients' ability to function. Professional providers can also unintentionally impede clients' efforts to achieve their goals by defining dreams as unrealistic, by giving messages that significant improvement is hopeless, and by being overly protective and discouraging clients from taking risks.

Major barriers to achievement for those with mental illness are the stigma and discrimination that pervade their lives. The stigma of mental illness is extremely powerful in North American culture. This results in a broad-based fear of people with mental illness, and this leads to discrimination in all areas of life. The stigma against mentally ill individuals also has profound negative effects on clients' families and loved ones, which can interfere with what may already be difficult relationships.

The grinding poverty experienced by many mentally ill individuals is another major obstacle to the pursuit of dreams. A lack of resources directly reduces opportunities. Living with extremely limited resources requires more than usual resourcefulness and creativity to maintain interdependent relationships and pursue productive activities. The poverty of many struggling with mental illnesses requires that they focus continuously on survival, and cannot even consider pursuing other goals. These impediments are similar to the obstacles to linkage described in more detail in Chapter 6.

These obstacles are quite daunting. It is not surprising, then, that some mentally ill individuals lose all self-esteem and give up hope. Some individuals also lose all motivation for change, and may find it too painful to allow themselves to dream. It is not surprising then that many individuals turn to alcohol and/or drugs for solace, even though this frequently leads to additional problems. Overcoming obstacles to the achievement of client goals can be as daunting to the professionals serving them as it is to the clients. Nevertheless, this must be an area of concern if community living is to be fully successful.

The Contributions of Psychosocial Rehabilitation and Mental Health Consumers

There is a need for further development of technologies, approaches, and interventions that will help with overcoming these obstacles and supporting clients to develop meaningful activities and relationships. However, important work has been done, which provides numerous clues for success that can be incorporated into the clinical case management approach.

The concepts of psychosocial rehabilitation and psychiatric rehabilitation have been discussed in the mental health literature for a number of years (Anthony, Cohen, & Farkas, 1990; Liberman, 1988; Vorspan, 1988). Additionally, mental health consumers have also written about the elements of recovery from mental illness, and about consumer participation in the development and delivery of services for seriously mentally ill clients (Sherman & Porter, 1991; Zinman, Harp, & Budd, 1987). Both the psychiatric rehabilitation approach and consumer involvement in the delivery of services offer valuable and complementary approaches to supporting clients in their efforts to achieve their goals and dreams in the areas of work and interdependent relationships. Both also describe a philosophy and/or principles of care that are consistent with those described in the clinical case management approach.

For example, Bachrach (1992) has outlined eight concepts that underlie psychosocial rehabilitation. These include (1) an individualized approach, (2) the provision of environmental supports, (3) supporting client strengths,

(4) restoring hope, (5) focusing on vocational potential, (6) incorporating the full array of social and recreational concerns, (7) full client involvement and participation in treatment, and (8) an ongoing process which incorporates many interventions in many settings. Anthony and his colleagues (1990) state that the principles of psychiatric rehabilitation are implemented through the provision of environmental supports and the acquisition of skills.

Deegan, representing a mental health consumer's perspective, states that psychiatrically disabled adults "are not passive recipients of rehabilitation services. Rather, they experience themselves as *recovering* a new sense of self and of purpose within and beyond the limits of the disability" (Deegan, 1988, p. 11). Deegan and other consumers insist that the most important component of the recovery process is hope (Lovejoy, 1982). Without hope for a better life, there can be no motivation for change and growth. Hope is essential for clients, for those who care about them, and for those who serve them.

Deegan suggests four requirements for programs to support client recovery. First of all, providers must understand that recovery is not a linear process. That is, not all efforts are successful, and steps forward are frequently followed by steps backward. Unsuccessful efforts should not be defined as failures but rather should be seen as a necessary part of a process to learn what can be successful. Because of this, there need to be "fail-proof programs" that continue to offer hope, support, and opportunities for change, regardless of the client's progress or lack of it. Second, it is necessary to see "each person's journey of recovery as unique." There must be numerous programmatic opportunities in which clients can participate in both provider- and consumer-operated vocational and socialization services. Deegan's third requirement is to acknowledge the unique gifts that consumers can give each other in the recovery process. Those who have suffered from mental illnesses and are recovering can provide understanding and hope, and can serve as role models in ways that professionals cannot. Therefore, it is necessary to incorporate consumers as staff within rehabilitative services. Finally, staff attitudes are a critical component of care. Helpful attitudes diminish the differences between the "normal and abnormal" or between "us and them," so that staff and clients can identify with each other in common life struggles (1988). These attitudes acknowledge the interdependent relationships between staff and clients.

It is not surprising that psychosocial rehabilitation programs incorporate case management into their activities, and that case management services include psychosocial rehabilitation approaches in their efforts.

Anthony and his colleagues (1988) describe case management as a necessary component of psychiatric rehabilitation. Case managers focus on the provision of environmental supports, which is one of the key aspects of the rehabilitation process.

Numerous case management programs incorporate the principles and activities of psychosocial rehabilitation and/or incorporate mental health consumers within their staff. For example, the Program for Assertive Community Treatment (PACT), developed in Dane County, Wisconsin, organized to provide comprehensive and continuous care, emphasizes vocational functioning and the development of other constructive uses of time for its clients (Stein et al., 1975).

The Strengths Model of case management focuses on supporting clients' strengths in order to attain and maintain successful community living. Rapp (1992) argues that successful community functioning requires utilizing all of the resources of the community. He also suggests that it is necessary to find a niche in the community in which the client's unique strengths will be utilized and appreciated.

Several case management programs have begun hiring mental health consumers as staff. Among the first of these is a program in Denver, Colorado, in which consumers work closely with clients' case managers to implement an individualized service plan (Sherman & Porter, 1991).

Utilizing the Clinical Case Management Approach

It is a premise of this discussion that successful community living for people with mental illness is enhanced when those who serve them integrate all of the technologies, approaches, and interventions that are available. This includes integrating traditional psychiatric treatment and social service approaches with psychosocial rehabilitation principles and consumer involvement.

Clinical case management is an approach that encourages the integration of all available technologies. The remainder of this chapter will describe how clinical case managers tailor multiple interventions to the needs and resources of particular clients, within the context of local environments, to support them in the struggle to achieve their dreams and goals.

General Considerations

There are several general issues to consider in the work to support client goals. The first of these is that the pursuit of dreams can be an end in itself.

Not all dreams are achievable, nor are they necessarily intended to be achieved. Client dreams that appear to be beyond reach do not always represent grandiosity.

For many people, dreams that may not be attained represent something to strive for and provide direction and meaning for their lives and work. For instance, many of the authors of this book share the dream of a time when there will be comprehensive services for all mentally ill individuals who need them, and when there will be interventions that will allow the most severely ill to live their lives with dignity and productivity. Although these goals may not be achieved in the lifetimes of these individuals, they provide direction for their lives and their careers. These dreams provide a framework for short-term goals and a rationale for day-to-day decisions in the work of these individuals.

It is important to remember that many things taken for granted today were once only dreams, and may have been ridiculed by many as being unrealistic. It is also important to note that some of the "dreamers" who achieved "unrealistic" goals suffered from mental illnesses.

Therefore, supporting clients' struggles to achieve their dreams can be as important as the attainment of them. It is this struggle that can provide meaning for their lives. It is through this struggle that smaller goals are set and attained.

The second consideration is that the struggle to develop meaning in life includes a very broad range of activities. In general it involves work and interdependent relationships, both of which are defined very broadly. Work includes not only full-time, paid employment but also part-time and volunteer jobs. However, for this discussion, it also means any productive activity that contributes to others. Interdependent relationships are those in which clients contribute as well as receive from others, and can involve those with family, friends, lovers, employers, co-workers, landlords, church members, mental health providers, other clients, and almost anyone else in the client's community. Meaning in life is also pursued through educational and recreational activities as well as expressions of spirituality and creativity.

The third consideration is that success in supporting life activities usually involves providing multiple interventions in a variety of settings. All psychiatric and human service interventions are helpful to some people some of the time. It is often necessary for case managers and others in the client's support system to continue to pursue the activities and combinations of approaches that will work for a particular individual. Success also requires that all of the resources of the community be available to support client activities and relationships.

The Clinical Relationship

As recounted throughout this book, clinical case management is dependent on the relationship between client and case manager. It is through this relationship that clients gain access to and use community supports. It is also through this relationship that clients learn to manage their illnesses and grow. This relationship, then, can be a powerful tool in supporting clients' dreams and goals and, therefore, in assisting clients to develop constructive activities and meaningful relationships.

With an individualized and flexible approach, the clinical case manager can support each client's "unique journey to recovery," as described by Deegan (1988). This journey must begin where the client is, rather than where others feel the client ought to be. That is, the journey must begin by acknowledging the clients' attitudes and feelings about themselves, their disabilities and needs, as well as their strengths and stated goals.

In providing comprehensive and continuous care, the case manager can provide the environmental supports and develop the opportunities for skill building, which underpin psychiatric rehabilitation, as defined by Anthony and his colleagues (1990).

Case Manager Attitudes

Although case managers will participate in a variety of activities and will implement a series of interventions with clients, their success in assisting clients to achieve their life goals is as dependent on the case managers' attitudes as it is on their skills. These attitudes include believing in clients, accepting the necessity for clients to participate in the rehabilitative process, and the ability to see the commonality between the clients' life struggles and their own.

Case managers must believe in their clients' ability to change and grow, as well as their ability to develop meaningful activities and relationships. It is only through this belief that case managers can have hope for their clients to improve. If case managers and others in the clients' lives do not have hope, it is much more difficult for clients to have hope for themselves (Lovejoy, 1982).

Belief in clients is not blind and does not ignore either the severity of their illnesses or the difficulty of their circumstances. It also does not mean believing that all severely ill clients will necessarily achieve the full range of functioning. What is required is a belief in clients' abilities to have improved relationships and additional meaningful activities. The belief must be in possibilities.

As indicated in Chapter 1, client participation is a principle of the clinical case management approach. It is also a crucial aspect of any rehabilitative effort. Whereas there may be some interventions that can be done to clients, and some practical supports that can be provided for clients, the journey to recovery can only be undertaken by clients. Encouraging clients to participate with efforts to support this process can be quite difficult; nevertheless, there is little useful that can be done without the clients' acceptance of and participation in such efforts.

One important role for case managers is to encourage clients to participate in developing meaningful activities and relationships; and it is equally important for case managers to recognize that they cannot move ahead without this participation.

A critical attitude involves accepting that the struggle of mentally ill clients is universal and not defined by disability or illness. The struggle to have productive and meaningful work, and loving and supportive relationships, is the struggle of all humankind. It is necessary, then, for case managers to recognize that there is more in common between them and their clients than there is separating them. The acknowledgment of this commonality may be what it takes for clients to have sufficient trust in their helpers to be able to participate in the efforts to help.

Providing Environmental Supports

Through the clinical relationship, case managers are in a position to participate with their clients in the effort to develop constructive activities. Case managers are also in a position to provide a series of environmental supports, skill development activities, and psychological interventions in multiple settings to pursue this effort.

Pursuing dreams usually requires satisfying basic needs of housing, financial supports, and so forth. For many clients it also requires treatment to stabilize psychiatric symptoms; treatment for medical, dental, and substance abuse disorders; or the resolution of legal problems. By implementing the broad definition of what is therapeutic, clinical case managers are in a unique position to organize a comprehensive response to these needs. With their ability to be mobile, case managers can develop these supports wherever and with whomever necessary in the community.

For example, a client who is homeless and suffers from hallucinations that cause him to strike out at others and, as a result, is in jail on assault charges, will most likely need a variety of practical supports and treatment services before being able to pursue a goal of paid employment. The case manager is expected to provide or coordinate what is needed so that the client will be in a position to pursue meaningful activities.

On the other hand, it is not necessary that all support and treatment issues be resolved before supporting the pursuit of life dreams. In the case of a young African-American man, the client's only stated goal was to find work, even though he suffered from delusions that were upsetting to his family, with whom he lived. Initially, the client refused to take medications. The case manager chose to support the client's efforts to find work, rather than wait until he accepted medications and resolved the difficulties with his family. The client was able to get part-time work cleaning up in a local grocery store. When difficulties he had with the owner threatened his job, the case manager was able to use this opportunity encourage the client to accept medications. This not only helped the client save his job but also consequently helped improve the relationships with his family, which may also have saved his home. This example illustrates that directly supporting clients' goals can make it possible for some to accept other supports and services that they need.

Supporting Skill Development

In addition to providing environmental supports, clinical case managers are directly involved in skill development. This occurs in a variety of ways. First of all, case managers work in the community with their clients. In doing so, they may directly help with such daily living activities as shopping and using public transportation. In the client's home they may help develop cooking and money management skills. In community settings case managers can assess what clients can do for themselves, and either provide skills training activities directly, or link the client to other skill development resources. Through the clinical relationship case managers model social skills for clients and also provide knowledge that clients need to succeed in the community.

Using the Relationship to Develop Relationship Skills

A major disability for many seriously mentally ill individuals is expressed in their limited capacity to establish and maintain interdependent relationships. Through the clinical relationship case managers utilize psychological understanding and interventions to develop clients' capacity to relate. As a result of the symptoms or vicissitudes of the illnesses or, in some cases, as a result of traumatic life experiences, many clients have either a paucity of relationships or dysfunctional relationships. Because the ability to relate is critical to the success of most client goals, this can be a major obstacle to their success.

The clinical relationship offers an opportunity to improve clients' ability to appropriately use and benefit from a positive relationship. The case manager becomes a constant object in a relationship that the client can trust because it is reliable, caring, and free from fear, abuse, or punishment. In this context the case manager can provide feedback to help the client reality test various experiences. The case manager can also support legitimate dependency needs, which is necessary in any interdependent relationship. Through the clinical relationship the case manager provides a positive emotional experience that promotes healing and growth. Finally, the case manager affirms the client's sense of self and the client's autonomy.

The case manager offers the client a primary relationship that, when successful, becomes a model through which clients can develop others (Kanter, 1985). By experiencing one supportive relationship, clients can be hopeful for more. Success in relationships can increase motivation for the pursuit of goals.

Assessing and Supporting Client Goals

It is in the context of providing practical supports and clinical interventions that case managers assess client goals and support client dreams. The assessment and support of dreams, goals, and aspirations require considerable skill and understanding.

Some clients have clear-cut goals and plans to achieve them. When this is the case, it is important for case managers to know when to get out of the way and not interfere with clients' pursuit of their goals. In these instances the greatest difficulty for case managers may be in overcoming their own discomfort in allowing clients to take risks. What is often helpful is for the case manager to provide encouragement and practical help while being available to give support if problems occur.

An example is when clients pursue romantic relationships. Not infrequently, clients become involved with people who have problems similar to their own. Case managers and others in the clients' support systems can be quite concerned that these relationships are not right or will cause harm for the client. Yet the drive for a significant relationship is as powerful among mentally ill individuals as it is for everyone else. Attempting to interfere with a client's opportunity for a romantic involvement is usually counterproductive. On the other hand it can be helpful to celebrate the client's joy and success at having the relationship. Practical support might involve information about where to go on dates, or to find privacy on a limited budget, or education about safe sexual practices. If problems are encountered, the case manager can provide emotional and concrete support as needed.

Some clients express not having any goals, either because they feel hopeless or because they simply have not thought about it. Others express goals that are not likely to be achieved, such as wanting to be an astronaut or a professional tennis star. Still others express goals that are socially unacceptable, such as wanting to use or sell drugs or harm others.

In each of these situations the case manager must consider strategies to help clients develop and pursue meaningful activities and relationships. The situation in which a client does not have or cannot express any dreams or goals may be the most difficult. Trying to understand why this is the case can be useful in developing the most appropriate strategy. Is it because the client has never been successful, or has been repeatedly disappointed? Is it because the client is preoccupied with survival needs and cannot see beyond daily concerns? Is it because the client is severely depressed? Of course, there are many possibilities, and just as many possible responses.

It is often helpful to look for small things a client might want to have or want to do, or small problems they would like to solve. Success with small needs or problems may lead to the identification of further or broader goals. For instance, a trip with a case manager to a local park reminded a client of previous pleasant experiences in the park. This led to future visits that the client made on his own.

It can also be productive to review the clients' strengths and abilities, as these may suggest possible productive activities in which the clients might have an interest. For example, a middle-aged women with schizoaffective disorder had a history of multiple hospitalizations. She expressed no interest in becoming involved in any activities or productive pursuits. Because she had received a Bachelor of Fine Arts degree in her youth, her case manager encouraged her to pursue her interest in drawing and painting. This pursuit provided her with something to do with her time, helped her get out of her room, and led to several friendships.

As discussed in Chapter 6, case managers can help motivate clients toward developing and implementing goals through a process of education and support.

Sometimes it is necessary to wait. Clients may need a more stable situation, or may need to develop more trust, or may need enough encouragement, or may just need time to consider what they want before they can clearly express their goals. As already noted, it is necessary to engage clients in a participatory process, which can only occur at each client's own pace.

Dreams are often fragile, and it is important not to squash them, even if they seem unattainable or inappropriate. What seem to be grandiose goals may simply be a self-protective response to low self-esteem. Even so, the content of these expressions usually represents an area of interest that should be considered.

For example, the goal of being a tennis star may represent an interest in tennis or sports, and suggests areas to be pursued in developing activities. Perhaps the client would like to play tennis with friends, or watch local matches, or read about the history of the game and its great players, or work in a sporting goods store. As discussed earlier in this chapter, unattainable goals can provide direction for one's daily activities.

Therefore, it is not helpful to discourage clients from their goals. Rather, it is more often helpful to find the small steps that they can take to pursue them. In experiencing success through small steps, many clients can set some realistic and achievable goals for themselves. To paraphrase the adage, each unique journey begins with a single step.

There are goals expressed by clients that case managers cannot support because they are illegal, unethical, or destructive. In these cases it can be useful to redirect clients to more appropriate activities, or wait for opportunities to develop. Even so, questionable goals can provide the motivation for clients to pursue constructive activities.

For example, a young male client in one program for seriously mentally ill individuals could only express a goal of wanting to smoke marijuana. However, he complained that his biggest problem was that he did not have enough money to buy as much marijuana as he wanted. Without condoning his marijuana use, the staff of the program stated that they could help him find a job, which would improve his financial situation, if he would participate in a vocational program. With this incentive the client did complete the program and obtained a paying job. He then had more money to pursue his goal. Interestingly, because of the demands of his job, his drug use actually declined (Kalinowski, 1992).

When working with clients to pursue their dreams, patience is the greatest virtue. The most useful case management principle when considering developing meaningful activities is that of providing continuous care. The recovery process is lifelong and is enhanced with ongoing support and encouragement.

One man who is active in the consumer movement was making a presentation to the families of psychiatric hospital patients. He described a long history of hospitalizations and life failures, which he attributed, in part, to noncompliance with recommended outpatient treatment. He stated that it was only the continued faith and support of his family that helped him eventually accept treatment, which eventually allowed him to pursue his goals. One of the participants expressed frustration with a daughter who had steadfastly refused to accept medications, and asked how long families must continue to be hopeful and provide support. This man responded that, in his case, his mother stood by him for 12 years before he accepted outpatient treatment.

As already noted, growth is not linear and it is studded with upsets and setbacks. These should not be seen as failures but rather as opportunities to learn. Continuity also means that clients cannot fail in the case management program and will continue to be served as long as they are willing to be. This means that case managers must also never give up on rehabilitative efforts, and must keep faith that clients can continue to grow and develop. It also requires that new approaches continuously be considered when previous ones do not work or no longer prove useful. Time is an ally and often rewards persistent efforts. One factor that works in favor of the process is that the client and the case manager mature in their relationship over time, and both develop additional skills and insight.

The Role of Mental Health Consumers

Mental health consumers can make significant contributions as staff in clinical case management programs, particularly in the area of rehabilitation. Deegan (1988) states most eloquently that disabled people have a unique gift to give one another:

> Their gift is their hope, strength and experience as lived in the recovery process. In this sense, disabled persons can become role models for each other. During that dark night of anguish and despair when disabled persons live without hope, the presence of other recovering persons can challenge that despair through example. It becomes very difficult to continue to convince oneself that there

is no hope when one is surrounded by other equally disabled persons who are making strides in their recovery! Hope is contagious and that is why it is so important to hire disabled people in rehabilitation programs. (p. 18)

As staff within case management programs, consumers perform many of the same activities and tasks as professional case managers. However, consumers have attributes and perspectives that allow them to make contributions that cannot be made by professional staff.

Mental health consumers have no difficulty in understanding the commonality between their plight and that of their clients, because consumer staff have had common experiences. This can be immediately understood by the clients and allows for empathy and bonding that are difficult for others to replicate. Consumers can also validate client experiences more effectively than professionals. Finally, the fact that consumer staff are working as staff in a mental health program is inspirational to many clients.

Mental health clients working as staff in case management programs are a powerful force against stigma. Those in the consumer movement have demonstrated a great deal of courage in publicly proclaiming their status as former patients. Through clear and compelling arguments for the need to reform mental health programs and service systems, they also demonstrate a deep understanding of the problems and describe useful solutions.

This courage and clarity of expression are clear evidence that mentally ill individuals have a great deal to contribute to the needs of other mentally ill individuals. If this is so, then it is also true that they have a great deal to offer in any human endeavor. These expressions can be most convincing, to both the general public and mental health professionals, that stigmatic responses are unjustifiable.

Within a clinical case management program, consumer staff will work within the context of a relationship and use many of the same principles and approaches described in the previous section of this chapter. The specific activities they participate in will be as varied as the needs of particular clients and situations. In one urban case management program, some of the activities consumer case managers have been involved in include taking clients to a variety of community resources to obtain items such as clothing, food, and furniture. They have also established linkages with the community agencies that provide these resources.

Additionally, they accompany clients to volunteer work assignments and recreational activities. They provide counseling, discuss medication compliance, and encourage attendance at other self-help programs. They assist clients in obtaining and moving into better housing; teach daily living skills; and set up medical and dental appointments and accompany clients to them. All of these activities are in the service of client recovery and rehabilitation.

A final benefit of hiring mental health consumers in case management and other mental health programs is that it provides jobs for clients of the mental health system. This, then, is part of the recovery process for these employees.

Mental health consumers now serve in a number of direct service roles in mental health services for seriously mentally ill clients. This is something that was merely a dream for some of these consumers only a few years ago. It was a dream that the majority of mental health professionals would probably have described as unrealistic.

Programmatic Supports

In addition to the work of individual clinical case managers and consumer case managers, there are structural supports within a case management program that can support rehabilitative efforts. These include providing group treatments and vocational counselors within the program.

Groups offer an opportunity for clients to share experiences and learn skills. Socialization groups in a case management program can be quite helpful in supporting clients' efforts to develop relationships and activities. The groups provide not only an opportunity to teach socialization skills but also an opportunity for clients to meet one another and establish relationships that can continue outside the group. Finally, if group activities occur in community settings, clients can learn to make use of community resources.

One case manager established a group for young Latino men, which initially met over meals in restaurants. The members then decided that they wanted to pursue other activities, so they have gone fishing, to movies, and to a club for dancing and woman watching. One of the members had a cookout at his home for the others. They organize activities outside the scheduled group meeting; and there are times when the whole group will schedule an activity without the case manager. Sometimes, two or more of the group get together. For instance, the two members who now like to go fishing will go with each other. This group has expanded both the range of activities and the confidence of its members.

Developing group activities can be a useful role for both clinical and consumer case managers. Job development and job coaching are specialized skills. It is useful, then, for case management programs to hire vocational counselors to assist clients in obtaining paid employment. Vocational counselors assess clients' preparedness for work and can assist in finding jobs, or in making referrals to pre-vocational or placement programs. They can also provide job coaching for those clients who do find employment, or consult with case managers about providing referrals or job coaching. Vocational counselors in case management programs work directly with clients and provide consultation to case managers. Because of their specialized knowledge, they also may be the best staff to develop relationships with vocational programs and employers on behalf of the case management agency.

Linkage and Advocacy

Supporting clients in their struggle to achieve their dreams and goals involves utilizing all available resources in the community. A major role for the case manager is to help clients utilize community resources to not only establish and maintain relationships but also find constructive ways to use their time. These resources include mental health and human service programs, such as day treatment programs, clubhouses, and vocational programs. They also include local educational resources, such as community colleges, local high school programs, and other training opportunities.

Both paid and volunteer work are found in a wide variety of settings. For example, in one case management program clients worked at a blood bank, in a bookstore, as a taxi driver, as a receptionist at a child's school, as a peer counselor on an acute psychiatric unit, as a clerk in a health center, and as a manager in a self-help center. Others made money through their own enterprise by providing housecleaning and window-washing services, or by selling such diverse items as cassette tapes and homemade meals on the streets, or by panhandling. Still others are involved in the political process and volunteer on advisory boards, participate on committees to coordinate services for the homeless, and organize rallies, letter-writing campaigns, and testimony to influence legislators about state and local health budgets. A number of clients raise or participate in raising their own children, or are involved with the children of relatives in such activities as organizing birthday parties for godchildren, buying presents for the children, or taking them to the park.

In developing recreational and creative activities, clients also utilize the gamut of community resources, such as parks, churches, movie theaters, museums, art centers, senior centers, and fishing holes. Some clients are able to find a niche in the community where they both give of themselves and receive from others. One client, who writes and performs rap music, volunteers in a music recording studio. In return for helping record other artists, he is allowed to use the studio. Another client helps out as watchman in a local grocery in return for lower prices on his purchases. The purpose of these examples is to suggest that there is no limit to the possibilities that are available to clients. The process of linking clients to community resources is described in detail in Chapter 6.

Despite the best efforts of clients and case managers, many mentally ill individuals do not lead their lives as fully as possible. There continues to be a need for more services to implement the technologies that are available, and for more effective technologies to support clients' efforts to attain their goals. The stigma of mental illness continues to provide unnecessary barriers for clients and providers alike.

It is incumbent upon case managers, then, to evaluate their efforts to determine how effective they are at helping their clients develop meaningful activities and relationships. It is also necessary that they experiment with new interventions and approaches that might improve their effectiveness.

Finally, as discussed in Chapter 7, one expectation of case managers is advocacy on behalf of their clients. Case managers must advocate with mental health administrators and policymakers for more opportunities and better technologies to help their clients to pursue their dreams.

References

Anthony, W. A., Cohen, M., & Farkas, M. (1990). *Psychiatric rehabilitation*. Boston: Center for Psychiatric Rehabilitation.

Bachrach, L. L. (1992). Psychosocial rehabilitation and psychiatry in the care of long-term patients. *American Journal of Psychiatry, 149*(11), 1455-1463.

Deegan, P. E. (1988). Recovery: The lived experience of rehabilitation. *Psychosocial Rehabilitation Journal, 11*(4), 11-19.

Erickson, E. H. (1950). *Childhood and society*. New York: Norton.

Goldman, H. H., Morissey, J. P., & Ridgely, M. S. (1990). Form and function of mental health authorities of Robert Wood Johnson program sites: Preliminary observations. *Hospital and Community Psychiatry, 41*, 1222-1230.

Jerrell, J. M., & Hu, T. (1989). Cost effectiveness of intensive clinical and case management compared with an existing system of care. *Inquiry, 26*, pp. 224-234.

Kalinowski, C. (1992). Personal communication. (Dr. Kalinowski is Assistant Clinical Professor, Department of Psychiatry, San Francisco General Hospital; and former Medical Director, Stanislaus County, California, Integrated Service Agency.)

Kanter, J. S. (Ed.). (1985). *Clinical issues in treating the chronic mentally ill: New directions for mental health services* (Vol. 27). San Francisco: Jossey-Bass.

Kanter, J. S. (1989). Clinical case management: Definition, principles, components. *Hospital and Community Psychiatry, 40*(4), 361-368,

Liberman, R. P. (Ed.). (1988). *Psychiatric rehabilitation of chronic mental patients.* Washington, DC: American Psychiatric Press.

Lovejoy, M. (1982). Expectations and the recovery process. *Schizophrenia Bulletin, 8*(4), 605-609.

Rapp, C. A. (1992). The strengths perspective of care management with persons suffering from severe mental illness. In D. Saleesby (Ed.), *The strengths model of social work practice: Power in the people* (pp. 45-58). New York: Longman.

Robinson, G. K., & Bergman, G. T. (1989). *Choices in case management: A review of current knowledge on practice for mental health programs.* Washington, DC: Policy Resources Incorporated.

Sherman, P. S., & Porter, R. (1991). Mental health consumers as case management aides. *Hospital and Community Psychiatry, 42*(5), 494-498.

Stein, L. I., Test, M. A., & Max, A. J. (1975). Alternative to the hospital: A controlled study. *American Journal of Psychiatry, 132*(5), 517-522.

Thompson, K. S., Griffith, E.E.H., & Leaf, P. J. (1990). A historical review of the Madison model of community care. *Hospital and Community Psychiatry, 41*(6), 625-633.

Vorspan, R. (1988). Activities of daily living in the clubhouse: You can't vacuum in a vacuum. *Psychosocial Rehabilitation Journal, 12*(2), 1-6.

Zinman, S., Harp, H., & Budd, S. (Eds.). (1987). *Reaching across.* Boston: Center for Psychiatric Rehabilitation.

13

Resolving Value Conflicts

ROBERT W. SURBER

Providing clinical case management services for mentally ill clients is challenging work. One can be physically depleted after a day of visiting a client in a hospital, meeting with another client's family in their home, and helping a third client move to a new hotel room. It can be emotionally stressful to work to bolster a client's motivation and instill hope while struggling to overcome the resistance of a day treatment program to accept the client. It is psychologically challenging to determine not only what a client needs but also how to use oneself and the clinical relationship to best meet those needs. Similarly, the behavior and needs of some clients raise issues that are difficult for the case manager because they raise conflicts with personal experience and values.

Some clients deteriorate or die, with even the best of care, through their unwillingness or inability to participate, through major medical illnesses and other disastrous events, and at their own hands. This is painful for everyone working with these clients, and may cause a personal reexamination of existential and ethical issues. This can also raise questions of societal responsibility, economic distribution of services and wealth, and the role and responsibilities of the legal system.

It is suggested here that this work can also challenge the basic beliefs and values of practitioners, the tenets of the mental health professions, and the expectations of the general public.

There are two major areas where the needs of the clients or the expectations of case managers can conflict with the values of the clinicians who provide the care. The first issue concerns the use of power and authority in the clinical relationship. The second involves working with a population that is dependent on others for meeting its needs.

Values provide a cornerstone for human relationships in general, and specifically for the relationship between provider and client in all human service fields. They provide direction and meaning for care providers. They help define the responsibilities of provider and client. They underlie the prescribed limits of the relationship which protect both parties.

The work with mentally ill individuals can cause conflict with values, both because of the needs of the clients and because of the expectations made of clinicians. As an example, the negative symptoms of schizophrenia can include apathy, amotivation, and withdrawal. When combined with the positive symptoms of hallucinations, delusions, and disordered thought processes, these symptoms can dramatically impede the individuals' ability to act autonomously to meet their own needs. This creates genuine dependence on others for help. On the other hand, the training of most mental health practitioners occurs within a culture that places a premium on independence. This bias toward independence can create a negative reaction or ambivalence toward individuals who are dependent on others for their needs. This can result in a real conflict between the needs of the client and the values of the care provider.

As another example, there are times when clients with serious mental disorders become so ill that they are a danger to themselves or others, or are unable to provide for their basic survival needs. These are times when society has determined, through legislation, that individuals should be cared for, even if they are unable or unwilling to accept care on a voluntary basis. It is the public mental health authority, and frequently case managers, who have the responsibility for implementing involuntary treatment. At the same time, the right of self-determination is a basic tenet of all mental health disciplines. Most mental professionals enter their field of practice because of a desire to help other people, and many define their responsibilities to include the empowerment of clients toward achieving their own goals. Forcing clients to accept care that they do not want can readily be seen as undermining self-determination and empowerment.

Involuntary treatment is usually provided in locked settings, where clients may be restrained, secluded, or not allowed outside of a restricted area without accompaniment. Clients may also be injected, against their will, with medications that can make them feel uncomfortable. When they are involuntarily committing a client, this may make mental health staff feel more like jailers and agents of social control than like helpers. The values of the clinician can be in conflict with the expectations of the role. These potential value conflicts confront case managers on a regular basis and can directly affect the course of care provided. The literature on psychotherapy suggests that one of the predictors of positive outcome is the therapist's ability to express empathy toward clients (Squier, 1990). If case management clients cause conflicts in core issues for the case manager, it will be more difficult to be empathetic and establish a positive alliance. If unrecognized, these conflicts can seriously impede the case management process. On the other hand, if they are recognized and handled well, they can assist case managers in understanding their clients and themselves and also improve the treatment provided.

This chapter will discuss the reasons why there is a high risk that these value conflicts will not be recognized and dealt with effectively, and how this can have detrimental effects on the case management process. It will then suggest how these conflicts can be recognized, understood, and resolved. The resolution of the use of authority in the clinical relationship is based on practical considerations. The resolution of the conflicts with the value of independence when working with a highly dependent population is based on philosophical considerations.

It is not suggested that these are the only value conflicts that can interfere with the work of a case manager. Indeed, value conflicts are common occurrences. Rather, this discussion considers two of the most common issues and suggests that it is part of the ongoing work to identify and resolve value conflicts that can impede one's effectiveness.

The Use of Authority in the Clinical Relationship

Case managers do have a lot of power and authority to influence their clients' lives. It is a premise of this discussion that authority exists in all helping relationships and must be used effectively as part of any professional intervention. However, there a number of problems that interfere with a case manager's ability to recognize, accept, and utilize this authority.

This section of the chapter will describe the types of authority that a case manager has, and how they are derived, so that this aspect of the role can be understood. It will then describe the issues that interfere with the recognition and use of authority. Finally, it will describe how value conflicts with authority may be resolved, so that authority can be accepted and used to further the goals of treatment.

Types of Authority

To use one's authority one must understand what it is, how it is derived, and what expectations are attendant to it. In mental health treatment, the provider's authority and power derive from several sources. Palmer (1983), in an article discussing authority in social service agencies, describes five types of authority. For the purposes of this discussion, this typology is being condensed into three categories: legally constituted authority, institutionally constituted authority, and personally constituted authority.

Legally constituted authority is defined as that which is based on legislation and is subject to review by the courts. In the mental health field, this largely involves providing involuntary treatment.

The power to confine individuals in a place they do not want to be, to strap them to a bed, and in some instances force substances into their bodies against their will is extraordinary in contemporary Western society. Police officers can incarcerate individuals but cannot not medicate them with force. Medical practitioners can sometimes provide treatment without consent, but only in emergency life-and-death situations when the patients cannot speak for themselves.

Many mental health consumers report that being forcibly detained and involuntarily treated can be very traumatic and may cause powerful and long-standing psychological repercussions (Campbell & Schraiber, 1989). This may be a major determinant in many clients' willingness to continue participation in mental health treatment when free to make their own decisions.

In invoking legally constituted authority, mental health professionals do not act as individuals, nor are they allowed the latitude of making judgments based on clinical opinions about what is best for the client. Rather, they are acting under the delegated authority of the local mental health authority and are carrying out the "will of the people" through a statutory requirement that care and treatment be imposed under certain circumstances. In most jurisdictions the criteria for involuntary treatment have to do with a person's impaired capacity due to mental illness and, as a result, exhibiting behaviors that are dangerous to self or others, or being unable to provide for basic needs.

When the conditions for involuntary treatment are met, mental health professionals, including case managers, are obligated to intervene in invoking this prescribed authority, to ensure that treatment is provided. Although one must make a professional judgment that the legal requirements are met, one cannot interpose personal judgments about client needs in making the decision to commit a client. For instance, if a client is seriously planning to commit suicide and otherwise meets the local criteria, the mental health worker cannot act on a personal belief that in this client's circumstances, suicide might be an honorable and appropriate solution to the pain the client is suffering. On the other hand, when the strict criteria are not met, the mental health worker cannot impose involuntary treatment in circumstances where the client might be best served by hospitalization.

By definition, legally constituted authority is limited in that there is an opportunity, if not a requirement, for review by the judicial system. Therefore, a judge or hearing officer will make a final determination as to whether such decisions are appropriate.

In summary, legally constituted authority is defined by statute, and those who invoke it are acting as designates of the local mental authority and not as individuals. This is prescribed authority that does not allow for decisions based on personal opinions and judgments. Finally, the decisions can be reviewed and overturned by the courts.

Institutionally constituted authority is that given to case managers to carry out the responsibilities of their positions in the agencies in which they work. This authority may be based on legislation but is not reviewed by the courts. Also, in utilizing this type of authority, a case manager is expected to make clinical judgments about what clients need and how best those needs will be met.

Institutionally constituted authority involves decisions about who receives care, how it is delivered, and what other resources are available to a client. Case managers make decisions about who receives case management services, under what circumstances, and how the case management process is to be implemented. Case managers can also determine access to other resources. For instance, it may be determined that a client who wants to be hospitalized can manage in a temporary shelter, or that money management is a requirement of receiving entitlements, so referrals are made or not made in keeping with these judgments. A case manager can also make access to resources conditional on client behaviors. For example, a case manager may require that the client demonstrate regular attendance and punctuality in day treatment before receiving referral to a vocational program, or remain sober for a period of time before being supported in an application to return to school.

Clearly, utilizing institutionally constituted authority can have a profound effect on clients' lives. Clients must usually accept case managers' judgments and decisions and they have no recourse through the courts. What is sometimes referred to as "manipulation" by clients is often a result of their understanding of the great power that mental health professionals wield in making resource decisions, and it derives from clients' clumsy, desperate, and ineffective ways of expressing their needs.

To summarize, institutionally constituted authority sanctions case managers to do their work and requires that they make judgments about not only client needs but also how resources will be utilized to meet those needs.

Personally constituted authority is derived from two sources. The first is the knowledge, expertise, and skills that mental health professionals have by virtue of their training and experience and use to evaluate clients' needs and deliver helpful interventions. The second aspect of personally constituted authority is the inherent personal qualities and characteristics that instill confidence in clients, inspire them to accept professionals' influence, and make them want to continue to work on resolving their problems.

The preceding chapters of this book make it clear that the ability to help clients understand their illnesses, to work with them towards managing them, and to utilize the community resources to support them requires considerable knowledge and skill. It is knowledge and skill that all professionals offer their clients. Therefore, the power to understand clients' problems and offer interventions to ameliorate them is inherent in all professional relationships. For clients to accept the power of the professionals' knowledge and skills, they must have faith that they can be helpful and faith in the professionals. There is evidence to support the notion that faith in the healer's powers makes a considerable contribution to the healing process (Ngokwey, 1989).

Personally constituted authority is an inherent aspect of the professional role, based on the professional's knowledge, skill, and ability to inspire trust. Unlike legally constituted authority and institutionally constituted authority, which are imposed on the clients, personally constituted authority must be bestowed on professionals by the clients.

To summarize, mental health professionals have considerable power and authority in relation to their clients. There is the power to provide involuntary treatment when circumstances warrant, the authority to determine access to resources, and the power to help clients with their problems.

Reluctance to Use Authority

Despite the considerable and broad-ranging authority that mental health providers can exert, there are a number of reasons why they frequently are not able to acknowledge it and utilize it well.

The first reason for not acknowledging it is a lack of awareness. Authority is a topic that is seldom addressed in professional training, even though it is inherent in all professional relationships. It is also seldom discussed in orientation programs, case conferences, and supervision sessions of those working with seriously mentally ill clients. This lack of discussion of power and authority over clients is not simply the result of oversight. Power is not talked about because mental health professionals are frequently uncomfortable with it.

This discomfort with authority can be due to conflicts within individual professionals. Most mental health professionals probably did not choose a career in the mental health field out of a wish to impose controls on other people. Although career motivations are many, it is likely that most individuals have chosen a mental health discipline out of a desire to be helpful to people in improving their lives and their health, not as agents of social control. In work with seriously mentally ill clients, this can create a mismatch between professionals' expectations of their work and what their work expects of them.

In some instances mental health professionals may have unresolved issues about authority figures that stem from their personal experiences. At best, these unresolved issues can also lead to a denial of authority implications in the clinical relationship; at worst, they can result in a misuse of power.

Another issue goes beyond the individual professional to the individuals' professions. The concept of self-determination is embedded in the principles of practice and ethical codes of the mental health professions. This is also evidenced in descriptions of psychotherapeutic orientations, which all require motivation for change and participation by the client in the treatment process. It is possible for clinicians to believe that the utilization of power is counter to the precepts of the mental health professions and their methods of practice.

Accepting and Utilizing Authority

Authority is inherent in all professional relationships, and seriously mentally ill clients have unique needs, which sometimes require that extraordinary powers be invoked on their behalf. Yet, mental health professionals are not prepared to accept this authority and may feel that its use is antithetical to the precepts and practices of their professions.

If it is not resolved, this dilemma can dramatically reduce a case manager's effectiveness. As discussed in Chapter 2, it is the case manager's relationship with the client that is the vehicle for change and growth. This relationship must be based on mutual expectations and trust. If case managers deny or do not accept the considerable authority that they do have, at least three difficulties arise. First of all, their ability to use their authority on behalf of their clients is limited. Second, they can possibly use their authority inappropriately, to the detriment of the clients. Finally, because the clients are usually fully aware of the power of the case manager, they will have difficulty trusting a clinician who denies it. This dilemma is resolved by understanding authority and accepting it as a tool that must be used effectively.

Because the first step in acceptance is understanding, the typology of authorities described earlier in this chapter should be understood by all staff working with seriously mentally ill clients. It is helpful to understand that authority is a necessary component in a professional relationship. It is useful to understand the purpose, derivation, limits, and expectations of all types of authority. With this understanding comes the realization that authority is something that must be used effectively in the clients' best interest and not be denied or avoided.

For instance, hospitalizing clients involuntarily is controlling their behavior, but it is not done out of a wish to strip them of their right of self-determination. Rather, it is done because they have lost their ability to make their own judgments without endangering themselves or others. In other words, external controls are imposed when internal control mechanisms have failed.

Although they might protest while being committed, a number of clients report in retrospect that they were helped by involuntary hospitalizations and that the hospitalization was necessary (Kane et al., 1983).

Acceptance of authority also comes from talking about it. For clinicians this can be done with peers and with supervisors. Discussing authority issues helps clarify the professional issues and the personal issues that may interfere with using authority effectively. To this end, it is helpful for supervisors to be alert for problems that case managers might have with authority, and raise them in supervision. It is an issue that is also productively raised in group supervision meetings, case conferences, and in-service training sessions.

To use authority effectively it must be an issue that is incorporated into the clinical relationship and the treatment process. It is usually best incorporated through openness and honesty, and it is necessary for case managers to be open and honest about it to themselves and to their clients. As an example, it is useful for the case manager to explain to the client, at the beginning of the relationship, the local requirements for involuntary hospitalization and how the case manager will implement these requirements when necessary. This should be done in a straightforward manner, using clear and simple language. It should convey the message that the case manager cares about the client and the client's well-being.

It has been argued that raising the issue of involuntary treatment early in the case management process will unduly frighten clients so they will not continue to work with the case management program. However, it is the experience of the author that being honest about commitment procedures actually helps with engagement. This is because the clients are usually aware of the commitment procedures and know that the case manager can use them. Knowing that the case manager is clear and comfortable with authority can help engender clients' trust. When told of the commitment procedures on the day they met, a woman with schizoaffective disorder told her case manager that she was glad to have someone to look out for her when she could not take care of herself. She just asked that the case manager not treat her meanly.

When a case manager does intervene in a way that goes against the client's wishes, either by providing involuntary hospitalization or in not supporting a client's stated desires, it is helpful to discuss this directly with the client. In doing so the case manager should check out the client's reaction and support the client's feelings. The case manager should also explain the reasoning for the intervention or decision, how the case manager understands the decision, and how, in the case manager's opinion, it was in the best interest of the client. When genuine, the case manager may express that the decision was made out of caring and concern for the client, even though the client does not like it. The case manager may need to acknowledge and accept that there can be a legitimate difference of opinion with the client, and may have to accept the client's anger.

When intervening to involuntarily commit a client, it is critical to take responsibility for the action. There is a temptation for case managers to put the responsibility on the physician who wrote the admission order, or the emergency service that implemented it, or the judge who approved it. While this may be true in a technical sense, it can be confusing and difficult for the client. Clients do have strong feelings about being hospitalized against their will, feelings that can range from embarrassment to rage. It is necessary for clients to express these feelings and work them through, and this is best done with those who make the decisions. If case managers take responsibility for their interventions, clients have an opportunity to work through their feelings and can more readily take responsibility for their behaviors.

Involuntary treatment is only a small component of care, even for those who are repeatedly hospitalized. The case manager's goal for most clients is to care for them voluntarily in the community. When clients are being treated voluntarily, it is also necessary for the case manager to use one's power openly and honestly. This means being honest about the case management program and the case manager's role. It includes being straightforward about what resources are available, how they can be accessed, and what criteria the case manager will use to determine how these resources will be used. It also means sharing knowledge and expertise about mental illness and its treatment, so that the clients can learn to manage their own illnesses.

By imparting knowledge, the case manager is giving clients the opportunity to participate in their own treatment. Client participation is one of the principles for case management services described in Chapter 1. Through knowledge and participation clients can empower themselves to direct their own lives. Client empowerment is a goal of case management, and case managers can support client empowerment if they are able to model the use of their own power, which can be accomplished only by understanding, accepting, and using it effectively.

Dependence, Independence, or Interdependence

The resolution of the problem of authority is to understand it as an inherent tool that must be accepted and used like any other tool. This is a practical solution. The problem of dependence requires a philosophical resolution.

Conceptualizing Interdependence

The concepts of individuality, individual responsibility, and independence provide the cornerstone of Occidental thought and tradition. Throughout the history of Western civilization, the individual has been determined the basic unit of society. Social order has been predicated on individuals assuming responsibility for meeting their own needs and accepting the consequences of their own behavior. Concomitant with the precept of the primacy of the individual is the concept of personal independence.

Individuals must function independently in order to meet their personal responsibilities.

The themes of individual responsibility and personal independence have provided the driving force for the development of the United States and are intertwined with every aspect of the dominant culture. For instance, the most important patriotic holiday celebrates the signing of the Declaration of Independence. This document represents more than one people demanding independence from the control and domination of another; it is also a declaration of the credo of individual independence, as expressed in the preamble, which states that among the inalienable rights are "life, liberty, and pursuit of happiness." Subsequently the concepts of "divine grace" as purported by the Calvinists, and "manifest destiny" in the nineteenth century, and more recently, "social Darwinism" have all provided justification for personal independence.

If the social ethic is to support and revere independence, where does this leave the disabled? What is the response to those who, by fate's hand, do not have the physical or mental capability to meet their own needs or fend for themselves, and, therefore, are dependent on others for their survival and well-being? Historically, the response has been ambivalent. The Old Testament admonishes that the gleanings of the harvest are to be left to the old and infirm. Traditionally, the church in Western civilization has played a major role in providing charity for the poor and disabled. This role continues through the delivery of a wide variety of social services by religious organizations in many communities.

A formalized role for government with the needy has been a more recent development. The Elizabethan Poor Laws passed in England in 1603 represented the first comprehensive attempt of government in the Western world to take responsibility for the poor and infirm. Two centuries later, the novels of Charles Dickens characterized the effect of these laws as more akin to penal servitude than benevolent charity. The Constitution of the United States of America states that one responsibility of government is to provide for the general welfare. However, it has been only in this century, and more particularly within the past 60 years, since the introduction of President Franklin D. Roosevelt's New Deal, that the federal government has considered that it is its responsibility to care for the dependent in our society.

Although it is in the best of Western traditions to provide for the old, the poor, and the sick (i.e., those who are dependent), the countervailing values of personal independence and responsibility create considerable ambivalence toward fully implementing these traditions. Helping the disabled is likely to leave a residue of pity, if not animosity. The themes of moral weakness, personal inadequacy, and downright laziness are inextricably intertwined with charitable efforts. This ambivalence to charity is found not only among the givers but also within the receivers. The ethic of independence is embedded within all individuals, the able and disabled alike. Those who find themselves in a dependent status often feel a diminished sense of worth and value at having to look to others for help.

The aspersions of accepting help fraudulently have fallen hardest on those with mental illness who often do not appear, nor necessarily act, disabled. This was illustrated by the policies of President Reagan's administration in the early 1980s. The stated policy was that the truly needy would not be hurt by the proposed cuts in social programs, with the implication that some were malingering on the welfare rolls and other services at the expense of hard-working citizens. The implementation of the policies was devastating for many seriously mentally ill individuals who were removed from eligibility for SSI because their disabilities prevented them from meeting increased bureaucratic requirements.

It is not surprising to find, among health professionals, ambivalence toward those who are dependent. As noted earlier in this chapter, the right of self-determination is embodied in the principles of professional organizations. This is directly derived from the credos of individual responsibility and personal independence. Many health professionals report that the greatest reward in their work is to use their expertise and skills in restoring individuals' functioning and independence. Mental health professionals' values and training focus on restoring functioning and independence and do not prepare them for working with those who have severe chronic dependency needs.

From this discussion it might seem that independence is good and dependence is bad. However, from another perspective it can be suggested that most people are highly dependent on others. In one sense individuals are dependent on others for the basic needs of food, clothing, and shelter. This is because in contemporary society not very many people grow their own food, build their own homes, and make their own clothes. Given specialized work roles and international markets, there can be literally hundreds of people from around the world who have been involved in creating the materials and designing, manufacturing, and distributing the clothes that most people put on in the morning.

In addition to physical well-being, people are dependent on others for their emotional well-being. Most individuals depend on their relationships with family, friends, and co-workers for support. Indeed, individuals frequently define themselves in terms of roles created by these relationships, such as spouse, parent, employee, friend, collaborator, advocate, and so forth. These roles provide meaning and rewards in life and require other people to play complementary roles. Mental health professionals are quite dependent on their clients, because without clients they would not have the same ability to earn an income. However, they are also dependent on clients for satisfying and rewarding careers. From this perspective, then, all people are greatly dependent on others for all basic needs.

On the other hand, many seriously mentally ill individuals could be viewed as highly independent. Many live out-of-doors and sleep under the skies. They eat from the surplus of our society, which can be found in the Dumpsters of our cities. They are unfettered by entangling human relationships and social expectations. To some they may be considered free spirits who are living out a romantic fantasy of total freedom and independence. However, it can also be suggested that their lives may best be summarized by the line from the song *Me & Bobby McGee*: "Freedom's just another word for nothing left to lose."[1]

The dichotomy between independence and dependence has been over-simplified to make the point that these concepts are not very useful in defining human relationships. More specifically, they are not helpful in understanding the relationship between mental health professionals and their clients. It is suggested that the concepts that should be considered in understanding these relationships are those of autonomous functioning and interdependence.

The interdependence of human relationships is central to Asian traditions. In Eastern thought the individual is sometimes described as an illusion. An analogy used to help understand this is that of a wave in the sea. As the wave crashes, droplets of water are formed. Although the droplets appear temporarily as individual entities, they inevitably fall back into the sea to become an indistinguishable part of the whole. Similarly, individual people are but temporal manifestations of the whole of the cosmos. In Asian cultures, then, the individual is not the basic unit of society. Rather, the family is the basic unit, and the individual is an interdependent part of the whole. That is, individuals depend on others, and others depend on the individual for the survival and well-being of all.

In Western cultures, the idea of interdependence is encompassed in systems theory, which suggests that the whole, the system, is greater than the sum of its individual parts. It also suggests than in any system there are interdependent relationships among all of the parts of the system, so that if one part is changed or altered, then all of the other parts will change.

The concept of interdependence is coming to the fore through the natural sciences in the relatively new field of ecology. Ecological thought is derived from systems theory and posits that there is an interdependent relationship among all living organisms, among all species of organisms, and among individuals within each species. From this viewpoint interdependence is not bad. Rather, it is an inescapable part of the human condition, and the concept of independence has little meaning. However, while every individual must depend on others, it is equally important that others be able to depend on each individual. Therefore, to participate in dependent relationships, all individuals need to function as well and autonomously as possible.

What is suggested here is that in working with seriously mentally ill clients, the goal is not to foster independence but rather to foster autonomous functioning, so that clients can participate fully in interdependent relationships. These are relationships in which they not only receive support and sustenance from others but can also give of themselves and be supportive and helpful to others. In interdependent relationships both parties depend on each other.

Supporting Interdependent Relationships

Through the concept of interdependence in the relationship between case manager and client, it becomes clear that it may not be helpful to discourage the dependence of the client on the case manager. Rather, it is often necessary to foster appropriate dependency on the case manager in order to create a secure and supportive environment in which clients can develop psychologically, grow interpersonally, and learn the skills to function more autonomously. In short, it is necessary to support genuine dependency so that the client can develop more autonomous functioning and consequently participate in more interdependent relationships.

One can find support in the psychiatric literature for developing interdependent alliances that support genuine dependence. Attachment theory posits that attachments, another way of referring to interdependent relationships, are necessary throughout life. From this view it is desirable for adults to be attached to each other. Indeed, the absence of attachment can indicate pathology (Ainsworth, 1972). Therefore, developing a relationship in which a client can depend on the case manager allows for the development of a psychologically healthy relationship. As described in

Chapter 12, the clinical case manager can model an interdependent relationship that the client may be able to generalize to other relationships.

Seriously mentally ill clients do have difficulty in establishing and maintaining useful attachments. Burnham et al., in discussing ambivalence in clients with schizophrenia, describe the "need/fear" dilemma. The dilemma is that a mentally ill client recognizes the deficits of the illness and understands the needs for help but also feels highly vulnerable and fears that the helper will take over and engulf the client (Burnham, Gladstone, & Gibson, 1969). Because many clients have experience with mental health services taking total control of their lives, it is understandable, in light of this duality, that clients are reluctant to become involved with case managers and other care providers.

Several authors have commented on the importance of supporting genuine dependency needs with seriously mentally ill clients. Watson (1983), in describing the working relationship with seriously mentally ill clients, has stated:

> Independence is not the opposite of dependency, but is achieved gradually through the satisfaction of various dependency needs. With a cultural premium on self-sufficiency, community mental health programs are all too likely to posit independent functioning, not as a long-term goal, but as a criterion for participation or for success of short-term helping efforts, without regard to where the client is on the developmental continuum. (p. 65)

Sable (1979) restates this concept as follows: "Workers worried about dependency needs may resist providing a secure base for the clients for fear that they will become overdependent." She goes on to state: "Such pressure for self-sufficiency may overlook the client's inborn natural striving to feel securely attached to another" (pp. 140-141).

Harris and Bergman (1984), in a paper on working with "revolving door" clients, argue as follows:

> Although clinical personnel must be careful not to foster unnecessary dependency, they must be able to allow for and respect the legitimate needs for dependency that do arise. Similarly, although autonomy is a goal that should be supported, patients should not be catapulted into situations containing demands for independence that they cannot handle. Establishing a balance between autonomy and dependency, and allowing that balance to readjust over time, is a difficult task. Increases in autonomy must parallel changes in the patient's psychological development. (p. 286)

To summarize, supporting genuine dependency needs is considered a necessary role for mental health professionals. One major area of disability for the severely mentally ill client is that of not being able to establish and maintain constructive human relationships on which to depend. It is, therefore, incumbent on case managers to offer stable, consistent, trustworthy, and supportive relationships on which clients can rely, so that they can develop the ability to function as autonomously as possible and participate in interdependent relationships. Bowlby (1973, p. 250) has stated this in terms that are quite appropriate in considering seriously mentally ill clients: "Paradoxically, the truly self-reliant person . . . proves to be by no means as independent as cultural stereotypes suppose. An essential ingredient is a capacity to rely trustingly on others when occasion demands [and] to know on whom it is appropriate to rely."

Note

1. *Me & Bobby McGee* by Kris Kristofferson and Fred Foster, © 1969 TEMI Combine INC. All Rights Controlled by Combine Music Corp. and Administered by EMI Blackwood Music Inc. (BMI). All Rights Reserved. International Copyright Secured. Used by Permission.

References

Ainsworth, M.D.S. (1972). Attachment and dependency: A comparison. In J. L. Gerwitz (Ed.), *Attachment and dependency* (pp. 97-137). Washington, DC: Winston.

Bowlby, J. (1973). Separation: Anxiety and anger. *Attachment and loss* (Vol. 2, p. 250). New York: Basic Books.

Burnham, D. L., Gladstone, A. I., & Gibson, R. W. (1969). *Schizophrenia and the need/fear dilemma*. New York: International Universities Press.

Campbell J., & Schraiber, R. (1989). *The well-being project: Mental health clients speak for themselves. Pursuit of wellness: Vol. 6.* Sacramento, CA: The California Network of Mental Health Clients.

Harris, M., & Bergman, H. C. (1984). Reassessing the revolving door: A developmental perspective on the young adult chronic patient. *American Journal of Orthopsychiatry, 54*(2), 281-289.

Kane, J. M., Quitkin, F., Rifkin, A., Wegner, J., Rosenberg, G., & Borenstein, M. (1983). Attitudinal changes of involuntarily committed patients following treatment. *Archives of General Psychiatry, 40*, 374-377.

Ngokwey, N. (1989). On the specificity of healing functions: A study of diagnosis in three faith healing institutions in Feira (Bahia, Brazil). *Social Science and Medicine, 29*(4), 515-526.

Palmer, S. E. (1983). Authority: An essential part of practice. *Social Work, 28*(2), 120-125.

Sable, P. (1979). Differentiating between attachment and dependency in theory and practice. *Social Case Work,* 138-144.

Squier, R. W. (1990). A model of empathic understanding and adherence to treatment regimens in practitioner-patient relationships. *Social Science and Medicine, 30*(3), 325-329.

Watson, M. A. (1983). *The working relationship in social work service to the chronically mentally ill.* Unpublished manuscript.

14

Implementing Clinical Case Management Services

ROBERT W. SURBER

This book is based on the experience of the Citywide Case Management Team, which operates in San Francisco, California. The other chapters describe what the staff of this team have learned about providing direct services to a population of seriously mentally ill adults. This chapter focuses on what has been learned about implementing and managing these services.

The first part of this discussion will describe the history of the Citywide Case Management Team, because the issues that this program struggled with in its creation and development are illustrative of the issues that will face many programs that serve this population. The chapter will then focus on the needs of case managers and will suggest methods to provide support for them.

History of a Clinical Case Management Program

The Citywide Case Management Team grew out of the frustration of the staff of the Department of Psychiatry at San Francisco General Hospital. The experience of the psychiatric inpatient and psychiatric emergency service staffs was that many patients were repeatedly admitted to acute services and were often transferred to long-term locked care, but when they eventually returned to the community, they received very little treatment or support. These individuals did not link to community treatment services, both because they were not welcomed by those services and because they did not seek mental health treatment. They often failed at linking with supportive services that they wanted because the behaviors or disabilities that resulted from their untreated illnesses created overwhelming obstacles to their receiving them.

One study of recidivists at San Francisco General Hospital during this period indicated that 6.5% of the patients were responsible for 23.7% of all admissions. Therefore, there were economic concerns about how limited resources were being utilized with little benefit, in addition to concerns about inadequate community treatment (Goldfinger, Hopkin, & Surber, 1984).

In 1981 the Northeast Mental Health Center, one of five community mental health centers in San Francisco, issued a request for proposals to take over the administration of a small case management program that served psychiatric hospital recidivists who lived in this center's catchment area. This was the catchment area that admitted the largest number of patients to San Francisco General Hospital. The existing program was designed to serve clients for 90 days, with the purpose of linking them to ongoing outpatient, day treatment, and supportive services. This program's staff was composed of paraprofessionals.

A physician and a social worker at San Francisco General developed a proposal that was radically different from the existing program. The proposal was based on the premise that effective work with clients with the greatest needs required staff with the greatest understanding of mental illness, the greatest skills in treating it, and sufficient time to provide comprehensive and continuous care. Therefore, the proposal included a professional staff with small caseloads of between 15 and 20 clients. This meant that each client would have an individual case manager, who would be responsible for developing and implementing a comprehensive treatment plan. A critical component of the conceptualization was that the work would occur through a trusting, supportive, and therapeutic relationship between client and case manager. Therefore, it was necessary that each client have an individual case manager to foster the development of this relationship.

The proposal also required that case management services be provided for indefinite periods of time and that the delivery of clinical services be integrated with the provision of practical supports. To this end, the initial proposal co-located the case management program within a mental health outpatient clinic that had the capacity to prescribe and administer medications for its clients. The program staff, known as the Northeast Recidivism Team, initially included three case managers.

Admission criteria for the program have always been based on recidivism to acute psychiatric services. Originally, the criteria were that the client be treated in an acute psychiatric inpatient service three times in the 12 months, or two times in the 6 months preceding the referral. The criteria have been broadened more recently to require only two inpatient admissions or five psychiatric emergency service visits in the 12 months prior to referral.

Staff have been expected to accept all referrals that meet these criteria. This has meant that clients could not be excluded for behavioral problems, or lack of motivation, or particular diagnoses, or substance abuse, or any other problems. Rather, staff have been expected to attempt to develop effective interventions for all clients who are referred. The only exception has been when the team has been full and not open for referral. During these times clients are referred to traditional outpatient services. This is because clients with such urgent needs cannot be kept on a waiting list.

Clients, of course, can refuse case management services, but staff are expected to make assertive but respectful efforts to involve them in the program. When clients who have refused care or who cannot be found reappear in inpatient or other settings, the case manager they have previously worked with will again offer services.

Within the first 2 years of its existence, the program was able to demonstrate that it was achieving its goals. One study demonstrated that clients utilized 50% fewer hospital days in the first year of work with the team, as compared to the year prior to admission (Williams, 1982). Another showed a reduction in hospitalization, as well as increased income and stable housing for the clients during the first 6 months in the program (Chafetz, 1988). Later, data showed that the program was successful at linking with 80% of the clients who were referred to it. Clients who had no history of linking voluntarily with outpatient treatment linked with the program at the same rate as clients who did have a history of utilizing outpatient treatment (Fariello, 1989).

Because the program serves clients that other mental health programs are reluctant to treat, and because it has been demonstrated to reduce acute care costs as well as improve the quality of clients' lives, the mental health administration has consistently increased funding to expand the program. This expansion has been both to serve more clients and to respond to special client needs. Eventually, the team added its own physician and nursing personnel to prescribe and administer medications within the program rather than depend solely on the host clinic.

A major program development occurred in 1984. At this time the San Francisco Department of Public Health consolidated five mental health centers into one mental health administration. The Northeast Recidivism Team was asked to expand to serve clients throughout the city. A decision was made to do this by hiring additional staff who were outstationed to several outpatient clinics throughout the city. The program was then re-named the Citywide Case Management Team.

This expansion created a number of opportunities, and problems, for the team. As the program's focus moved from serving clients living only in the urban center to those living in neighborhoods throughout the city, staff had to learn to engage and treat a broader client population. In residential neighborhoods clients were much more likely to live with and/or have the support of families. This required a change in approach for many clients to involve their families and educate and support them so that they could better support the clients. As families often provided help in practical needs, such as housing and income, many case managers had to find other client goals to work with in engaging them. One goal that many clients expressed was for paid employment.

Expanding throughout the city created both the responsibility and the opportunity to develop a staffing pattern that reflected the diversity of San Francisco. This meant recruiting additional African-American staff, bilingual and bicultural Asian-American and Latino staff, and staff from sexual preference minorities. The fact that many of the clinics into which staff were being outstationed already focused on specific minority populations made many of the new positions more attractive to minority candidates.

There were significant problems in incorporating the case management staff into traditional outpatient clinics. The case managers were not always well understood or accepted by the professionals in the clinics. Some thought the work of case managers to be beneath professionally trained staff, and some thought the integration of practical and psychotherapeutic issues to be clinically inappropriate. Many found that having lower functioning clients who may not be well kempt, may create disturbances, and are not required to keep regular appointments to be disruptive for their clinic program. These issues have been dealt with by incorporating the case management staff into the host clinics and sharing some clinic responsibilities, such as serving as officer of the day; by participation in staff meetings and other clinic activities; and by educating clinic staff in case conferences and informal discussions. Host clinic physicians also treat many of the case management team clients. Over time, the case managers have generally been accepted in the clinics and respected for their ability to effectively treat a difficult population.

At the same time that case managers have had to become comfortable in a host clinic, they have had to be integrated into their own program. This has created an ongoing tension for staff that has had to be continuously addressed through efforts at providing support and team-building for the case management staff as a whole.

Although the original conceptualization of the program proved to be basically sound, and has been demonstrated to improve clients' lives, no one is completely satisfied with the overall effectiveness of the program. Some clients cannot be engaged into care, some cannot live effectively in the community, and some do not satisfactorily pursue their goals. Therefore, staff have continuously strived to improve the services. In this regard, the program has been seen as a laboratory in which staff are encouraged to experiment with new approaches to respond to unmet needs.

There have been a number of specific issues and needs that have had to be addressed in caring for the team's clients. One that was identified early on was that of substance abuse. A majority of the team's clients have used drugs and/or alcohol to the degree that it interferes with their care and treatment. Because of their mental health problems, these clients are usually excluded from substance abuse treatment, and because of their substance abuse are excluded from many mental health services. Therefore, the staff needed to develop expertise in treating both disorders concurrently. This required staff training in assessing and treating substance abuse, developing substance abuse education and treatment groups, identifying and working with 12-Step programs that would accept mentally ill clients, and advocating for these clients to receive the supports and services that they deserved.

Many of the clients of the program were unable to develop social relationships, and consequently languished in their hotel rooms with few activities to ameliorate their symptoms and enhance their lives. Yet many were also too low functioning to either be accepted into or utilize the socialization day treatment programs that were available. In response to this need several members of the case management staff developed a socialization group that taught socialization skills and provided socialization opportunities. Another case manager has established a Latino men's group in which the members organize social activities. Yet another staff member organized a weekend camping trip for several clients.

As noted above, the case management program was designed to accept all clients who met the recidivism criteria. An unexpected problem developed when some of the clients referred were not allowed to enter host clinics because of previous violent, threatening, or disruptive behaviors. Some of these clients could be seen in community settings; but with others, it was too dangerous for case management staff to see them alone in the community. The program responded by locating a case manager in the Psychiatric Emergency Service at San Francisco General Hospital, a setting that provides security for both clients and staff.

In addition to working with hospital recidivists, the program has recently developed a position for working with severely mentally ill clients referred from the county jail. This position was funded as one component of a multiservice package to divert mentally ill clients from the jail into community-based care.

Another example of innovation is the recent development of the peer case management project. Peer case managers are consumers of mental health services who have been hired to work with clinical case managers to assist in the implementation of clients' service plans. In implementing this project a committee of professional staff, mental health consumers, and members of the families of mental health clients worked together to define the role, design an orientation and training program, and recruit and select the peer case managers. Members of the committee have developed a process to provide ongoing support to peer case managers as they implement the role. Peer case managers work collaboratively with clinical case managers to implement specific aspects of the treatment plan, and work independently in leading mutual support groups. The specifics of the role will continue to develop with experience.

It is the experience of most of the program's staff that the program has been quite successful at helping clients live stably in the community. However, many staff are not as satisfied with their efforts to support their clients' attempts to pursue their goals of work, constructive activities, and establishing meaningful interdependent relationships. The life-enhancement project is reviewing how well the team as a whole is succeeding in these areas and developing linkages with community resources and activities within the program to improve its effectiveness.

The history of the Citywide Case Management Team demonstrates that there is no correct way to implement a clinical case management program for seriously mentally ill clients. When this program began, no one would have envisioned that it would eventually have staff located in nine separate clinics throughout the city. No one considered the need for a safe and secure setting for clients whose behaviors excluded them from traditional outpatient clinics. No one imagined that mental health consumers would be hired as staff to provide direct services. What this program has tried to do is both respond to local needs and take advantage of the opportunities that have arisen to meet those needs.

There are distinct advantages and disadvantages to the program's criteria for admission, its treatment approach, and its organizational structure. For example, by treating only acute care recidivists, the team reduces acute care costs in the city and has been afforded the flexibility to develop innovative approaches. The easily measurable admission criteria have also protected the program from being flooded with referrals and have prevented other services from referring clients for whom they have clear responsibility. On the other hand, these clear criteria are necessarily arbitrary, and many clients who need case management services are denied them.

The individual approach has made it possible to develop an ongoing clinical relationship that is extremely flexible and allows for practical, psychological, and interpersonal interventions to be made singly or concomitantly, as needed. It also makes it possible to have a number of case managers (one or more) in several program sites. However, relying heavily on an individual case manager can cause problems of discontinuity when the case manager goes on vacation or leaves the program.

Placing staff in a number of clinics has had a number of advantages, which include maximizing local resources, enhancing the program's ability to hire an ethnically diverse staff, and locating case managers near the clients and families. Nevertheless, case managers have sometimes felt isolated and not fully supported by or incorporated into their own program. The decentralization of staff has also made it impossible, thus far, to develop 24-hour-a-day or 7-day-a-week support for clients. This might have occurred by now if all 30 staff were located at one site.

These examples are cited to illustrate that there are a number of choices to be made in implementing case management services, and that there is no one best choice. The question, then, is what criteria to use in making program design decisions? Bachrach has noted that model programs that have been successful in one community have often not worked as well in other settings. She suggests that rather than attempt to transplant programs as a whole, it may be more effective to implement a new program that is based on the principles of the original model and is then adapted to local conditions (Bachrach, 1988).

In developing the Citywide Case Management Team, the program decisions have been guided both by the principles described in Chapter 1 and by local circumstances. As with any complex effort, there have been many challenges and struggles in creating, developing, and maintaining this case management program. In responding to these struggles, the leadership has stood firm on the principles and has been very flexible in working out the details. For instance, the program has resisted every bureaucratic or funding expectation that could limit either the time that clients can remain with the program or the breadth of interventions provided, because of the principles of continuous and comprehensive care. Due to the need to develop culturally competent services, the program has often delayed filling vacant positions until bicultural and/or bilingual staff could be recruited.

On the other hand, great flexibility has often been necessary. In order to maintain the support of the mental health administration and maintain funding, the staff have made every effort to meet burdensome documentation requirements to maximize revenues, to work collaboratively with other services, and to respond to other requests.

A great number of program design elements have been made in response to local opportunities and resources. That the program serves primarily acute care recidivists is due to the fact that this was the population that the original funding source wanted to serve. Similarly, the project to serve clients referred from the jail grew out of the wish of a member of the Board of Supervisors to reduce jail overcrowding by developing human services, rather than building another jail. The hiring of peer case managers was possible, in part, because of the interest and support of local consumer and family organizations. A recent expansion occurred because of an opportunity to divert funds to the program from a contract for acute hospitalization. Therefore, the program exists and has been able to grow because it has seized the opportunities to obtain new resources or broaden its operation as they have become available.

The other determinant of program decisions has been a lack of community resources. Staff have developed methods to serve clients with substance abuse problems and have implemented socialization groups because other options were not available to meet these needs. Therefore, the program design is based partly on what other programs or individuals cannot or will not do to meet client needs.

Had those who wished to develop case management services in San Francisco in 1980 insisted on one particular service model with rigidly defined interventions, the Citywide Case Management Team would probably not have grown as it has, might not be as responsive to client needs, and might not exist at all. By founding its program on a series of principles that have been implemented flexibly, and by making use of available resources in responding to local need, the team has flourished.

Conversely, a clinical case management program in another community will likely be organized quite differently because the context in which it develops will be different in terms of local priorities, available resources, and client needs.

Providing Support for Case Managers

It is the staff who make a clinical case management program. It is only through the skills, abilities, and resourcefulness of case managers, and other staff who provide direct care, that clients are served. It is necessary that staff have the resources to do this work. These resources include practical support, administrative support, and staff support and development.

Practical Support

There a number of practical resources that case managers require to do their work. The most important of these is time. It takes considerable time to engage clients and develop and implement a comprehensive and individualized service plan. It also takes time to identify and utilize natural supports, such as family, friends, landlords, pastors, and employers.

Case managers can only have the time they need to adequately serve each client by being responsible for small caseloads. When caseloads become overly large, case managers focus on client crises out of necessity and cannot proactively respond comprehensively to client needs that could increase functioning and avert crises (Reinke & Greenly, 1986).

There is not an absolutely correct caseload size. It has been suggested that the optimal size for a clinical case management caseload is 15 clients (Harris & Bergman, 1988). It is the experience of the Citywide Case Management Team that the optimal number varies over time. While developing a new caseload, a case manager may only be able to manage a few clients who have recently been released from acute hospitalization. During this period it is necessary that a case manager's supervisor carefully monitor how quickly the caseload increases. On the other hand, a case manager who has been working with clients for a number of years may be comfortable with a caseload of more than 20. In general, a full-time case manager has been able to manage a caseload of between 15 and 20 clients, when most of them have been on the caseload for a period of time and there are only a few newly referred clients. In situations of great client need and few community resources, the number may be lower.

Another critical need of case managers who work with a seriously mentally ill clientele is very close access to psychopharmacological treatment. Because most case managers are not physicians, or nurses, or psychiatric technicians, they cannot prescribe or administer medications. Yet, medications are often critical to a client's ability to live successfully in the community.

Whether the physician and nursing personnel work within the case management program or whether they are hired by a separate agency, it is particularly necessary that they work in a hand-in-glove relationship with the case manager. This includes close communication about client needs, wishes, treatment history, and medication response, including side effects. This also includes medical personnel who support the principles and approaches of the case manager, who are flexible in their approach to medication treatment, who are willing to see clients at unscheduled times and in community settings, and who are respectful of client wishes.

Many of a case manager's activities must occur in a variety of community settings, and case managers must have the mobility to be where they are needed. This requires ready access to transportation through a program car or van, the ability to reimburse staff to use their personal vehicles, or public transportation. This also requires administrative support and program flexibility for case managers to be where their clients need them, when they need to be there.

A very helpful concrete resource is cash. Most case management clients are very poor and have few economic or social resources to manage unexpected situations. What would be a minor problem for many people could be a catastrophe for those with a serious mental illness. The availability of a loan or a small cash grant to buy food, or clothes, or a room for the night, or bus fare, or other supplies can be enormously helpful to clients and, on occasion, can avert a hospitalization.

Administrative Support

Case managers work within an agency and within a community context. Their success is as dependent on the support they receive for themselves and their clients as it is on their individual efforts. Of course, the concrete supports described above and the staff support described later in this chapter require administrative support.

However, the administration of a case management program also has the responsibility to support access to community resources for case managers and their clients. An individual case manager's ability to advocate with many human service bureaucracies is limited. An agency, such as a case management program, has a greater ability to advocate with other agencies or providers for an individual client or groups of clients. Case managers must be able to call on their supervisors or program director to intervene when their own efforts are not successful at meeting client needs.

It is also necessary for the leadership of the case management program to respond to unmet client need, both at higher administrative levels and through the political process. This means directly approaching or utilizing the case management program's parent organization to reach the larger human service establishment or the local political establishment, to encourage existing services to be more responsive to seriously mentally ill clients or to develop new services that respond to unmet need.

Another administrative responsibility is to evaluate the efforts of the case management program. Case managers wish to serve their clients well and need objective measures that evaluate their program. Data from objective measures is needed, along with the subjective experience of case managers and clients, to have an overall view of the effectiveness of the program. This feedback is necessary for case managers to continue to improve their services.

The administration has an additional responsibility to define clear expectations and boundaries for case managers and their role. It is imperative that case managers know what they are expected to do, what support they will receive to do it, and the limits of that support. This includes who they will serve, how they will be referred, and the general parameters of the interventions. They must also know what is expected of them in terms of relationships with other agencies and community resources.

It is particularly important to address the issue of personal safety for case management staff. In general, this involves emphasizing that the case managers' safety is of paramount concern, and that they either must not enter or must leave situations if they feel any concern for their own well-being. This also involves incorporating safety training into supervision and training sessions.

Finally, the administration must endeavor to shield the staff from as many burdensome bureaucratic expectations as possible. In this era of overbearing documentation requirements, this can be difficult. Nevertheless, with diligence some of the mandates that come from above, reducing the time to serve clients, can eventually be mitigated or reversed.

Staff Support and Development

To provide optimal care to clients, the staff of a case management program require direct support in a variety of ways. This begins with recruitment and continues through their careers with the program. Recruitment and selection of case managers and other treatment staff is critical to the success of the program. These individuals must meet a number of criteria, including a genuine interest in working with seriously mentally ill clients, enthusiasm for providing a broad array of interventions in community settings, knowledge of mental illness and its treatment, skills in engaging reluctant clients, and the ability to use themselves to provide clinical and practical interventions. It is also necessary to have bilingual and/or bicultural staff who reflect the ethnic diversity of the clients and can communicate effectively with the clients. In short, a case management program must be able to recruit the best of mental health professionals.

Unfortunately, case management is frequently not viewed as a highly desirable role for many mental health professionals. This is for a variety of factors, such as misunderstandings about the skills required to perform this role, stigma toward seriously mentally ill clients, fears about working with unpredictable clients in unsupervised settings, and often low pay.

A number of factors can increase a program's ability to recruit well-qualified personnel. The first is a good salary and benefits package. Unless case managers are compensated at a level that is competitive with other mental health professionals, it will be extremely difficult to either hire or retain the best available candidates.

It is also helpful, in recruiting well-trained and highly qualified staff, to emphasize the clinical knowledge and skills required to perform this work. Candidates need to know that their training and skills will be valued, and that they will have the opportunity to develop these skills while incorporating them with new approaches. Similarly, many candidates will want to know that there are opportunities to take on additional and higher-level responsibilities as their abilities develop. One of the best recruitment tools is to expose candidates to an existing staff who are enthusiastic toward the work and challenged by it.

It is not always possible to hire staff who meet all of the criteria described above. In making choices, it is necessary to remember that the essential criteria are an eagerness to care for disenfranchised clients and an interest in integrating complex clinical and practical interventions. Knowledge and skills can be taught, but caring attitudes and enthusiasm cannot. From this perspective it is sometimes a useful strategy to hire recent graduates who are challenged by a new approach. This approach to recruitment requires strong supervisory capabilities.

Recruiting bilingual and/or bicultural staff requires additional strategies to those already described. It is important to remember that staff from ethnic minority backgrounds have varied career goals. Some wish to work primarily with clients from their own ethnic background, while others wish to work with a culturally diverse clientele. Therefore, to respond to the goals of different individuals, programs must be prepared to be flexible in terms of client assignment.

Some minority professionals are attracted to a setting where they do not feel isolated in terms of being token members of a minority population, or by being the only ones who are interested in serving clients from their own ethnic group. It can be helpful to create work settings where minority case managers can work in groups with others of a similar background who are interested in serving a particular client group. Working collaboratively in a setting that focuses on a particular minority population encourages the development of approaches that are responsive to the specific needs and resources of that ethnic group (Zatzick & Lu, 1991).

Recruiting minority professionals and bilingual professionals requires patience and tenacity. There are fewer of these individuals in most communities and they may be heavily recruited by other agencies. It is helpful to advertise broadly, and it is often necessary to wait for some time to fill a vacant position that is slated to work with ethnic minority clients or clients who are monolingual or more comfortable being served in a language other than English. There are many legitimate pressures that make it difficult to wait to fill positions. Nevertheless, these must be weighed against the need to hire staff who have the knowledge and skills necessary to provide the most effective services.

There is little point in recruiting the best available staff if they do not remain with the program. Considerably more effort needs to be spent in maintaining and developing staff than in recruiting them. It has been acknowledged throughout this book that the clinical case management role can be a very difficult one that challenges case managers in many ways. It is also a role that takes considerable knowledge and skill, if not wisdom. All case managers, then, will make mistakes in judgment, will have clients do poorly, will become frustrated, and will question their abilities and themselves.

The primary support that a case manager needs is supervision. This includes having a primary supervisor who will meet regularly with the staff member. Generally, this will be for at least an hour a week, or more often when the staff member is new, or as needed when the case manager is struggling with a particular issue.

The supervisor is responsible for seeing that the case manager not only develops the ability to deliver both practical and clinical interventions but also meets all of the administrative requirements of the program. Because this is a lot to ask of one individual, the supervisor may want to make other resources, such as readings, trainings, or consultants, available to the staff member.

Group supervision is a necessary adjunct to individual supervision. In group supervision the staff discuss case material and clinical issues with one another. As with any group process, case managers learn that the problems they struggle with are shared by others, that they have something to contribute to their peers, and that there a number of helpful ways to approach any issue.

Some of the best support for mental health professionals comes from their colleagues. Case managers should be encouraged to discuss their clinical problems and practical concerns both with colleagues within their own program and with staff in other mental health programs.

In-service training is a necessary component of staff development. When in-service training sessions are provided regularly, such as for a half day each month, they become a tangible means of support as well as an opportunity for staff to learn. In-service training sessions can be didactic presentations, process discussions, or a combination of both. They can be prepared and led by staff of the program or by outside experts. Topics for training should be based on staff needs identified by both the program leadership and the staff. These topics might address specific knowledge areas, such as substance abuse assessment and treatment, approaches to working with families, psychopharmacology, work with HIV-infected clients, and diagnostic issues. The topics could also address community resources by inviting staff from other agencies to describe their programs, or to develop strategies to work more collaboratively with these programs. Finally, the topics might include internal program issues, such as refining the approaches of the service, managing stress, or dealing with the loss of clients.

In order to remain with the program, case managers need to feel that they are growing and developing new skills. One very gratifying activity for many case managers is the opportunity to train others in this role. Providing clinical internships for mental health trainees not only helps to prepare professionals for work with seriously mentally ill clients, but also challenges their staff supervisors to continue learning and developing their skills. Similarly, some case management staff members wish to share what they have learned in doing this work by making presentations at professional meetings or publishing in professional journals. Case managers should be supported in their desire to utilize their expertise by having the opportunity to train students or by being encouraged to present or publish their work.

Just as the purpose of a case management program is to support clients in achieving their goals and dreams, it must also support case managers in achieving their goals and dreams. If the program supports staff in their efforts to learn and implement new techniques, to serve additional populations, to continue to learn and grow, and to achieve their career aspirations, they will be most likely to remain with and further develop it.

References

Bachrach, L. L. (1988). On exporting and importing model programs. *Hospital and Community Psychiatry, 39*, 1257-1258.

Chafetz, L. (1988). Recidivist clients: A review of pilot data. *Archives of Psychiatric Nursing, 2*(1), 14-20.

Fariello, D. F. (1989). Unpublished data of Citywide Case Management Team, San Francisco, CA.

Goldfinger, S. M., Hopkin, J. T., & Surber, R. W. (1984). Treatment resisters or system resisters?: Toward a better service system for acute care recidivists. In B. Pepper & H. Ryglewcz (Eds.), *New directions for mental health services: Advances in treating the young adult chronic patient* (pp. 17-27). San Francisco: Jossey-Bass.

Harris, M., & Bergman, H. C. (1988). Misconceptions about use of case management services by the chronic mentally ill: A utilization analysis. *Hospital and Community Psychiatry, 39*(12), 1276-1280.

Reinke, B., & Greenly, J. R. (1986). Organizational analysis of three community support program models. *Hospital and Community Psychiatry, 37*(6), 624-629.

Williams, E. (1982). *An investigation of hospitalizations for clients pre-entry and post-entry to the Northeast Recidivism Team.* Unpublished manuscript.

Zatzick, D. F., & Lu, F. G. (1991). The ethnic/minority focus unit as a training site in transcultural psychiatry. *Academic Psychiatry, 15*(4), 218-225.

PART IV

Epilogue (A Case Study)

15

Sí, Se Puede *(Yes, You Can)*

VICKI KELLER

"My girlfriend just dumped me. My family won't speak to me. I'm being kicked out of the residential treatment center and I have no place to go. I don't even have enough money to buy a pack of cigarettes. I stopped my meds because I'm not a mental patient. My counselor at the day center is on vacation and no one there will help me. I'm not ever going back. I think I want to jump off the Golden Gate Bridge."

Hopelessness, rage, and fear were the warp and weave of the tapestry of crises in which I first started working with Juan. Everything he said was colored with expletives, tears, pounding on the desk, and digressions that just did not make sense. How was I ever going to engage someone so desperate and overwhelmed? How could I do it quickly enough before he became truly suicidal, and carefully enough to allow trust to develop?

I just had to be direct: "So you're afraid I will abandon you, too?" A pause, a nod, some tears, and when the shaking subsided, I knew something had started. Would it be a nightmare or an adventure? What was I in for, and was I up to it? Was he up for it? Whatever it was to be, I made a commitment. We were in it together, and I would learn whether my skill, determination, and luck would have any power to help.

I had actually met Juan 2 months before, in the acute inpatient psychiatric ward of the county hospital where he had been admitted involuntarily for the fifth time in 2 years. He had been brought in by the police after assaulting his brother and threatening his brother-in-law with a knife. He was referred to Citywide Case Management because he was an acute care recidivist and because the outpatient clinic was reluctant to accept him due to his violent history and substance abuse.

On the ward Juan looked younger than his 21 years. He was suspicious and guarded, with a thin veneer of forced politeness. The distrust in his eyes at times gave way to a pleading glimmer of hope. He adamantly denied any psychiatric problems, blaming his hospitalization on vengeful family members, sadistic police, and then on his drug use. He was agitated and had to leave the interview twice to smoke a cigarette and then use the toilet.

Before the interview I had met with the treatment staff to gather history and determine how he could be treated in the community after discharge while ensuring everyone's safety. History from staff, records, and Juan himself showed that violence was directed mainly at family members during arguments or while under the influence of drugs. At that point, to be cautious, I made the decision to see him only in public areas, such as a treatment facility or an entitlement office. If outreaches were necessary I would do them with a partner or with the police.

During the initial interview I explained our services, framing them as assistance to avoid further hospitalizations. Juan identified a lack of housing and money as his most pressing needs. I did not confront his denial of psychiatric problems directly but did make explicit my expectations of nonviolent behavior. Juan was agreeable to the plan of a halfway house, and a date was set to accompany him to the entitlement office. He reluctantly make a verbal contract for taking medication, for sobriety, and for no harm to self and others. It was clear that much of his agreeableness was due to his eagerness to leave the hospital, but the expectations connected with the offer of help needed to be clear from the beginning. I anticipated aloud with him that he might break the contract but that I would expect him to live up to it, not as a matter of morality but as a pragmatic path for achieving his goals.

I gathered fragments of information over the next months, but it was an arduous process to digest and formulate them into a coherent whole. Juan was born in rural Mexico, the youngest of 10 children. His earliest memory was of his mother leaving (for the United States) when he was 4 years old without saying goodbye or telling him. His father was older than 60 when Juan was born, and Juan describes him as a bingeing alcoholic who was verbally and physically abusive. At age 12 Juan ran away to live with his grandmother in a large city, but spent much of his time in the streets. When he was 15 he was brought to San Francisco, where his mother and several siblings were already living. Initially, he lived with his mother and siblings for about 9 months. He described his mother as extremely strict,

religious, and authoritarian. Juan could not tolerate her rules and regulations. He also tried living with a brother and a sister and their families.
Juan did poorly in school and began using drugs. This is when his contact
with the mental health and legal systems began. He was treated for almost
a year at the adolescent unit of the State Hospital, where he learned
English and received educational credits. After discharge he worked for
short periods at several jobs, terminated by being fired or being hospitalized.
He stopped medications and dropped out of mental health treatment
whenever he started feeling better, and never really connected to any
services. He also hastened his relapses by episodic polysubstance abuse.

Working with Juan was never easy. His story was fragmented, confusing, and contradictory, making it difficult to get a grasp on the most
significant problems. His presentations from session to session, and from
one service provider to another, were remarkably variable. Thus, it was a
continuous and constant process of assessment. His records reflected this
variability of presentations. He had been given diagnoses of schizophrenia,
bipolar affective disorder, schizoaffective disorder, adjustment disorder,
conduct disorder, major depression, and substance abuse disorder. The contradictory information in the records and the lack of symptom substantia-
tion (i.e., a psychological evaluation indicated that he was a diagnostic
dilemma with no evidence of mood or thought disorder, but he was given
a provisional diagnosis of schizoaffective disorder) alerted me to the
possibility that Juan might have a borderline personality disorder. Most
of Juan's contacts outside of his stay at the State Hospital had been when
he was in an acute crisis phase. He had never really connected to any service
provider long enough for a longitudinal assessment to be made. The
intensity and quantity of negative affect that former treaters demonstrated
was also a clue to a possible diagnosis of borderline personality disorder.
Although the diagnosis was confusing initially, what was clear was that
certain types of treatment had not been effective with him. Juan had been
written off as "just another chronic schizophrenic" and treated off and on
with medications, crisis intervention, and in day treatment. He relapsed.
Others insisted that only interventions uncovering and dealing with his
early abuse were indicated, ignoring that his ego defenses were not currently
sufficient to help him work through the trauma he experienced. He
continued to decompensate. Juan was also refused medications and psychotherapy by others until he completed a substance abuse program and
had been clean and sober for a determined amount of time. Again he
decompensated.

For the first years, much of the work was focused on the here and now, based on the assumption that no real psychological work could be done until basic needs were met. Juan's housing was in constant jeopardy. He had several suspensions for verbal aggressiveness with staff and residents at the residential treatment program. He was allowed to return only after much intense advocacy. The fact that I had a good professional relationship with the staff, based on years of experience, was useful. I think our mutual frustration with Juan was tempered by the understanding that none of us had sole responsibility, and we trusted that each would do what was needed to carry out the treatment plan.

In spite of this, in the end, Juan had to be discharged for drinking and breaking a window in a fit of anger. He had almost completed the program, and discharge plans were under way. He later revealed that he was experiencing discharge as rejection, rather than a success, but it took a long time before he could admit that he sabotaged the process.

After being kicked out prematurely, Juan adamantly denied the need for any kind of supervision or structured living situation. The only placement he would accept was a hotel room. I helped him find one, and then he insisted on changing hotels several times. After several months of this he finally found a rented room on his own. I had underestimated him, but I had been convinced that he would immediately decompensate without some kind of supervised living. He did not do so, and I was always to remember this lesson as I helped him to reality test of each of his goals over the next years. He has remained in this same room now for more than 3 years. Juan's ability to achieve residential stability does not signify that he was emotionally stable over these years, but it did provide a basic grounding for him to resolve crises at a higher level than mere survival.

Medications were an integral part of the treatment. Juan had never been compliant with medications for any significant period on an outpatient basis. Most of the medications he had received had been prescribed when he self-presented in crisis at an emergency unit. I linked Juan with an experienced Latino psychiatrist in the clinic where I was based. Juan related to him as a father figure in the most positive sense. Juan was able to hear advice and information from him that he had not been able to hear from me or other clinicians. Juan responded to the psychiatrist's philosophy of maintaining the lowest possible dosage, and education on effects and side effects. Over a period of time he became more compliant when given some control to use the medications on an as-needed basis, with consultation. A systemwide plan was enacted to redirect Juan back to us whenever he self-presented at psychiatric and medical emergency rooms, seeking medications. Initially, he would frequently take extra doses, state that he had lost his bottle, or complain that his medications had been stolen. Through coaching by the psychiatrist, I was able to do a great deal of monitoring of medication compliance and side effects between appointments. I was also able to schedule crisis appointments in response to Juan's complaints. The flexibility of the psychiatrist in being available to see Juan during crises helped reduce noncompliance and prevented rehospitalizations. Juan felt cared for and listened to. The psychiatrist was also attentive to the variability of symptoms with which Juan presented. Over several months, and trials of several classes and dosages of medications, Juan found that a low-dose neuroleptic worked best in controlling his anxiety, fearfulness, poor impulse control, and overwhelming emotions. The psychiatrist and I communicated briefly before and after most sessions, so that the psychosocial events influencing symptoms and compliance were shared, and the treatment plan and messages given were consistent between the two of us. This was tremendously important because Juan tended to stress certain pieces of information variably with each of us. We emphasized to Juan that we would work as a team to treat him.

Juan's minor medical complaints, both real and psychosomatic, were addressed jointly by the psychiatrist and me in terms of assessment, referral, linkage, and continued monitoring and education. For example, once his eye swelled shut and Juan attributed it to the medication. When medically evaluated, it turned out to be an infection and easily treated. We had to teach him how to distinguish between oversedation by medication and being in a relaxed or depressed mood. Juan worried about having AIDS, convinced that the heart palpitations, sweaty palms, and trembling he experienced after an argument with his family meant that he was going to die.

Juan needed to be able to use his trust in us to form yet another relationship with a medical practitioner. The communication between the psychiatrist and the physician was essential to obtaining and maintaining these medical services. Although his HIV status turned out negative, we were able to use this crisis to correct Juan's misconceptions concerning AIDS, to provide general health education, and to begin looking at Juan's patterns of self-destructive behaviors, that is, having unsafe sex. Juan was not initially comfortable in discussing issues of sexuality with a female; however, the psychiatrist was able and willing to provide sex education and condoms.

Within the medical-psychiatric continuum was also a need to focus on substance abuse. Juan had used PCP, cocaine, marijuana, and alcohol. From the beginning a concerted effort was made, by all treatment providers involved, to educate Juan on the effects of these substances. He initially responded to these interventions negatively, interpreting them as attempts to control him. As we began to link his substance use with his goals of having work, a nice apartment, and a girlfriend, he saw the intervententions less as a judgment on him or an attempt to control him. Rather, he began to see the choice to be made by him between achieving his dreams or continuing on the same downwardly spiralling path. He resisted encouragement to attend Alcoholics Anonymous until he was helped to find a Spanish-speaking group close to his home that had many young Latino male members. This was important because he was lonely and desperate for contact. He had previously associated primarily with his drug-using friends at the beginning of the month when his check arrived. Being on money management services was helpful in breaking this pattern. What also helped was spending a night in jail while intoxicated—it really scared him.

The focus on relationships was the heart of the work that Juan and I did together. Initially, there were poor impulse control, inappropriate behaviors, and violence to be contended with. Juan was given a firm message that he would not be rescued from the consequences of his behaviors, even if that meant he would go to jail. Since he revealed that most incidents occurred because of his fear and anger that others were trying to control him, I stressed my belief that he could and would control his actions and thus the consequences. I emphasized that the ground rules included that we would treat each other with *respeto* (respect). His acute sense of victimization tinged by paranoia gradually diminished as we tediously, incident by incident, linked his control in each altercation with the outcome. He has continued to have innumerable verbal conflicts but has also walked away from many provocative and escalating situations. He has not physically assaulted anyone since he hit his brother, which led to the hospitalization when he was referred to me. Although he has become rageful at me, the psychiatrist, and the clinic secretary, he was able to either leave the building or take a time out, and he never threatened to hurt us.

In addition to our mutual safety, there were many factors to consider in forming a viable therapeutic relationship. Juan trusted no one, and not without some cause, but he was also vulnerable, needy, and dependent. He alternated between being angry, devaluing, demanding, tearful, depressed, confused, and helpless. Help had to be offered in a way that acknowledged his prioritized needs, yet could not be perceived by him as intrusive, controlling, or irrelevant. The safety net had to be woven tightly enough to contain him, yet loosely enough to let him move and breathe.

Concrete assistance, such as help in obtaining financial resources, housing, money management, and translations, and giving basic straightforward information, did provide that initial link with Juan. He was motivated to be as independent and competent as he could, but during his periodic crises would regress to being dependent, helpless, and entitled. We spent much time negotiating what I would and would not help him with, and why. I had to assess each request for concrete assistance, what it meant, what he was really asking for, and what would be the effects on his self-esteem and our relationship. For example, he did not understand the Social Security bureaucracy and felt that the presence of an authority could be more effective, especially when it was their error. So I did accompany him to the Social Security office. After several times of role modeling, he was able to do this independently if I explained the papers he brought to me. There were times when he had problems with the landlord and demanded that I rush immediately to fix them. But when I attempted to explore the problem further, he would get angry and storm out of my office. When he returned to the next session, acting as if nothing had happened, we would discuss it further. At this point he was more amenable to exploring his role in causing or mismanaging the problems. Initially, he would spend his weekly check on clothes and drugs, or give it away, and then come demanding an advance on the next week's check. He often left angry when I would not do so. Over time he was given more of his money to manage, and finally the entire check was turned over to him when it became clear that he would and could provide for his food, shelter, and clothing.

Initially, I was uncertain how Juan would respond to a clinician who was Anglo but Spanish-speaking, as I am. These issues were explored at the beginning and over time. Juan told me that he felt my being Anglo would counteract the discrimination he felt and pave the road for better access to services. Both in terms of concrete advocacy and in discussing acculturation issues, Juan was able to use me as a culture broker. Initially, he insisted on speaking English, then gradually began using more Spanish as the therapy progressed to more psychological issues. This gave us a lot of freedom to role play interactions that he would have to make with English-speaking agencies, and also to touch some of his earliest feelings that were accessible only in his primary language. I took the stance that he was an expert on his own culture and made it clear that I wanted him to teach me about it, to better understand him and to help him understand himself. We actually had a lot of fun with language. He would often ask me to define a word for him in Spanish to improve his English vocabulary, or would ask how to pronounce a particularly difficult word. We both laughed at some of my grammatical or pronunciation errors, and he taught me much street slang that I am sure I would not have learned elsewhere. The ambiance that we created around making mistakes, laughing at them, getting corrected by the other, trying again, and moving on was something that I tried to ensure would permeate throughout the sessions. I tried to let him see making mistakes in language, like making mistakes in his life, did not make him a bad person. He was forever free to continue to grow and change and did not have to be bound to the mistakes and the pains of the past. However, this also depended on his admitting his errors and consciously making efforts to correct them. Would he choose *as asi es* (that's the way it is) or *las cosas cambian* (things change)?

Juan related to me both as the mother who abandoned him and attempted to control him and as the fantasized mother who would nurture, love, and take care of his every need. Group and individual supervision, as well as constant consultation with the psychiatrist, helped me immensely when I could feel myself either ready to give up in frustration or wanting to rescue him. It was hard to find the ever-changing delicate balance between dependence and independence, abandonment and rescuing, activity and waiting that Juan needed at each moment. Over time he learned to express his needs more clearly, and I learned more about his verbal and nonverbal cues. Juan several times described his experience of our relationship as that I have been "his right arm and his left arm." This is a much more poetic expression of the process that we call the therapist functioning as an auxiliary ego for the client.

Woven into the work of our relationship was the focus on his family. When I met Juan he was estranged from every member of his family. They were angry at him for his behaviors toward them. Juan was in much pain due to this rejection, but was also angry, feeling he had been mistreated by them in return. My usual focus is to involve the family in treatment whenever possible, to support the family in their caregiving, and to teach coping strategies in order to bolster the client's support system. However, in this case, a decision was made with Juan not to include them directly, because he was still furious at them and they also refused to attend family meetings at the hospital prior to discharge.

Even so, the spirits of the family members were frequently invoked in the sessions. Therapy focused on the issues of anger and loss, ranging from the recent rejections to the first abandonment by the mother and abuses by the father. The tears flowing out from under the anger were truly heartbreaking but cathartic. From this Juan's own sense of self began to coalesce. His sense of inferiority, badness, incompetence, unlovability, anticipated victimization, betrayal, and rejection diminished imperceptibly over time. He kept informed about his family through mutual friends and acquaintances, and eventually decided to contact the ones he felt closest to and who had the least amount of rancor toward him. His ability to determine that he deserved another chance and love from them, and his decision to forgive them as well as apologize for his own behavior, was a spiritual transformation for both of us. The resiliency and the process of healing the heart are as miraculous as any sunrise or childbirth. Part of Juan's effort to bridge the gap with some family members was the motivation to support a brother who was hospitalized for depression and suicidality. Given the amount of bitterness he felt some family members had toward him, taking that first step for Juan was a courageous act of love, as well as an act of desperation, because of his sense that there was nothing left to lose. These feelings were so strong for him that he needed no therapeutic intervention, other than a witness, to make them manifest.

With another brother, he initially tried to reestablish the connection by lending money. The brother did not pay it back, and Juan was afraid to jeopardize their tenuous communication by asking for it. He risked his housing and lost several pounds because he could not afford to eat. I had to confront him on this, but also realized that it was important for him to demonstrate that he had something to give in return for the love and support he so desperately wanted from them. I let him know I understood the value of mutuality and also helped him identify what else he had to give.

While attempting to rebuild the relationships with some family members, Juan was also determined to find a girlfriend. Much education had been done with him regarding sexuality, contraception, and disease prevention. He has not always practiced safe sex. I have frequently done reality testing about his adolescent sense of "nothing can happen to me." His relationships with women have to this date been unsatisfying. They have been chaotic, fraught with heated arguments (but no violence) and deception. Some have been purely sex. He is still trying to get a sense of what he wants in a relationship with a woman. We both agree that much long-term work needs to be done in this area. In addition to our discussions, I have often redirected him to consult his peers, to help him see where he fits on the continuum of normality of feelings and behaviors for someone of his age and culture in these times.

This has helped increase his support system. In San Francisco the community of Latino mental health clients is small and well connected. Some of his friends are, or were, on my caseload. They talk and share information and perceptions of me and other providers. I am careful to maintain confidentiality, but I also use my knowledge of this network to enhance clients' support systems. They have heard from each other how I have helped and set limits on other clients, and have also relayed their concerns about their peers' decompensating. When one client is progressing, the others take heed and have hope that they can also do the same.

While Juan was prioritizing his goal of finding a girlfriend, I also stressed that he not ignore other aspects of his life. I was concerned about how he spent his time. I knew that unless he had some structure to his daily activities, he ran the risk of having increased symptoms. The challenge was to help him find something that was challenging without being too stressful. After Juan left day treatment he went on to take English classes. His goal was to get his GED, and then work or get vocational training. I reminded him of his reported goals when he missed classes to be with his girlfriend or because of discouragement. He wavered between wanting to get a job to buy the latest fashions and electronic music equipment, go on dates, and so on, and sticking in school so that he would be able to eventually get something other than a dead-end job. Often I had to carry the hope for him that he was good enough to want more out of life. He had dreams of being a carpenter or mechanic. We weighed many factors, such as history of both successes and failures of working, goals and readiness to relinquish the safety net of SSI (public entitlement), what the relationship between self-esteem and identity and work was for him.

Juan's English had improved tremendously and he dropped out of English classes. He felt he was not ready to take GED preparatory classes, fearful especially of math. We have been exploring and problem solving for months. Recently he revealed he was "working under the table." He stated he had not told me before because he was unsure if he could handle the job and did not want to jeopardize his SSI.

The concomitant stresses of working, finding out that an ex-lover may be pregnant by him, and having arguments with a temporary roommate all led to his first hospitalizations in 4 years. He began to have insomnia, became depressed and anxious, and experienced auditory hallucinations and intense fearfulness. He was hospitalized voluntarily for a few days. He agreed to restart the neuroleptic medications and move into a crisis house for further stabilization. I had to advocate for him to return, even after several years, because he was remembered as a troublemaker. The staff hardly recognized him and were able to see him in a new light. They put much effort into helping him regain the progress he had made over the recent years.

Over the past year Juan and I had mutually agreed to reduce our sessions from biweekly to weekly, then bimonthly. When I first met Juan his attendance was erratic. Then he seldom missed a session for several years. Over the past months he has missed more appointments, giving excuses about having other obligations. I did not press the issue because our theme was individuation, and it seemed healthy for Juan to want to rely less on the mental health system. It became clear to both of us that, although his increasing independence needed to be supported, he was not ready to decrease the frequency of contacts so much. Juan and I agreed to have daily sessions for this crisis period, then return to weekly ones. He had been explicit about his ambivalence regarding mental health treatment. On the one hand, he did not want to need treatment; on the other, he could articulate how it had helped him and the problems he was currently dealing with. His positive experiences with treatment, and his pride over his growth, contributed to his being able to ask for help while in crisis, though he had waited too long, until he was actually decompensating.

Juan is far from cured. But we both feel hopeful that he has a future to look forward to and that therapy will be one useful tool in getting there.

Juan still does not know who he is or where he is going. On the other hand, how many 25-year-olds do? Work and love are still the basic issues.

Juan recently looked at me in puzzlement and joy and stated that it meant a lot to him that I "had not given upon him, no matter what." I guess I passed his test. Now he has to pass his own.

Sí, se puede, Juan—Yes, you can.

About the Contributors

Evelyn F. Balancio, M.S.W., received an her master's degree from the University of California, Berkeley. She is Assistant Clinical Professor at the Department of Psychiatry, University of California, San Francisco, and a Clinical Supervisor and the Assistant Director of Training for the Citywide Case Management program. Her professional interests include treatment and delivery of services for dually diagnosed substance abusers and homeless mentally ill individuals. She is also interested in cross-cultural issues in assessment and treatment.

Deborah Begley, M.S.W., is a Licensed Clinical Social Worker who has been with the Citywide Case Management Team since 1989. She works from the Psychiatric Emergency Service at San Francisco General Hospital. She received a B.S. degree in psychology from Radford University in Virginia and a master's in social work from the University of California at Berkeley. She has worked in both psychiatric inpatient and outpatient settings, as well as in chemical dependency programs. Her professional interests include countertransference issues and dual diagnosis clients.

Valerie Roxanne Edwards, M.S.W., earned her A.B. in psychology and her master's degree in social work from the University of California at Berkeley. She was a Supervisor for the University of California at San Francisco's Citywide Case Management program. She is part of the Adjunct Faculty of New College of California and part of the Clinical faculty of UCSF. Currently Ms. Edwards is the Director of Westside Crisis and Outpatient Services in San Francisco.

David F. Fariello, M.S.W., has worked with Citywide Case Management since December 1980 and currently serves as the Program Director. He received a master's in social work from California State University at Sacramento in 1976. Professional interests include working with treatment resistant and difficult-to-manage clients and treating dually diagnosed clients. Additionally, Mr. Fariello serves as an oral examiner for the California Board of Behavioral Science Examiners and as a reviewer for *Hospital and Community Psychiatry.*

Jeralyn Jones, M.D., is a graduate of Southwestern Medical School. She completed her psychiatric residency at California Pacific Medical Center. Following residency she worked as Medical Director of Citywide Case Management in San Francisco. She is currently in private practice in Boise, Idaho. Her interests include women's issues and working with chronic mentally ill people.

Vicki Keller, M.S.W., is a Clinical Supervisor who has worked with Citywide Case Management in San Francisco since 1985. She received her master's degree in social work, with an emphasis on community mental health, from the University of California at Berkeley. She received her B.A., majoring in social work and psychology, with a minor in Spanish, from the University of Iowa.

Allan F. Leung, Ph.D., is a psychologist and Assistant Director of Citywide Case Management, a program of the University of California, San Francisco. He received his doctorate from the California School of Professional Psychology, Berkeley, California. His interests include the provision of responsive community mental health services to the chronically mentally ill, cross-cultural clinical issues particularly as these affect Asian-Americans, the training of mental health professionals and students, and the treatment of character disorders.

Carlos E. Morales, M.S.W., currently a Forensic Case Manager with Citywide Case Management, holds a master's degree from the University of California at Berkeley. He is active in alternatives to and diversion from traditional criminal justice models for severely mentally ill individuals. He is also involved with developing and implementing affordable housing options for low-income persons. He participated on the peer case management implementation committee and is an advocate for professional and consumer collaboration in the delivery of services.

Shirley Powers, M.S., is a licensed Marriage, Family, and Child Counselor, is Assistant Director of Citywide Case Management, and has been with the program since 1985. She received her master's degree in counseling from San Francisco State University. She maintains a private practice in San Francisco.

Susan Scheidt, Psy.D., is an Assistant Clinical Professor at the University of California, San Francisco, and Unit Chief Attending Psychologist on the Latino/Women's Focus Inpatient Unit at San Francisco General Hospital. Dr. Scheidt was the program psychologist for Citywide Case Management for 2 years. One of her main areas of clinical expertise is psychoeducational interventions and support to families with seriously mentally ill relatives.

Robert W. Surber, M.S.S.W., is Deputy Chief for Community Services and Associate Clinical Professor with the University of California, San Francisco, Department of Psychiatry, at San Francisco General Hospital. He received his master's degree from the University of Wisconsin at Madison in 1969. He is interested in developing clinical approaches and service systems for multiple-need client populations, such as those with mental illness, substance abuse disorders, and/or HIV infection.